The Synergy of One

Creating High-Performing
Sustainable Organizations
through Integrated
Performance Leadership

Also Available from ASQ Quality Press:

From Quality to Business Excellence: A Systems Approach to Management
Charles Cobb

The Executive Guide to Improvement and Change
G. Dennis Beecroft, Grace L. Duffy, John W. Moran

Quality into the 21st Century: Perspectives on Quality and Competitiveness for Sustained Performance
International Academy for Quality

Office Kaizen: Transforming Office Operations into a Strategic Competitive Advantage
William Lareau

Creating a Customer-Centered Culture: Leadership in Quality, Innovation, and Speed
Robin L. Lawton

Developing New Services: Incorporating the Voice of the Customer into Strategic Service Development
Caroline Fisher and James Schutta

Customer Centered Six Sigma: Linking Customers, Process Improvement, and Financial Results
Earl Naumann and Steven H. Hoisington

Principles and Practices of Organizational Performance Excellence
Thomas J. Cartin

The Change Agent's Guide to Radical Improvement
Ken Miller

The Change Agents' Handbook: A Survival Guide for Quality Improvement Champions
David W. Hutton

To request a complimentary catalog of ASQ Quality Press publications, call 800-248-1946, or visit our Web site at http://qualitypress.asq.org.

The Synergy of One

Creating High-Performing
Sustainable Organizations
through Integrated
Performance Leadership

Michael J. Dreikorn

ASQ Quality Press
Milwaukee, Wisconsin

The Synergy of One: Creating High-Peforming Sustainable Organizations through Integrated Performance Leadership
Michael J. Dreikorn

Library of Congress Cataloging-in-Publication Data

Dreikorn, Michael J., 1961-
  The synergy of one: creating high-performing sustainable organizations through integrated performance leadership / Michael J.Dreikorn.
    p. cm.
  Includes bibliographical references and index.
  ISBN 0-87389-605-X (hard cover)
  1. Leadership. 2. Performance technology. 3. Organizational behavior.
I. Title.
HD57.7.D74 2003
658.4'092—dc22
                              2003016294

© 2004 by ASQ

All rights reserved. No part of this book may be reproduced in any form or by any means, electronic, mechanical, photocopying, recording, or otherwise, without the prior written permission of the publisher.
10 9 8 7 6 5 4 3 2 1

ISBN 0-87389-605-X

Acquisitions Editor: Annemieke Hytinen
Project Editor: Paul O'Mara
Production Administrator: Barbara Mitrovic
Special Marketing Representative: David Luth

Sponsored by The Aviation, Space and Defense Division of the American Society for Quality.

ASQ Mission: The American Society for Quality advances individual and organizational performance excellence worldwide by providing opportunities for learning, quality improvement, and knowledge exchange.

Attention: Bookstores, Wholesalers, Schools and Corporations: ASQ Quality Press books, videotapes, audiotapes, and software are available at quantity discounts with bulk purchases for business, educational, or instructional use. For information, please contact ASQ Quality Press at 800-248-1946, or write to ASQ Quality Press, P.O. Box 3005, Milwaukee, WI 53201-3005. To place orders or to request a free copy of the ASQ Quality Press Publications Catalog, including ASQ membership information, call 800-248-1946. Visit our web site at www.asq.org. or qualitypress.asq.org.

Printed in the United States of America

 Printed on acid-free paper

Quality Press
600 N. Plankinton Avenue
Milwaukee, Wisconsin 53203
Call toll free 800-248-1946
Fax 414-272-1734
www.asq.org
http://qualitypress.asq.org
http://standardsgroup.asq.org
E-mail: authors@asq.org

Dedicated to sound ethical leadership

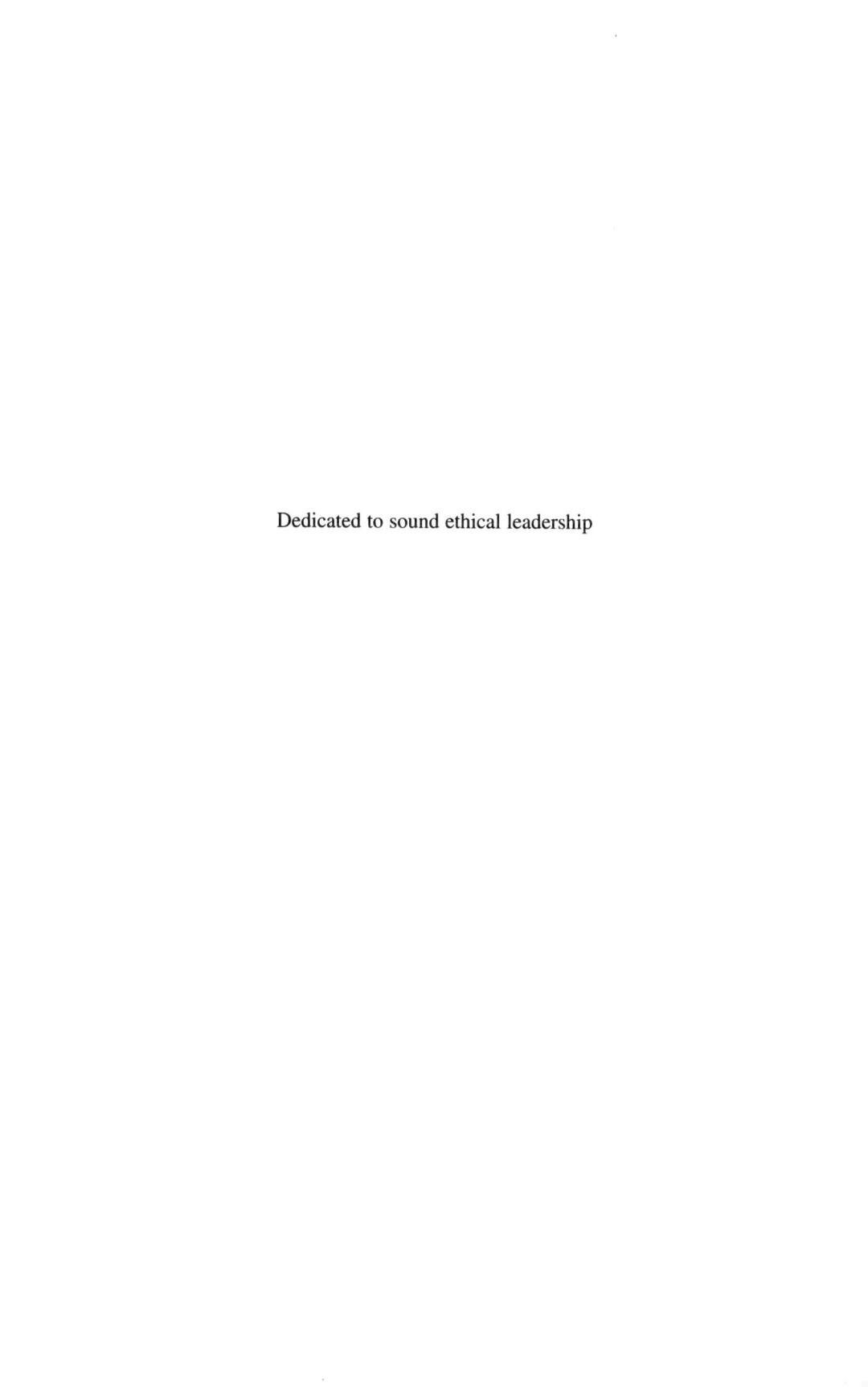

Table of Contents

List of figures ix
List of tables xi
Preface xiii

Chapter 1   An Introduction to IPL 1

Chapter 2   Integration 15
   The Theory of Integration 16
   An Integrated Organizational Structure 24
   Deciding on the Structural Design 39
   The Notion of Decentralization 40
   Authority through Reporting Lines 42
   Defining a Common Direction 46
   Integrating Initiatives 49
   Systems of Routines and Chaos 52
   System Validation 60
   Feedback and System Design 63
   Summary 63

Chapter 3   Performance 67
   Defining Organizational Performance 69
   Aligning Performance Metrics 75
   Aligning of Organizational Resources 80
   Summary 86

Chapter 4 Leadership **89**

    Visionary Leadership 90
    Contextualized Leadership (understanding) 94
    Glaubwürdigkeit (Believability) 96
    Managing Leadership Abilities 97
    Leading for an Environment of Dialogue 101
    The Psychology and Motivation of Dialogue 104
    Rewarding Performance and Behavior 107
    Summary 112

Chapter 5 Making IPL Work **113**

    Understand It 114
    Be Decisive 115
    Create a Sense of Urgency 116
    Create a New Mental Model throughout the
      Organization of What Will Be 117
    Create a Real Plan for Action 118
    Design for Incremental and Frequent Successes 122
    Take Massive Action 123
    Continuously Measure Engagement 123
    Communicate Frequently 124
    Stay True to the Plan 125
    Summary 126

Chapter 6 Conclusion **127**

Appendix A VISION Center Networks **131**

    The VISION Center Concept 131
    Setting Up a VISION Center Network 139
    Modular Aspects of the VISION Center Process 143
    Supplier Accountability Process 144
    Supplier-Funded Over Inspection 148
    Quality in Development Processes 149
    Integrated Project Selection 150
    Demonstrating Value 151
    Summary 154

Appendix B Integrated Knowledge Management **155**
   Taxonomy of Knowledge Capability 157
   Identifying Types of Knowledge 161
   Macro Knowledge Mapping 162
   The Integrated Knowledge Management Matrix 166
   Knowledge Management Measurement 170
   Evaluation of the Capability Level 173
   Assignment of Work in Accordance
      with Knowledge Capability 174
   Capability Development 175
   Using the Integrated Knowledge Management Matrix 177
   Value-Stream Knowledge Assurance 181
   Summary 184

Glossary *187*

About the Author *193*

References *195*

Index *205*

List of Figures

Figure 1.1	The IPL model.
Figure 1.2	The responsibility of leadership.
Figure 2.1	As your environment changes so must you.
Figure 2.2	Schwandt's organizational learning model.
Figure 2.3	Parsons's four functional prerequisites.
Figure 2.4	Entropy and homeostasis.
Figure 2.5	Organizations must find balance.
Figure 2.6	Traditional organizational structure.
Figure 2.7	Life cycle macro business processes.
Figure 2.8	Example of the concept phase.
Figure 2.9	Example of design process map.
Figure 2.10	Example of production process map.
Figure 2.11	Example of service process map.
Figure 2.12	Sample of IPMT roles and responsibilities.
Figure 2.13	Example of an integrated organizational structure.
Figure 2.14	Dotted-line versus solid-line reporting.
Figure 2.15	Integrated organizational structures.
Figure 2.16	Organizational members must have requisite knowledge.
Figure 2.17	Initiatives and performance expectations must be integrated.
Figure 2.18	Three levels of waste.
Figure 2.19	Organizations must leverage the power of the pen.
Figure 4.1	The four characteristics of leadership in IPL.
Figure A.1	VISION center network model.

List of Figures

Figure A.2	The VISION concept.
Figure A.3	VISION center product evaluation process.
Figure B.1	The integrated knowledge management model.
Figure B.2	The integrated knowledge management model worksheet.
Figure B.3	The integrated knowledge management matrix.
Figure B.4	Sample checklist for ensuring supplier's and partner's knowledge.
Figure B.5	Organizations must be aware of multiple value streams.

List of Tables

Table 2.1	Questions for determining organizational structure and process value.
Table 2.2	The four orders of value.
Table 3.1	Campbell's list of effectiveness criteria.
Table 3.2	Strategic constituencies.
Table 4.1	The vision-span structure for leadership.
Table 4.2	The six psychological human needs.
Table A.1	Sample roles and responsibilities of a VISION center technician.
Table A.2	Example of VISION center work.
Table A.3	Sample cost-avoidance formula.
Table B.1	The major categories of knowledge.

Preface

For years, I have pondered the notion that regardless of what happens in an organization, those happenings are always at the determination of leadership. I realize that we can't hold specific leaders in an organization accountable for every little thing that occurs there. However, it is the leadership of the organization who make choices on system design, capital investments, training investments, priorities and measures, and business strategies. The people in the organization typically behave in the manner leadership sets forth for them; and customers will be treated according to the way the organizational system has been designed to perform, provided the system is adhered to.

This book is about understanding the dynamics in organizations and treating business interactions as integrated processes that can be defined and managed as a holistic organism. To facilitate this understanding, I introduce the concept of integrated performance leadership, which combines aspects of various sciences and theories to bridge the gap between academic postulation and the realities of organizational practice. In short, the concept is simple: when an organization understands the expectations of its customers, the dynamics of its internal and external environment, the interrelatedness of its business processes, and the influence of leadership, it can design systems and grow people to ensure a sustainable existence. Customers can be satisfied, organizational members can have their human needs met, and investors can have their performance expectations satisfied. A lot of this is truly common sense, but I am amazed at how many organizations are focused on incredibly short-term results at the expense of long-term survivability. I would like to share with you just such an experience, where a very large organization truly missed the mark from both its customer's perspective and that of its employees.

Not so long ago, I undertook a journey from Hartford, Connecticut, to Osaka, Japan—a business trip. It was an early morning flight with connections through Chicago and San Francisco. I felt well prepared for the trip. My assistant had carefully mapped out my itinerary and had confirmed all of my connections and hotel accommodations. The team I had assembled for the business aspects of the journey was ready for the week of action that was before us. We had prepared ourselves with content for our upcoming meetings and had performed a number of dry runs to ensure our message would be understood by our foreign meeting partners. The journey started very early in the morning. A light rain was falling as we left our homes for the airport, and the dawn had yet to break. The team was ready and on its way.

Our first surprise of the trip was finding a 45-minute wait to get through security. Given the security situation following September 11, it should have been expected, and yes, my assistant did tell me to get there two hours early. But of course, being the world traveler that I am, I thought one hour was sufficient. And it barely was—clearly, my error. As I proceeded through the metal detectors of security, the buzzer went off, as I expected it would given my preference of belt buckles. The process required me to go through a side screening, which I did not mind at all. As a matter of fact, I was quite pleased that security was so thorough. Meanwhile, my laptop computer, computer bag, and leather jacket remained on the x-ray machine conveyer belt as other passengers' personal items piled up on top. Given that my shoes also triggered attention, the special screening process took a few minutes longer. As luck would have it, other passengers were lining up for the special screening because they too had set the detector off. I do want to make an important point here: I am not complaining. The airlines and airport were doing the right thing, and I was happy to oblige. I would suggest, though, that the security processes be matched with their capacity requirements. There were only two lanes open for the primary screening process and one screener for the special process. The potential for my laptop to be damaged or stolen while we were separated didn't give me a warm fuzzy feeling, either. But we have slowly learned to accept such conditions in our daily lives.

It did start to become apparent, though, that I was doing business with an airline that performed its processes in isolated steps and not as an integrated enterprise. Although my departure gate was right next to where the special screening process occurred and I know the gate attendant saw me go through that, as I was attempting to check through boarding, I again drew the lucky screening number and was subjected to a special security screening. Now, my appearance is not one that I thought would trigger special emphasis, but what the heck, I'm a team player and I played along with this with a smile. Yet it did come to mind that, as I went through the very same process as previously, the sampling method might not be providing the yield that the airline and airport security had intended. I was thinking, "You know, they could have stamped my ticket or provided some other control method to provide them with a broader sample." Nevertheless, in a few minutes I was on board the plane with five of my colleagues on my way to Japan eager to conduct business. Or so I thought.

My understanding of how an aircraft is prepared for flight is that the pilot and crew undertake a series of preflight checks to complement the activities of the ground crew in ensuring that everything is in good working order. We were all comfortable in our seats and rolling toward the runway, but we shortly found ourselves parked on the ramp. After considerable time had passed, the pilot announced over the intercom that he was experiencing a technical difficulty with the onboard computer and was trying to get it back online. He broadcasted a number of times over the next hour telling us about various restart procedures he was trying and that he was attempting to get authorization to fly to Chicago without the computer functioning. During this time, passengers were allowed to use the restroom and stretch. We could even use our cell phones to reschedule connecting flights if necessary. However, there was no service provided to any class of passengers as to connecting flight information or rebooking. When I asked for such information, I was told the airplane had no communication with the customer service organization and that I had no other choice than to sit tight. Eventually the pilot notified the passengers that the plane would be returning to the gate for maintenance and fuel—a decision that, in my opinion, could have been made at least an hour earlier. As we approached the gate, the pilot found that there were no open spaces, so we again faced a wait. As we sat in the chilly early hours of Hartford, our persistent pilot continued to attempt to restart the computer and was actually successful. And no, I did not hear any swift kicks to the instrumentation. We were now on our way to Chicago and other connections—over an hour late.

As we neared Chicago, I attempted to get information about our connections. Would we make our next scheduled flight? If not, did the airline have other options available for us? If the airline could not provide us with connections on its scheduled flights, could it coordinate with other airlines to ensure we were in Japan to conduct our business as planned? We had trusted this airline as a business partner to enable our business success, and I did not have the impression it cared. Other than telling us which gate our next connection would leave from before we arrived, the attendants had little other information of value for my team and myself. By the time we arrived in Chicago, we had missed our connection by five minutes. That connection should have had at least six domestic first-class passengers traveling on to Osaka via San Francisco.

Upon disembarking the plane, we were met by a customer service representative who was able only to direct us to the customer service counter. The agent there was friendly and was able to process my entire team. When I complemented her ability to get us on another flight, she gave the credit to the central booking group. My immediate thought was that something was going on behind the scenes in the way of integration, which was satisfying. We marched on to our new gate assignment and found it with 40 minutes to spare. However, to our surprise we found that we did not have seats assigned and would have to wait on standby to see if something opened up as we got closer to flight departure. I began to rethink my thoughts of this airline being integrated.

If you have ever flown long distance, you may have experienced the "escaping travel day phenomenon." As the hours, and frequently just minutes, tick away, especially those before noon when traveling west, precious alternative options evaporate. Where you could have made a flight if you had moved quickly, the opportunity is gone in five minutes. So you can probably imagine my growing anxiety and frustration. The disconcern of the gate agent only added fuel to our already heated emotions. As luck would have it, my team and I made it on the flight to San Francisco. However, the first-class seats we paid for were now dispersed throughout the plane as economy. Nevertheless, we were traveling in the right direction.

I was trying to make the most of the next leg of our journey, though I was crammed into a seat whose dimensions were smaller than mine. Thoughts of design occupied my mind. Just which customers did the engineers have in mind when they drafted the dimensions for this seat? As the door closed, 20 minutes late because of a late crew member, I was already thinking about the next transfer. The plane was taxiing toward the runway when a weather front hit and delayed all aircraft from taking off for about an hour. Again, the prospect of missing our long-scheduled business meetings started to bounce around in my thoughts. In the name of safety, the pilots made the right decision to keep the plane on the ground until the weather cooperated; however, had we left on time, the weather front would not have affected us.

The eventual takeoff was a bit bumpy, but we were finally headed toward San Francisco. The flight attendants were friendly, and during the flight I found an opportunity to share my morning experiences with them. I appreciated their sympathy but would rather have had a bigger seat. In conversation with the flight attendants, I asked if they could find out if we were going to make our connection. During the flight I asked a couple of more times, and I was assured they were looking into it. Wanting to ensure our travel success, I gave my assistant in Hartford a phone call from the plane. I have to say that my assistant, Lisa, is fabulous. Here we are on a Saturday, the weather is beautiful in Hartford, and Lisa is calling the airline to see what it is doing to help us. About an hour after my first call, I called my assistant back and learned that the airline had already rebooked us on a flight—which would have been wonderful, but it was for the following day. This meant we were going to miss some of our critical business meetings in Japan. The great disappointment was that the airline had done this before we ever left Chicago. I found these facts out in the third hour of a four-hour flight, not from the airline but rather from my assistant, Lisa. The concepts of honesty and disclosure came to mind and how this particular airline was not exercising any.

Armed with new information, I advised the helpful flight attendants of the situation and solicited their help with the "Company." Oddly enough, the term *Company* was theirs and not mine, which gave me the impression they did not feel like integrated members but rather only participants in its activities. Unlike on the earlier flight, this crew had some sort of communications with their ground organization (which I think the other crew had as well but were not concerned about their customers, as this crew was). They could even send and receive faxes, which they shared with me later in the flight. Because of the tardy crew member and weather delay, we were going to miss our connection by only 15 minutes but no amount of pleading would convince the Company to hold the plane. In addition to my team of six, two additional passengers were attempting to catch the same plane to Osaka. I must complement the flight attendants and pilots of this flight because they gave it their all to get the Company to help us out. The crew asked the Company to either hold the scheduled plane or find seats on another airline leaving the West Coast to anywhere in Japan. We would figure out how to get to Osaka if they just got us on the island. The fax they shared with me later conveyed to us that although the Company was looking for other flight options, holding the plane was not an option. We arrived in San Francisco safe and sound but without any connections. The airline had a customer service representative waiting for my team and me but not for the other two passengers. This was clearly a case of the squeaky wheel getting the grease. And boy was I squeaking, but in a nice way. I knew the individuals were not responsible for a system of the Company that had forgotten what customer service was about. So I treated them with respect and professionalism but also made it clear that we were not satisfied with the Company's service and that the Company was affecting my business—quite significantly, I might add.

At the Company's customer service desk in San Francisco, we met Nelson. Nelson was obviously an employee of the Company who had faced hundreds, if not more, of stranded travelers. He knew all of the processes and procedures and had one focus—the customer. This Company employee believed in the airline and was doing everything in his power to turn the situation around. Notably, Nelson did not refer to the airline as the "Company." He acknowledged the fragmented systems, and he had created numerous work-arounds through his years of experience. Thoughts of waste and employee dissatisfaction came to mind as Nelson exercised his talent. In the end, there was nothing Nelson could do to help us get to our meetings in Japan on time.

Nelson's courtesy and concern were disarming, and he provided us with options for going forward—though on the following day. The standard accommodations of meals and room were offered and accepted, and then it came to collecting our luggage for the evening. Surprise, our bags did not make our last flight! So we had lunch and waited for the flight that Nelson had assured us our luggage was on. When we went to collect our luggage, the employees working the luggage claim couldn't find them. As we discussed the possibilities, one of my team members noticed his bag behind a cage outside their office. We communicated this fact to the employees, but they did not believe us. My entire team walked out to the cage and recognized their own bags, and we began a debate with the Company representatives about the possibility of those bags being ours. Even when the cage was opened and the bags placed before us, the employees refused to accept that they could be our bags. Given the evidence of baggage claim tickets, we headed to the hotel with our luggage. I must report that Nelson was able to coordinate our accommodations, and the rest of the evening was without event. Sleep and dinner were our final priorities for the day. The following day we checked in for the last leg of our flight and were finally on our way to Osaka without further event—except for one positive note: Nelson made sure we were upgraded from business class on our international leg to first class—all six of us.

My reason for sharing this dreadful experience is not that it was a unique, newsworthy event. But rather, such service has become everyday practice, and we have been conditioned to tolerate it as normal. Consumers are confronted with "companies" that have organized themselves in collective fiefdoms, as opposed to organizations that focus on delighting customers. Many companies have become so internally focused that they have forgotten that all money comes from customers and work performed by employees who should be knowledgeable and satisfied. Given other options, customers will choose to spend their money where they get the greatest value, and employees will choose better environments in which to work. The exemplary airline employee, Nelson, was trying to satisfy, despite the Company indiscretion, and possibly delight the six stranded customers. Unfortunately, the airline was incapable of delighting any customer because of its disconnected system. We finally made it to Japan, and we were able to coordinate a revised schedule with our Japanese business associates, but we should not have had to. Sure, we could have left a day earlier, but that would have added unnecessary cost to my business, not to mention more time away from our families. I look at a service organization such as an airline as part of my business plan. I can either count on it being there to help me make my plan, or it is not part of it. This is the concept that I try to convey in the following chapters: the aspect of integration and the choices an organization's leadership makes relative to integration that directly affect performance and sustainability.

I have intentionally not named the airline because I respect its history and believe it can again become great. But to do so, that airline must make a choice. It is a leadership choice to redesign its systems so that knowledge is shared at the speed of customer expectations. For example, before leaving the gate in Hartford, the pilot should have already known the onboard computer was not operational. That fact could have been provided to technicians and corrective actions taken. Okay, let's say it could not have been noticed until the second engine was running and we were headed toward the runway. A response should have occurred, and maintenance options should have been quickly considered. Additionally, passenger flight itineraries should have been reviewed for impact and alternative travel options developed. Given some delays are not preventable, even enroute, the airline could have had a communications system connecting the plane and the ground to advise passengers of rebookings before they ever arrived at their connecting destinations.

The objective here is to reduce customer anxiety by apprising them of the situation. The concept here is to establish integrated systems that facilitate expected performance. Given the extent of technology available today, there is no reason we, as consumers, should not demand this level of service. The misunderstanding in Chicago with the customer service agent and the gate agent should never have occurred. If seats were not available, we should not have been told they were. Though the system was local, it was obviously dysfunctional. The same scenario is true for our delays leaving Chicago. Even if no rebooking options existed, the airline should have informed us of that while still enroute without my having to call my assistant to find out. I'm sure that if I hadn't called Lisa, I would not have learned about our missed flights until I met Nelson. That's not fair to Nelson or to us.

I firmly believe that in an era of fierce competition where all prices are similar, the company that will win is the one to which customers return to spend their money. Given the choice, I will always spend my money with a provider of services or products that I can depend on. What use is a low price if the cost is high? This book presents the notion of integrated organizations that are that way because their leadership made conscious decisions to design them as such. As a result of integration, their overall performance for customers, as well as their financial performance, is better than companies that are not integrated. The ordeal the airline put us through not only cost us time and disrupted our business, it also cost the airline in additional handling charges and accommodations. Such additional costs are purely waste and loss of shareholder value.

1
An Introduction to Integrated Performance Leadership

Imagine sitting in a top-level board meeting where the future of the company is being strategized. The president is sharing vision and objectives and each of the senior profit and loss, functional discipline, and department leaders is taking notes and engaging in discussion. Just before the meeting breaks up, the president asks, "Everybody got it?" And, of course, the response is positive. As the meeting adjourns the senior leaders of the organization go their individual ways to enact the strategy. However, unless all the leaders have processed the discussion through a common framework of understanding, the likelihood of a synergetic deployment is low. Typically, the sales department will go off and do its thing, engineering its, procurement its, quality its, and so on. Moreover, if the structure includes program management, that could increase the variation within the functional disciplines. Does this sound familiar? If so, it most probably means you gained your experience in an organization that was not integrated in terms of its systems, understanding, culture, resources, accountability, and leadership.

Consider the airline I described in the Preface and the kind of communication and system opportunities it had, and then consider your organization in the same light. Just how different is your organization from that airline? Are the business processes of the organization well defined and integrated so that the needs of its members and customers are met? Are your people knowledgeable in the work they are responsible for and empowered to execute, as Nelson was? If you think they are, how do you know that? How is organizational performance defined? Is there more internal competition for resources than there is external competition for market share? Does your organization focus primarily on short-term results or on long-term sustainability and growth?

If we integrate the systems and management direction through a framework of integrated business processes, the result is a higher probability of influencing organizational performance through consistent action. By clearly and consistently defining performance metrics throughout the organization and ensuring that there is a consistent understanding of expectations, action, and interrelatedness at all levels of the organization, we will have greater synergy and commitment to a common objective. And when we have visionary leadership that can balance transactional (aptitudes of commerce) and transformational (growth of people) leadership styles with vision and contextual knowledge, we then have the structure for predictable and sustainable performance with continuous improvement and growth. It is critical that organizations, and especially their leaders, understand the interrelatedness of the organization and understand the roles and value that each member provides within it. We must also understand how our structures and processes relate to the creation of value for the customer. After all, "All money comes from customers." Especially when customers have the discretion to spend their money elsewhere, they need to be continuously convinced not to. In addition, leaders must recognize and understand the interrelatedness of environmental influences and the organization. As market conditions and regulations change, so must the skills, processes, and strategies of our organization. Otherwise, the organization runs the risk of becoming extinct.

We are all familiar with the operation of a vehicle. You put gas in it, turn on the ignition, and go. It's as simple as that, right? Well, there might be a bit more to it. Subjecting the car to some sort of maintenance routine, such as changing the oil, checking the air pressure in the tires, and occasionally changing the filters and spark plugs, provides some assurance that it will continue to perform as intended, or even start. The notion of *operation* is based on a number of assumptions the manufacturer makes during the design process. For example, a sports car may have a tight suspension, a powerful engine with close tolerance gearing, and a low profile to the ground. These design characteristics allow it to perform in tight turns and with great speed on a prepared road surface. The vehicle is enjoyable to operate on windy roads and at high speeds. On the other hand, a sports utility vehicle (SUV) may be designed significantly differently than a sports car. An SUV typically has a powerful engine like a sports car but considerably different gearing and torque. The suspension and road clearance also is considerably different than that of a sports car; it frequently has enhanced shock-absorbing features and higher ground clearance to better manage its environment.

These differences allow the SUV to perform on and off the road within predictable performance parameters. The design of the vehicle allows the operator to drive the vehicle only at slower speeds, compared to the sports car, but it allows the operator to go places the sports car operator cannot.

Each vehicle is designed for a specific purpose and to operate in a predetermined environment. Moreover, the designers must take into account the broadness of their operating environments. This includes accounting not only for desired performance characteristics but also for compliance to laws, regulations, market signals, cost of materials, size of roads, traffic, and any other attribute that can possibly influence the performance of bringing the product to market and its sustained operation by the customer.

Each individual copy of a sports car or of an SUV can be considered a *system*. It is pretty much a self-contained system, but by no means a closed system. A closed system is one that is not influenced by anything outside of its internal environment. Social systems such as organizations are influenced by the external environment and are considered open systems. The engine responds to the inputs of the driver and transfers converted power to the drivetrain and tires. More advanced vehicles have sensors that monitor the performance of the vehicle and adjust the system to obtain ultimate performance in the suspension and power distribution. Whether the system is that of a sports car or an SUV, each will perform as designed for its specific purpose, provided it is maintained and operated in the appropriate environment and assuming it has been designed and constructed with the capabilities of sustained performance—again, assumptions that are made during design and validated at later points.

From a design perspective, vehicles are produced in accordance with assumptions made by the manufacturers. Assumptions are created through market-feedback analysis, experience, and sometimes crystal ball prediction. To create value for a customer (the source of money), the assumptions must be consistent with what the customer will be willing to pay for. In some cases, where organizations are heavily influenced by engineering leadership, assumptions may not necessarily be based on the needs or desires of the customer but rather on a bias for technology development and technocrat ego. Designing products or services that no one is willing to pay for is a sure way to lose market share and it is an indication of a disconnect between the organization and its environment.

The outputs of these assumptions are the systems we operate every day—our cars and SUVs. Now, as the owner of a system, we have the ability to either maintain the vehicle in the same configuration as delivered by the manufacturer or modify it to meet our unique needs. We could consider ourselves the leaders of our own little microsystems. We determine what grade of fuel we replenish our system with, how often we will perform preventative maintenance, and whether we garage the vehicle when not in use. So, as the leader of the system, we determine whether we maintain or modify its design, what type of energy we interject to sustain it, and when we need to adjust and refresh aspects of the system to ensure a long life. We are also in control of the signals we send to the system for action. We can drive it hard or drive it lightly, and the balance of maintenance and replenishment will contribute in determining longevity. The harder the vehicle is driven, the more attention it will require to sustain expected performance. A vehicle that is operated lightly may look good but probably is not fulfilling its intended role of economical transportation. We must find a balance between performance expectations and system attention and capabilities.

I use the example of the car as a system to illustrate that most things in life are established as systems. I could also use a biological example, the human body. It too is designed for certain performance abilities that we can choose to modify for performance needs or desires. Such modifications can be through diet, supplements, exercise, and in the extreme case, surgery. With the exception of uncontrollable environmental influences, these are choices that are made by the owner of the system—you and I.

We should look at organizational systems in the same light. We design them to perform certain functions. Whether the function is telemarketing, governing, delivering professional services, or large-scale design and manufacturing, they are still open social systems. Organizations are designed to perform in certain environments, such as regional or global, and to focus on customer segments, such as an industry-specific segment or the general population. The reason we do this is to be more accurate in providing value to the customer. We also design subsets of the organization that we frequently refer to as departments or divisions. We do this so that we can divide the work and focus the organization into more manageable segments to meet specific customer needs. Conceptually, this is done to make the organization more efficient and to create greater value.

For example, we traditionally establish a human resources division, or suborganization, to focus on recruiting and, hopefully, training/learning and development. We may establish an engineering or product development division if we intend on designing products and a manufacturing department to produce such products, and we continue to create functional suborganizations that focus on the practices of their discipline (for example, legal, procurement, quality, sales, and so on). In creating these suborganizations, we create procedures and policies to govern the functions of each and to direct the execution of work. The organizational structure begins to resemble the batch-production processes of a traditional manufacturing organization. We create suborganizations that require stops and starts in our business processes—precluding the possibility of continuous flow and elimination of waste.

When we add layers of management to the soup, and each organizational discipline establishes its own definition of what *good* looks like, the organization becomes confusing. Think about the car example and having more than one person trying to operate the vehicle. It is common for organizations not to be integrated in their steerage. Human resources may define good performance in terms of quotas of new college graduates recruited into the organization, a certain number of hours of training per employee, or the meeting of diversity objectives. The engineering department may establish performance metrics that measure the number of postdesign release changes to determine whether the department is meeting its objective of first-time quality, or it may look at on-time release as a measure of process quality. The production department may focus on the number of defective parts per million to measure its ability to control process variation or the cost per hour per employee to measure its productivity. But what most organizations rarely do is look at themselves as holistic systems that must function in unison to ensure overall performance.

The larger the organization, the higher the probability that it has grown many suborganizations that all measure success differently—which may be acceptable if the measures are integrated to achieve holistic performance. An organization that perceives itself as a holistic system integrates the functionality of its various unique characteristics with the aim of a common vision and common performance expectations and holds it all together with balanced leadership—visionary leadership. Can you imagine the power train (engine, transmission, and axle) in your car having different performance objectives than those of your brakes? It's essential that they perform together to ensure the safe operation and longevity of the overall system. My experience with the airline leads me to wonder how each of the individual parts of that organization is measured for success.

Integrated performance leadership (IPL) is a term I'd like to introduce that describes the constructs of organizational interrelatedness and system design, integrated organizational performance measures, and leadership influence over and in a system. IPL combines various academic theories of management, performance, and leadership into a single stream of thought. Each of these diverse academic perspectives is grounded in a research protocol that binds the construction of theory into a manageable process so that it can be applied for testing. The individual elements of a theory are made up of bits and pieces of thought streams that are referred to as *constructs*. In IPL, the three major constructs are integration, performance, and leadership (see Figure 1.1). However, I will introduce various supporting constructs to tie the streams together.

For example, it is important that we maintain focus on the customer when discussing the concept of IPL, so that the organization maintains a perspective of real value creation and promotes its ability to become a competitive organism, which Womack refers to as a *lean enterprise* (Womack and Jones 1996). A lean enterprise is one that truly understands the needs of the customer and has aligned all of its value-creating business processes to be waste-free and responsive. To *align* business processes to organizational objectives is to ensure the defined actions (processes and procedures) of the organization do not conflict with each other, gaps are identified, and action is leveraged throughout all aspects of the organization to create value in products and services for the customer. Greater efficiencies can be realized when the organization *synchronizes* its business processes so that its various parts are interacting with each other at a common pace and with little or no wait time in hands off. And still greater productivity will be realized through the *integration* of business processes where the lines of functional hands-off become blurred and the organization performs as one. The result is a highly competitive organization with a high potential for survival and success. IPL does not compete with the lean enterprise concept, but rather provides an integrative framework for the enterprise to become lean. IPL applies this concept as an organizing construct to help bind the three major constructs together. In this case, and as is discussed in more detail later, the construct is more closely aligned with the ideas of adaptation, requisite variety, and entropy.

Figure 1.1 The IPL model.

Because organizational improvement initiatives typically address a limited aspect of organizational dynamics and performance, leaders may not be focusing on creating sustainable organizations and may actually be wasting time and money in their efforts. In bringing the three main constructs (integration of organizational systems, clear definition of performance measures, and leadership) together, I hope to demonstrate that most organizations ignore most, if not all, of them when seeking to grow their business or even just trying to survive. Take, for example, the organization that seeks to improve the quality of its services or products. Most of the time it will apply some popular tools such as statistical process control or measurement of quality turnbacks. But the organization will rarely look at the influence of the internal or external environments of process performance, let alone the influence of organizational leadership. And those that do use such quality improvement tools to find the cause of poor performance typically do so in isolation from the rest of the management system. This may be a case of managers suffering from tunnel vision or shortsightedness or of managers just doing the best they can within the dysfunctional systems of the organization.

Many organizations that focus on aspects of leadership typically do so in an isolated and unconnected fashion. For example, when a production cell in a manufacturing organization has a high rejection rate, more often than not the local production cell leader (first-line manager) is the one who catches grief for poor performance. Rarely does the organization look more inward and evaluate the various signals that cell leader is receiving from elsewhere in the organization—namely, from senior leaders. The cell leader may be measured on various metrics to differing degrees at the same time, and the weighting of those measurements may alter minute by minute—especially at the end of the month when the books are closed out and financial performance is reported externally. The cell leader may be pressed to meet a delivery expectation, and the message from organizational leadership may be "I don't care how you do it, just get the product out the door." And leadership should be conscious that such signals need not be spoken out loud. Leadership behavior often speaks louder than words. At the same time, the cell leader may be pressed to resolve some quality issues prior to being allowed further processing of the product. Plus, the cell leader may be expected to participate in a number of other organizational activities that divert that leader's attention, focus, and valuable time.

The foregoing example weighs the measures of financial and delivery performance against the measures of quality and customer satisfaction against the cultural norms of teaming. The point is that the organization frequently sends messages to its membership that may be difficult to make sense of and may lead to organizational frustration and perhaps paralysis. In this case paralysis is the organizations inability to take effective or efficient action because of ambiguity and uncertainty—not knowing what is important or what to do next. These conflicting messages can be considered the arrows of organizational fragmentation.

Consider each signal as an arrow targeted for delivery to the organization. The ones that are bigger and occur more frequently are the ones that people typically respond to. Since product or service quality arrows often take more time after the event to be delivered to the internal organization, they usually don't have the same immediate impact as cost and delivery. However, where there is direct interaction with customers (as in the airline adventure described in the Preface), customer feedback is quicker, sometimes instantaneous, and therefore reaction and correction should be quicker if the processes are designed to facilitate such. To prevent paralysis, it is critical that organizational members are empowered to take action and that they know which action is appropriate. If properly designed, the systems of the organization facilitate quick action and organizationwide learning.

Put yourself in Nelson's shoes (remember, he was the airlines representative who saved the trip described in the Preface). Imagine how much more productive you could be as a contributing member of the organization if you were not constantly attempting to triage the fallout of disconnected systems. Imagine how much more cost effective the airline would be if it were not performing volumes of unplanned work. Imagine the influence on customer loyalty if both business and leisure travelers thought of their favorite air carrier as dependable. And finally, imagine your own organization and the frustration that exists because of systems that compete internally and do little for employee engagement.

Only when an organization has put its various performance goals through a filter of leadership determination and a funnel of structured sensemaking can it truly understand which way is up. It is also important to ensure that the messages that are sent are consistent, that they don't vary because the end of the month is looming. Inundating the lower levels of the organization with competing or conflicting signals only creates huge amounts of waste. Work is started and stopped, and flow is lost. People struggle to figure out what is important and what is the acceptable action for the moment. Integrated performance leadership addresses the need for the organization's business goals and strategies to be completely integrated into its culture, so that the organization not only understands but also believes in the desired performance. The big picture of what is expected is provided to the organization by its complete integration into the organization's culture and systems and through alignment of organizational resources. It is up to the leadership to create that big picture and contextualize it for the organization's various elements through systems and consistent behavior. But that does not mean you should divide the big picture into smaller snapshots and say, "Here's yours" to the various organizational departments. IPL requires that the organization's people understand how they as individuals and as subset collectives contribute to the organization's success. Ahhhh, success. This, too, must be defined and should be an integral centerpiece of the big picture.

Measurable success is addressed in the *performance* piece of IPL. Success means different things to different organizations. For example, Amazon.com could be defined by stockholders as a very successful company, but at the time of this writing, it has not yet turned a profit. Success for Amazon means growing the business (growing the top line), gaining market share, and doing so by developing consumer confidence. In defining the performance expectations of the company, Amazon shares with its members a vision of diversification and process streamlining so that they may reinvest in their mutual futures. Organizational members understand the big picture and know how they, as individuals and collectively, contribute to organizational performance. Leadership has established internal systems to support the performance expectations of the organization and actually eliminate the possibility of flawed localized leadership. For example, if someone is directed to "get the product out," they can do so only within the performance expectations of the organization. The leadership of the organization has established internal systems to foster the performance they desire, and in turn they have created an organizational culture that emulates those desires for fast and reliable performance. You need only to watch one of Amazon's television commercials to see that it focuses on making the output of its services a value proposition to the customer—and one that is greater than any competitor's. I do not mean to imply that Amazon has engaged in the concept of IPL, but from the vantage point of an outside observer, it has placed its focus on creating value for the customer and establishing the internal systems to ensure sustained performance.

So what is the *leadership* piece of IPL all about? If we design a system to perform in a certain manner, shouldn't that reduce the need for leadership to effective management of the existing routines? Absolutely not! Leadership is key to organizational success. To return to the car example, the leaders of the manufacturer define the design of the vehicle and contextualize it to the intended operational environment—sports car versus SUV and on-road versus on-and-off-road operation. They anticipate a market need and provide for such. As owners of the vehicle, we decide to maintain or alter the vehicle to perform to our unique needs, including our unique environmental situations. As *managers,* we would only maintain the vehicle within the specifications of the manufacturer. The result would be normal operation within a predictable state of decay. As *leaders* of this system, we can opt to upgrade or modify in response to changes in our environment and our performance needs. This will prolong system deterioration and may even result in the creation of a totally new system to serve new needs. For example, because of desire or need, the owner of a car can change the car so much that the only remaining artifact of the original car is its hood ornament (that is, company logo). Such is also true in organizational settings, especially given the many mergers and acquisitions we see today. The important element here is that as leaders of systems and people, we make choices that can influence both short- and long-term success and survival.

In organizational settings managers ensure the continuation of the day-to-day functions of the organization. Leaders, on the other hand, understand the big picture of the organization. The big picture is the overall vision, overall objectives, and a clear understanding of how each of the integrated subparts contributes to overall success. It also includes a clear understanding of the organization's internal and external environments as well as of where the organization is heading, and not just in the here and now, but for years out (See Figure 1.2).

The organizational system that is completely integrated and whose measures of success are absolutely linked and led by individuals who can anticipate the need for change and ensure such in an integrated fashion is not common. Why is this so? Probably because we get caught up in trying to make the short-term numbers and fail to recognize and understand (or purposely ignore) the long-term implications. And that is most likely the result of the influences of Wall Street and the day-to-day expectations of analysts

Figure 1.2 The responsibility of leadership is to make sense of organizational signals, to communicate direction and vision, and to facilitate understanding.

for big headlines and numbers from companies. We may also fail to perceive the need for change because we make organizations so complex that the only way to understand what is to be done is to slice and dice the organization into suboptimal pieces with little perspective of the whole.

The secret to success is to understand the market and to deliver what it needs at the most competitive price. To enable that objective, leaders must ensure that the organizational design and performance expectations are understood and are not overly complex. Integrated performance leadership addresses the complete organizational dynamic with the objective of reducing organizational complexity and increasing capability, and in turn reducing waste in materials and action. The more complex an organization's design, the greater the probability that it will fail and increase the number of times work must be processed. We could look at the writings of quality leaders such as Deming (1972, 1980, 1986) and Juran (1969, 1974, 1992) to understand how variation is the enemy of quality performance and, in turn, customer satisfaction. Deming (1980) claims that 85 percent of all nonconformances are attributable to an organization's system design.

Based on my own observations in organizations (albeit not totally scientific), I believe that 99 percent of all nonconformances and system failures are the fault and responsibility of leadership. After all, it is the leadership's responsibility to design, maintain, and change the organizational system. It's also leadership's responsibility to secure resources and design workflow so that workers can effectively and efficiently perform their functions, to ensure that other leaders have the capacity and capability to lead in the fashion appropriate to the desired culture, and to ensure that employees have the skills and knowledge to perform within the system. This needs to be supported through the processes of both hiring and training. The other 1 percent of nonconformances could be attributed to nature—stuff sometimes happens that shall just remain unexplainable or uncontrollable. Because of its rarity, this 1 percent should never be used as an excuse in organizations.

But in the spirit of keeping it simple, we can look at Darwin's theory of evolution. You either have a system that meets the environment you are in or the system will cease to exist—it's only a matter of time. An organization's leaders must understand the current and future environments they must perform in or they will not be around to play the game. In the social sciences, this is referred to as *requisite variety*; I will return to that in the next chapter. The events of late 2001 and 2002, where business leaders felt they could ignore the laws of the social environment and get away with it are an excellent example of the need to maintain congruency between the actions and behaviors of leaders and the environment. Who would have thought that companies the size of Enron, Arthur Andersen, and Global Crossing could be brought down by the unethical behavior of a few top leaders? Unfortunately, the environment responded with more laws, greater scrutiny, and loss of consumer trust.

In today's world, trust is becoming more and more important and confidence and integrity more valued. Citizens need to trust that the various governmental agencies will ensure their security and welfare. Investors want to trust that corporate leaders are engaging in ethical behavior. Employees want to believe that the organizations they work for care about them and have a sustainable business model for the future. And customers want to have the confidence that they will receive what they have paid for. The reality is, if you don't plan and control for these expectations, they will not be met. There must be more responsibility throughout all of our social systems, and we must bring defined processes to our actions to achieve our desired outcomes. Granted, advances in technology, such as the concept of disruptive technology (the replacement of existing technology with a completely new solution) (Christensen 1997), will always attract attention, but unless those advances can deliver what people want or need, they may have little value or application. The organizations that will have the competitive edge are those that can deliver according to the needs of their customers and sustain their business through a competitive cost structure and a healthy organizational culture.

Organizations that seek to influence the performance of their people must understand the relationship of behavior to performance. If behavior does not align with performance, the organization cannot create the intended customer value. To influence behavior, organizations must recognize that people behave in accordance with what they believe or understand to be correct. The belief structure of a person is based on understanding—that is, that which they have personalized and with which they make meaning. The ways in which an organization communicates appropriate and consistent understanding to its people become critical to success. Whether that is done through training, procedures and policies, verbal communication, or leadership behavior, the method is something an organization can control through a process perspective. The more fragmented these vehicles are, the more out of control behavior, and in turn performance, will be. A type of communication that many organizations don't recognize as powerful is the environment in which they allow their people to perform. The environment is itself one of the more powerful communication tools because it is constant. Whereas a procedure or verbal communication delivers its message at the time it is read or spoken, an environment is there when you look up or turn around. Recognizing the power of organizing direction and of understanding and influencing behavior is clearly a choice of leadership—to do it or not.

The following chapters speak to the various dimensions of IPL, namely the aspects of a social organization and the need for integration; the need for defining what good looks like or for establishing the definition of performance expectations, including the alignment of cost and resource accountability; and the aspects of leadership—its influence throughout the organizational system, and its relationship to performance and customer focus. The appendices address the challenges of implementation and provide examples of tools that can help improve organizational performance.

I discuss the concept of managing organizational knowledge throughout the book. To facilitate the understanding of treating knowledge management as a process, I introduce the concept of *integrated knowledge management* (IKM) as an integral tool of IPL. I also introduce the VISION (verify, investigate, standardize, integrate, optimize, no recurrence) process as a pragmatic methodology for integrating the resources of the organization in performance challenges and continuous improvement. The VISION process is not intended to compete with other quality tools or methodologies in practice today, but rather it provides an integrated platform to bring the various tools of an organization together for great effect on performance.

I've written the book for a wide audience. Practitioners are provided tools, senior leadership is provided pragmatic *so what?*s, and the academic community is provided the references upon which the concept is structured. Given this approach, a different style of writing is applied in attempt to provide a blended vocabulary of substance. I encourage any reader who finds a particular area of IPL of interest to consult the reference material and develop a deeper understanding of the theories. It is this comprehension and ability to share understanding that makes leaders believable.

2
Integration

In Chapter 1 we discussed the aspects of a system and the need for that system to be integrated and focused on the customer. We considered the construct of system integration in such a manner as to illustrate that without it we have suborganizations functioning either in isolation of the greater organization or as inefficient contributors to the holistic organization. The truth of the matter is, if an organization does not have the characteristics of integrated business processes and synergy in action, then it is generating significant waste and suboptimizing the creation of value for the customer. Consider our airline example of mass system confusion and generation of waste—not to mention customer dissatisfaction. The responsibility of leaders is to their people and to the organization. With such responsibility, it is essential for a leader to understand why integration is important and a little behind the theory. After all, as a leader one must be able to help others understand why something is important and help them contextualize it and apply it in practice to change their own situation and make it become personal.

In this chapter I address aspects of system integration related to the following:

- Constant change (requisite variety)

- Organizational structure (synergy in resources)

- Reporting lines (dotted versus solid)

- Communicating vision and direction (one voice)

- Implications for culture (harmonized action and understanding)

- Tools for integration and the management of variation (statistical process control, Six Sigma, and the like)

- A defined system of action (policies and procedures)
- System validation, including performance measures (making sure the system works)
- Feedback mechanisms (proactive evaluation)
- Changing the system of defined action (integrated change)

This chapter is by far the longest in the book. The concept of integration is very broad and touches on people, leadership, processes, environment, and finances. I offer numerous references to other works in this chapter, and the reader is encouraged to consult these other works to gain an even deeper understanding of the concepts discussed.

THE THEORY OF INTEGRATION

Many researchers who have focused on organizational system design have some link in their research to the theory of evolution. Darwin put it quite simply when he said that the survival of an organism depends on its ability to change in response to the evolving environment (see Figure 2.1). His research focused on the various aspects of biology that either facilitated system evolution and fostered continued existence or did not and ensured extinction. From those observations the term *requisite variety* was established, which means that a system has sufficient capabilities to recognize the need for change and to integrate new characteristics or capabilities into its being to sustain its existence.

Figure 2.1 As your environment changes so must you or suffer the consequences of extinction.

In the world of sociology, Darwin's research has been expanded to relate to organizational infrastructure and performance and an organization's ability to recognize and adapt to changing environments. This area of thought is referred to as *social Darwinism*. If you learn nothing else in reading this book, remember the concept of social Darwinism. Either an organization can recognize the need for change and can integrate change, or it will cease to be an organization. One must recognize the changing needs of customers before there are no customers. Equally important for an organization to recognize is that over time it may have drifted away from meeting the needs of the customer and complying with the expectations of the environment. This is referred to as *environmental creep*—is gradual and frequently not obvious until it is too late. As for those leaders who don't appreciate the need to understand change, they should be prepared to experience the concept of being irrelevant.

One of my favorite illustrations of this concept is the boiling frog. If you were to attempt to place a frog in a pot of boiling water, it would most probably jump out of it immediately. The sudden shock of temperature change is obvious and undesirable. However, if you were to place the same frog in a pot of cool water and gradually allow the temperature to increase, it would most likely not notice the increase and perish. The challenge for an organization is to establish processes for scanning its environment constantly to preclude becoming a cooked frog.

A major shortcoming of most new performance improvement concepts is that they are rarely based on science, theory, or research. They are frequently repackaged tools created according to fad or are incomplete abstractions from theory. And if they are based on theory and science, they may be influenced by one single frame of reference. This is where integrated performance leadership significantly differs. IPL attempts to recognize benefits from various ontological frames of reference to better understand the diverse factors that influence organizational performance. IPL has deep roots in the fields of sociology as well as education, psychology, management, quality, operations, and of course, business. IPL takes theories and models from the various fields of science and brings them together as an integrated path of thought.

As leaders in organizations, we each typically have a pedigree that represents one clear path of science that provides us a lens through which we perceive the world. For example, procurement leaders will have a foundation of learning in business or economics. Engineering leaders typically have a background in technical sciences, and lawyers, in jurisprudence. Each discipline is typically bound to a community of science, research, and understanding that has framed its perspective, which is rarely a holistic perspective of the complete organization. It is important that we create a bridge across the various fields, to create an integrated perspective to applied theory and to empower leaders to engage in broader forms of thought and action. In this section, and throughout this book, I discuss various models and concepts. The objective is not only to provoke readers to think but also to provide a frame of reference to theory so that readers can pursue research for their own needs.

For example, researchers such as David Schwandt (1993; Schwandt and Gundlach 1992) and Peter Senge (1990a; Senge and Sterman 1992) have written about organizational learning and leadership in great detail, each emphasizing the importance of systems and behavior in the organization. Schwandt's organizational learning model (see Figure 2.2) is a primary consideration in IPL because it provides a framework for organizing the sense-making processes of the organization to foster a process of learning and retention. This is an important aspect of organizing in that as organizations make sense of what's going on around them, they make business decisions.

The better or more comprehensive the sense-making processes are in an organization, the more aligned decisions will be with the actual needs of the business. Given the dynamic characteristics of Schwandt's model, the process of organizational learning becomes alive and measurable. Considered as a process, it can be managed, controlled, and integrated into the routines of the organization. The individual constructs of *environmental interface, action/reflection, meaning and memory,* and *dissemination and diffusion* can be perceived as destinations, and the interchange media as the active processes that link the constructs. For example, the construct environmental interface would contain a number of mechanisms for collecting new information. These could include participating in industry forums or listening to comments from customers. This information may need to be acted upon, and that action is determined in the action/reflection construct, but it's not enacted there. The construct dissemination and diffusion, which relates to the specific act of integration and is implicit in leadership discretion, enacts the appropriate actions. The meaning and memory construct is employed throughout the process to account for the resident knowledge and to update such accordingly. I offer this model not to make you an expert in organizational learning processes, but rather to develop a perspective that the organization can be viewed as a system of interchange and major constructs. Recognizing that these are established in each of our own organizations allows us to map our processes of action and account for performance and variance.

As organizations gain a clearer picture of their processes for action, they typically find that they suffer from fragmentation and suboptimization. Peter Senge (1990) argues that the main dysfunctions in our institutions are fragmentation, competition, and reactiveness, which are caused by human society's conditioning of being able to conquer the physical world. That is, we

The Dynamics of Organizational Learning

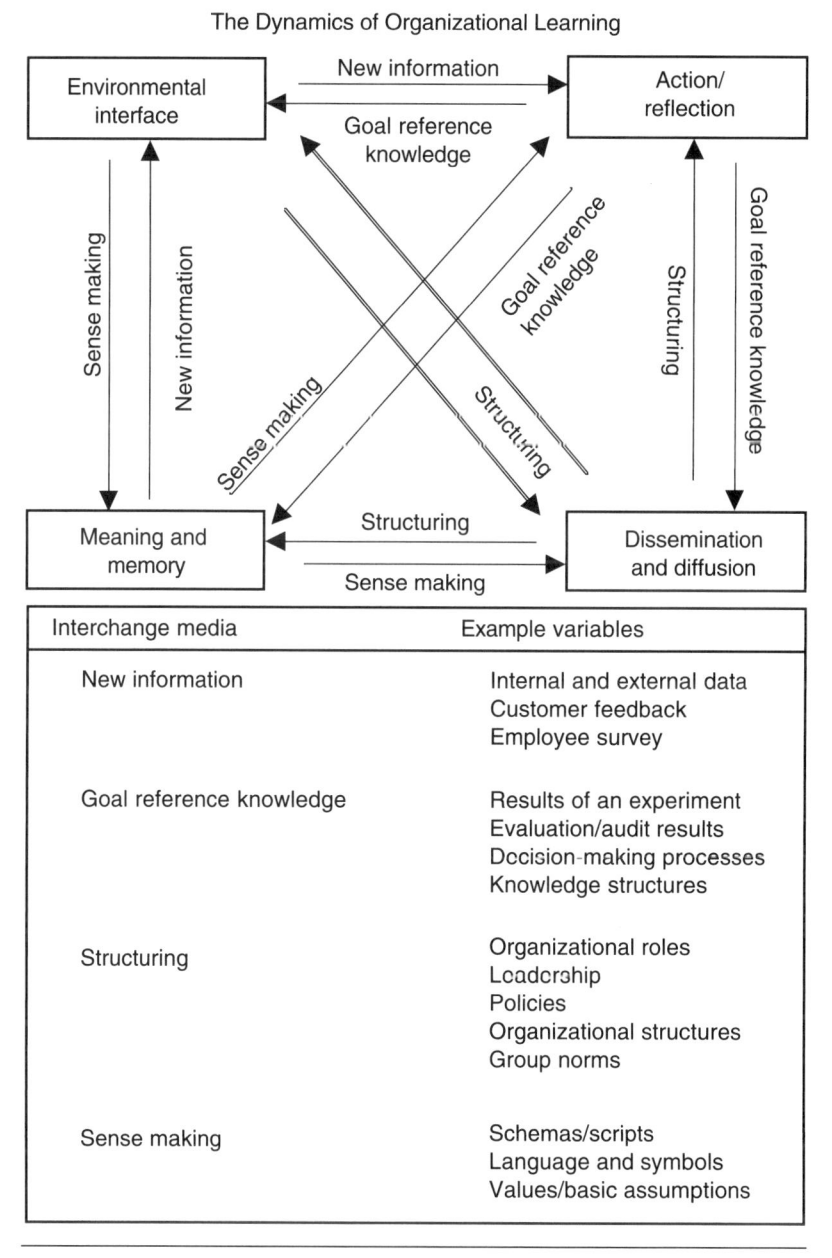

Interchange media	Example variables
New information	Internal and external data Customer feedback Employee survey
Goal reference knowledge	Results of an experiment Evaluation/audit results Decision-making processes Knowledge structures
Structuring	Organizational roles Leadership Policies Organizational structures Group norms
Sense making	Schemas/scripts Language and symbols Values/basic assumptions

Figure 2.2 Schwandt's organizational learning model.

have evolved to compartmentalize our thought processes and our recognition for what we are accountable for. He further suggests that fragmentation is the cornerstone of what it means to be a professional, so much so that we call ourselves "specialists." Because organizations are not integrated with respect to knowledge capability, we depend on individuals with great depth, and possibly little breadth, to perform work in silo organizations. It is when we are able to integrate the work needs of the business with the knowledge capabilities of the organization, and treat that as a process, that we finally break through and think as a whole as opposed to a collection of functions. This is where leadership comes in.

In his consideration of leaders' roles, Senge (1990b) suggests that a leader should be a designer, a steward, and a teacher to the organization and its members. These leader traits include the responsibility for ensuring learning through personal action and system design, which includes the processes of integration. As is discussed in Chapter 4, leadership is about making choices, making decisions, and taking action.

When organizations take action, that action must be targeted and with a specific intent in mind. Aimless effort is equal to waste. However, the science of organizing can be confusing, giving one a vast amount of opinions to choose from. The art is in recognizing what is science and what is opinion. IPL takes from many different scientific disciplines, but one of the more influential is the seminal work of Talcott Parsons and his theory of action. Parsons (1937, 1951, 1959, 1960, 1983) wrote from the 1930s to the 1980s on the dynamic nature of organizations and suggested that action within an organization be considered in four constructs, which he referred to as *functional prerequisites*—adaptation, goal attainment, integration, and pattern maintenance. Parsons's (1960) thesis on organization allowed the collective organization to be studied as a social system of interchange—as a process of integration. Schwandt later built upon Parsons' work with his organizational learning model. Using the social action system as the culture construct provides social action variables amenable to measurement. Again, once measurement potential exists, then we have the opportunity for treating the system as a process that can be controlled and improved. Parsons also refers to the individuals within the system, who have responsibility for action, as *actors* (Bluth 1982). In IPL, the actors are leaders, regardless of where they find themselves in the organizational strata.

If we look at Parsons's functional prerequisites (see Figure 2.3) we can see in the model that he addresses the need for an organization to adapt to its changing environment through the *adaptation* construct, without which he predicts the degrading of an organization's integrity, and eventual failure. As noted in the discussion of social Darwinism, the organization must have requisite variety to sustain its existence. Parsons also addresses the

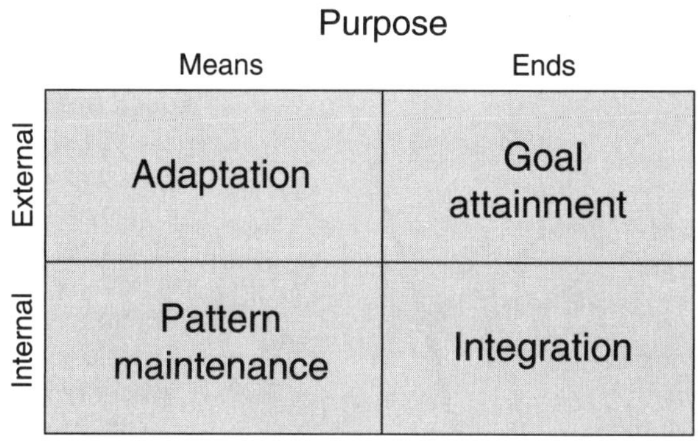

	Purpose	
	Means	Ends
External	Adaptation	Goal attainment
Internal	Pattern maintenance	Integration

Figure 2.3 Parsons's four functional prerequisites (theory of action).

need for explicitly defining goals and understanding how to get there. Parsons does that through his *goal attainment* construct. This usually takes the form of procedures that direct the day-to-day actions of the business and heavily influence the processes of sense making. Within the goal attainment construct we would also find aspects of the work environment and culture that influence the ways in which the organization engages in sense making.

Ensuring that the organization has an established synergy is addressed in the *integration* construct. This is where the ingredients of leadership are key in determining what actions will occur in the organization. To reduce waste, synergy is a must, as is the need to establish a homeostatic condition within the organization—a sense of balance. In a truly homeostatic environment, a system has realized a balance of all the internal elements; if the system were closed it would continue forever without the need to add additional energy. *Closed systems* are those that are completely isolated from any and all external influences. Closed systems do not and will not ever exist in the realm of social systems, so we need to understand the aspect of having to add energy to and realign our open systems to maintain or strive for homeostasis (see Figure 2.4).

The more homeostatic, or balanced, an organization is, the fewer resources are needed to sustain performance. Take, for example, a ball. In itself the ball has no energy to roll. However, if an input is provided to the ball it can move in a direction. However, the forces of nature, such as friction and gravity, will cause the ball to slow and eventually stop—this is referred to as *entropy*. The more energy that is provided the ball, the more movement it will have. If dependable and constant energy is provided as inputs to the ball, and it can maintain a constant movement and direction, then it has achieved a homeostatic condition—for the time being.

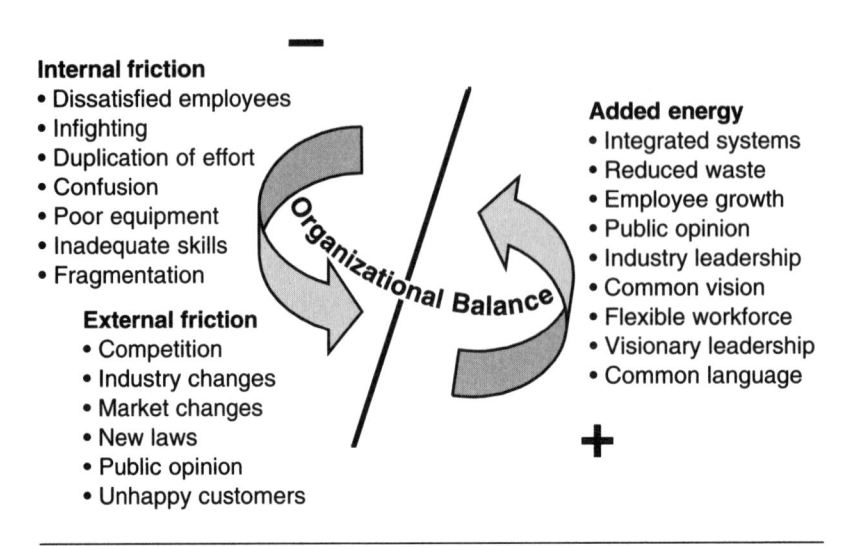

Internal friction
- Dissatisfied employees
- Infighting
- Duplication of effort
- Confusion
- Poor equipment
- Inadequate skills
- Fragmentation

External friction
- Competition
- Industry changes
- Market changes
- New laws
- Public opinion
- Unhappy customers

Added energy
- Integrated systems
- Reduced waste
- Employee growth
- Public opinion
- Industry leadership
- Common vision
- Flexible workforce
- Visionary leadership
- Common language

Figure 2.4 Entropy and homeostasis.

Now picture an organization with all of its bits and pieces, and try to imagine it as a ball attempting to maintain momentum to go somewhere. If there are bumps on the ball, it will not go straight. If the ball is too heavy, it will require significantly more energy than other balls to move forward. And if the ball cannot hold itself together as a single unit or will not follow a predictable path because of defects, it will loose its ability to function as a ball altogether and actually will require a different kind of energy to ensure movement. One additional aspect of this organizational ball is that if no one wants to play with it because it does not meet their needs or interest, it will not have a purpose and will not receive the needed energy to roll. Take, for example, an American football in a basketball game. One cannot bounce a football with any certainty that it will come back to its intended hand. So the football will have no application for the environment. However, if the football's owners were influential in changing the environment, they could create a new game, either within the basketball court environment by simply changing the rules or, with more difficulty, by changing the perception of the players and spectators, or they might create an entirely new venue for the ball altogether. What is implied here is changing the environment. To do so in nature is nearly impossible but doing so in social systems is clearly a matter of choice, influence, and knowhow.

Parsons (1937) addresses the need for maintaining balance within the organizational system through his *pattern maintenance* construct. In it the organization continuously monitors its environment and makes changes in system design, memory, or established goals to ensure survival. How many times have we seen organizations become complacent because of their temporal success, only to fall on the proverbial sword because they did not recognize the need to change? Recall our automobile system example. Up until the late 1970s, most cars were powered with leaded fuels that provided a lubrication characteristic to the car's engine. With the passing of U.S. legislation to protect the environment, leaded fuels were to be phased out in all new production vehicles. This required many manufacturers to modify the delivered systems of their vehicles to provide engines that functioned on unleaded fuels. Though few, if any, manufacturers were caught off guard by this change, some were better prepared than others. Those that were designing well in advance of the law change were able to deliver efficient vehicles with predictable performance. On the other hand, those that were not as well prepared found that either their designs did not enjoy high reliability ratings or they were forced to procure engines from the companies that got it right. Thus is illustrated the need for an organization (and in this case, a complete industry) to continuously monitor its environment for change and adapt to it appropriately (see Figure 2.5).

Figure 2.5 Organizations must find a balance with their internal and external environments.

In the following pages I address the various aspects of organizational integration. As you plan for integration, it is important to address vision, business planning, structure, and systems to ensure consistency in expectations and messages while maintaining a focus on establishing value for the customer. Keep in mind the theoretical references that we have discussed when you think about your own organization and how it is organized to ensure that waste is minimized, learning maximized, and processes integrated.

AN INTEGRATED ORGANIZATIONAL STRUCTURE

The purpose of an organizational structure is to create a method of deploying responsibility and accountability throughout a social system to most efficiently execute the action for which the organization was created. In most cases, an organization is created to provide value to customers who are willing to pay for that value. However, in public settings the purpose of the organization is to provide services of value to its society—safety and economics. In both cases, the organization's purpose is to provide value. Let's look at a common structural design of an organization in the private sector. Most have a president, a series of vice presidents, a number of directors, an abundance of managers, a scattering of team leaders, and a population of doers (see Figure 2.6). At the level of the president there is an overall expectation for performance. The business metrics the president looks for are those that provide the greatest value to the stakeholders of the organization. Typically, for publicly owned private-sector companies, these are

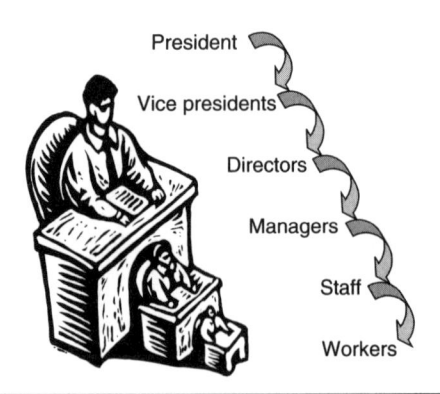

Figure 2.6 Traditional organizational structure.

the metrics that will impress Wall Street the most—top- and bottom-line performance expectations and results. We'll talk about performance metrics in the next chapter.

The president typically maintains an executive council made up of a number of the senior process or profit-and-loss owners in the organization, typically at the senior or executive vice president level. They each bring to the company a field of knowledge and a way of seeing things. Simply because they are human and have undergone education and training, these functional leaders are biased in their methods of interaction and interpretation. Rarely do we find an organization whose senior functional representation is willing to see the organization as a holistic entity as opposed to functional subparts. And even if those people espouse the expectation of working as one company, as when they deploy initiatives such as integrated product and process deployment/development (IPPD), they rarely know how to operationalize such initiatives and resort to linkages as opposed to integration.

At the next level down on the organizational ladder are the directors and managers, who are heavily influenced by their immediate leadership and will either perform within a functional stovepipe or an integrated system. That all depends on system design, how we measure success, and how we choose to lead. Visualize boats leaving a harbor. Initially, they all appear to be sailing in the same direction, yet each may be a couple of degrees off in its heading. As the boats travel further from the point of origin, their slightly different courses give them significant distance from each other. The same is true in organizations. However, the closer we get to the actual work of the organization, the higher the probability that we may find ad hoc collaboration in the organizational system. Out of the need to meet the immediate production or service needs of the organization, localized teams will have a greater tendency to work together. This typically arises more out of necessity than out of system design, and it poses a high risk for the organization—particularly in the area of sustainability. As the signals of leadership vary and the localized objectives are modified, the ability to sustain informal integration and collaboration becomes compromised. If not integrated in purpose and action, lower-level teams may actually erode organizational performance by meeting their localized objectives at the expense of the success of the whole. Unless integrated, the aggregates of the individual successes will rarely equal the performance objectives of the whole.

Because leaders become more insulated from the actual work of the organization as they rise higher in the organizational hierarchy, we typically find that integration becomes looser the higher you go. It is frequently acceptable for senior leaders to say that they will leave the details to the lower levels of the organization to figure out. But if the senior leadership is allowed to vary in their vision and direction, it is unlikely that any action can be effective and sustainable—cost, delivery, or quality. The execution of work can be treated as an integrated process only if the organization thinks in terms of executors of integrated business processes. Variance in purpose and understanding must be treated as something that must itself be controlled and eliminated.

So what can an organization do to ensure integration? We must purposefully design its business processes for organizational integration. The practice of maintaining functional departments for specific skills and responsibilities may still be appropriate in many industrial settings, but definitely not to the degree that most companies are structured. It is important to maintain functional leadership and expertise in areas such as engineering, sales, human resources, and quality, but the workforce need not be stovepiped.

The objective of any organization is to be nimble, efficient, consistent, and fast in its actions. For-profit organizations want to convert their energies into revenues as cost-efficiently as possible so that the measurable value of the organization increases. Not-for-profit organizations wish to meet the intent of their charter so that services can be provided when they are needed most—for example, the Red Cross in times of disaster. Governmental bodies seek to deliver services and structure in the most efficient manner to their citizens while maintaining the protocol that governs them—as in the case of the Constitution and laws of the United States. To enable such capabilities, resources and leadership signals must be integrated through robust and well-understood processes. To provide one cookie-cutter solution for organization design is not prudent. Depending on the organization's culture, its population, whether it is in the private or public sector, its products, and so many other variables, the organization must find its own way to organize to ensure success. However, the only way to manage an organization effectively is to treat organizing as a process.

Recognizing that organizations can structure themselves in a number of different forms, I'd like to focus on five major organizational constructs: *life-cycle business processes, value streams, functional leadership, cost centers and the supply chain, and communities of practice.*

Life-cycle Business Processes

Every organization's business processes have life cycles; organizational leaders should acknowledge this early, as well as the need to think in terms of an integrated business. The product or service that is provided does not care what department an individual reports to; all that is important is that the processes executed in creating value are capable. To keep the concept of life-cycle business process simple, lets consider the work of the organization in four specific phases: concept, design, production and delivery, and service. In each phase, a number of processes occur depending on the maturity of the product or service. For example, in the *concept* phase of a new product, a number of activities will be occurring that may not occur for a more mature product. For a new product the organization may engage processes to determine customer interest, whereas for a mature product it may be looking for customer feedback for potential product improvements.

By identifying the processes that have to happen in the organization to ensure that it can meet customer expectations, as well as those processes that ensure long-term survival, and mapping them to the phases of the life-cycle business processes, the organization gains an understanding of the interrelated nature of its business. This creates a level of visibility that cannot be created otherwise. Then, questions of *who* and *how* can be asked of a process, as well as *when* and *why*. Who is doing this process, how and when is it being performed, and why are we doing it? Can it be done in a more robust and cost-efficient manner? Has the process been fragmented as a result of our functional thinking? If we had a clean sheet of paper, how would we align and deploy the processes of the business? These are all necessary questions we need to ask of the alignment and design of the organization's business processes, and more than just once. This should be done periodically to ensure congruency between organizational alignment of processes and the needs of the business environment.

Figure 2.7 provides an example of a *life-cycle business process map*. Although work activities exist that will be logical for the phase alignment, the concept that a process is deployed throughout the complete life cycle is also important—this speaks to the *when* of the questioning. A process may have aspects that are deployed over multiple phases, and the *when* question exposes the timing to ensure they are planned for. Additionally, feedback mechanisms between phases provide bridges of communication around process design and performance. For example, if in the servicing phases of the life cycle the organization receives feedback from customers regarding the product or service, that feedback needs to find its way back upstream in the life cycle to ensure that not only corrective actions but also preventative actions are taken. If the feedback suggests that a business process is flawed, there is no reason to suspect that that business process will not yield more problems for existing and future products unless changed. So, in mapping the business processes, consider how bridges are created between the phases. In the organizational learning model discussed earlier, this would be considered *interchange media*. One additional consideration is that of human capability in the life cycle. In a later chapter, I'll introduce the concept of integrated knowledge management, which blends in with this mapping

28 Chapter Two

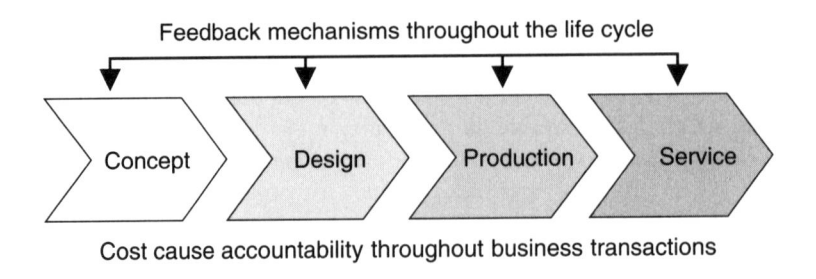

Figure 2.7 Life cycle macro business processes.

process and ensures that corporate knowledge is aligned with business processes. But what the organization must consider in its deployment of business processes are the methods of ensuring that people have the requisite knowledge and applied capability to deal with what is expected of them.

In the *concept* phase, the organization undertakes the processes of marketing, understanding customer requirements, alignment of design and production capability, contract review, internal audit, and any other process that aligns early in the business cycle prior to the actual design of the product or service. Herein resides early opportunities for deploying quality tools for mistake proofing and establishing capable processes for subsequent actions. An ounce of prevention is worth much more than a pound of rework. Organizations should consider as early as possible how they intend to execute the potential products and services, and not wait until later. To commit to a customer and then fail is much more costly than making the early investment in establishing capability. Figure 2.8 illustrates how this phase could look. However, each organization needs to use its own terms and processes in this alignment.

The *design* phase is where the organization creates the actual design of what will be produced. For example, here an insurance organization constructs a policy product with specific requirements for eligibility and terms of claims. Or a product manufacturer considers technology applications and validation processes. However, technology readiness should not be addressed in this phase. The concept phase is the point at which such conceptual decisions are made, prior to a major investment and commitment to customers. Again, investment in ensuring process and design capability in this early phase will prevent costly rework in later phases. Figure 2.9 provides a sample of a design process map.

The *production and delivery* phase addresses the actual execution of work that generates revenue for the organization. Some of the processes include production planning, where work instructions are created; first-article

Integration 29

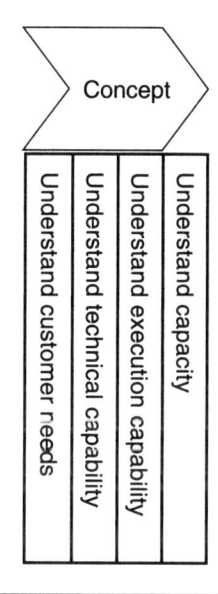

Figure 2.8 Example of the concept phase.

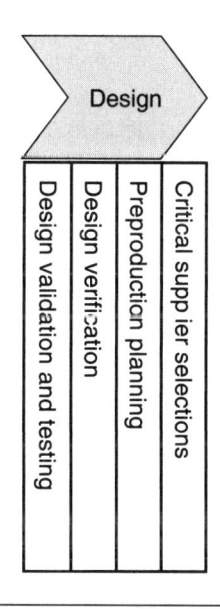

Figure 2.9 Example of design process map.

inspections; tooling; training; nonconformance handling; process capability; testing; packaging; handling; and shipping, as well as many others. This phase is typically longer than the two previous ones in that the production of the product will usually run longer than its concept and design. This brings with it greater need for consideration for sustainability of the processes, particularly with regard to capability and capacity. Ideally, once learning has occurred around capability and capacity, that learning will be transferred upstream to influence the business models in the concept and design phases.

As an example of the processes that occur during the production and delivery phase, consider the work of a hospital. The primary purpose of the hospital is to provide care (service) to its patients (customers). The doctors, nurses, receptionists, lab technicians, administrative support, janitorial support, security, marketing, and other support staff are all elements of an integrated macro business process. There are also external members who are important to the success of the macroprocesses of the organization, such as ambulance crews transporting incoming patients and paramedics administering emergency care in advance of hospital doctors. Ideally, the organization has mapped out the various work activities of the hospital and understands the interrelationship of the processes and has ensured that expected skills match resident skills. These interrelationships must effectively manage the transfer of knowledge and appropriate alignment of accountability. Incidents of the wrong limb being removed in surgery or the incorrect drug being administered because of poor process control should never occur. Performance data from important work processes must be continuously monitored, and near misses must be treated as if the event actually occurred. Learning during this phase must be integrated wherever possible in the business processes of the organization, the further upstream the better. For example, as learning occurs about a specific treatment, that knowledge needs to travel upstream to the design phase to ensure that standard treatments throughout the hospital are updated and improved—or even further upstream to be integrated into the university learning system to ensure future caregivers have the latest knowledge.

In the production and delivery phase, standard protocols would be revised and hospital members trained in changed processes. The members accountable for supply logistics would be advised of potentially changed drug requirements so that they can modify their procurement plans. And the integration goes on to consider any possible interrelationship with change in the work processes. Accountability must be clearly managed as well. For example, if the hospital expects that patients will not wait longer than 20 minutes for any given visit, who in the organization is responsible to ensure this doesn't occur? It's only based on my experience, but I think most hospitals don't manage this process much at all. There must be identifiable accountability for all aspects of the business processes; if not, they will not be controlled. Figure 2.10 provides a sample of a production and delivery process map.

The *service* phase offers a great opportunity to understand the value the organization is creating for the customer. This is also a phase most organizations neglect as a learning tool because they treat it as a separate profit-and-loss center as opposed to an integrated business process. Take, for example, the service center at a car dealership. In the service phase the organization can interact with the customer while providing services to support the product. Information on reliability, user friendliness, applicability, cost, timeliness, and so on can be gained and should be sent upstream to the other business processes. Yes, the service phase does represent a significant opportunity for the organization to grow its revenues, but the returns of knowledge are potentially even greater. Developing the capability to predict customer needs and desires can contribute to developing products quicker than the competitors. Updating designs to address customer complaints or concerns in a timely fashion can prevent the customer from looking elsewhere for the product. Understanding the challenges the organization subjects the customer to in conducting business can prompt better relationship processes that increase ease and convenience in interaction. If you don't think this last point is important, consider why banks are now located in

> Production

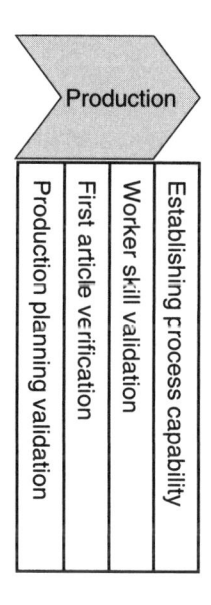

- Production planning validation
- First article verification
- Worker skill validation
- Establishing process capability

Figure 2.10 Example of production process map.

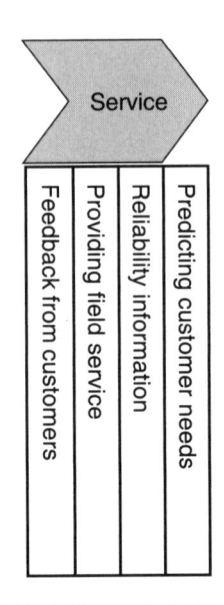

Figure 2.11 Example of service process map.

The Service phase includes: Feedback from customers, Providing field service, Reliability information, Predicting customer needs.

supermarkets—to make doing business with them more convenient. Imagine the potential for hospitals to reduce malpractice insurance claims if they actually understood what happened to their customers weeks, months, and years after services were provided and modified practice based on this learning. Figure 2.11 is a sample of some typical processes in the service phase.

Throughout the process definition activities you will ask the who, what, when, how, and why of the process. I suggest that you identify which organizational functions contribute to the execution of the process. This will further display the interrelated nature of the process among functional disciplines. The next step in process definition and deployment would be to align the procedures that describe the work, ensuring that they are aligned by process and not function.

Value-stream Structure

Another way to perceive the actions of an organization is as an integrated value stream. A *value stream* consists of the specific activities required to design, order, and provide a specific product from concept to launch, from order to delivery, and from raw materials into the hands of the customer (Womack and Jones 1996). Not unlike the perspective of the life-cycle business process map, but focused specifically on the product or service that is being delivered to the customer, a value-stream structure offers us a well-defined understanding of where value is being created and by whom. In most organizations, the value stream would be at a business level that represents a profit-and-loss entity and would itself contain multiple contributing value streams. It is when the organization considers itself as an overall enterprise of interrelated process and multiple value streams that it begins to think in terms of leveraging its actions and working toward becoming a lean enterprise. Some people have formed the odd perception that the term *lean* implies that the organization is bare bones. This is not true at all. A lean organization is one that has removed wasteful action from its business processes to ensure that the greatest value is being created from its investments. A lean organization should be one that is not only capable but also sustainable. For this reason, it is important to consider not only the aspects of work that contribute value directly to the customer but also those identified in the business processes of the life cycle model that ensure enabling actions, such as knowledge capability.

An organization can contain a number of business units, with some being defined as profit-and-loss entities (P&Ls for short). Conceptually, a P&L should be responsible for all the cost generators and investment factors that contribute to either financial profit or loss. Within a single P&L, there could also be multiple value streams depending on the diversity of the P&L's product portfolio. Overall, the P&L should be responsible for ensuring that all aspects of its value streams have the capability and capacity to do the job. Where most companies fall down in this model is in the alignment of resources, which I discuss in more detail in the following chapter. The elements of the value stream should be structured so that they are optimized for the execution of work. The juggling begins when multiple P&L leaders send signals to a single value stream. Clearly, providing a single model in this book that will work for every organization is impossible. However, the emphasis on visibility of capacity, capability, and expectations is key, and they must all be bound through accountability structures. In designing the organizational structure around value streams, one must consider what structural components are responsible for in work and who is responsible for the resources.

Some organizations that have initiated lean methods in their business processes also employ a structural process called integrated product and process development/deployment (IPPD) and have established integrated program management teams (IPMTs) to manage value stream. Depending on the type of business the organization operates in, it may focus its energy on products, projects, or programs. For example, in a large insurance company the structure may be developed around life, medical, and auto, which are products. But a software development or a jet engine–manufacturing organization may be structured around a program (for example, a specific word-processing package or a new-generation strike fighter). Whether the team is structured around a product or project is irrelevant; what is important is that it has the organizational freedom and structure to monitor overall performance of processes as they relate to delivery of value to the customer. Whereas the functional disciplines provide leadership within their field as a point of integration across the organization, the IPMT provides organizational integration through product focus. Figure 2.12 describes some of the typical functions of an IPMT. In many cases they would have responsibility for the financial spends throughout the organization so as to prevent cost overruns as well as to provide early indicators of performance misses. This means the IPMT typically has funding responsibility throughout the value stream to ensure success for the product, program, or project. As Womack and Jones point out in their book *Lean Thinking*, where one slice of the value stream may appear efficient and possibly even world class, in the broader view the value stream may be moving cost up or down the stream. The IPMT has the integration responsibility to eliminate waste throughout the entire value stream and to maintain a balance among the lines of business as well as with other IPMTs.

Within an IPMT there should be representation from every discipline necessary to develop, deploy, and maintain the product or program, but the team doesn't need to be as large as an army. This means that during the design phase there should be representation from the quality organization looking to mistakeproof the processes prior to deployment, procurement to address any sourcing issues prior to production, production to ensure that design and process capability are aligned, customer support to address service and maintainability issues as early as possible, and, of course, the design or engineering function to conceptualize and define the product but also to integrate the lessons learned from previous products to prevent the need for relearning.

Depending on the complexity and size of the product or service, an organization may need to create levels of responsibility within an IPMT structure. For example, a large, complex piece of equipment may have logical design modules that can be treated as sub–value streams. Though they are part of the greater value stream, the sub–value streams would focus their efforts specifically on the module they are responsible for. The same is true at the component level and at the part level.

The IPMT does not execute the actions or the work of the organization; it leads, manages, and ensures that all of the actions in the development and delivery of the deliverable product are accomplished and are consistent with the needs of the customer. The work resides within the line business, cost center, or supplier tasked with the aspect of the product applicable to them. Caution is advised here with regard to leadership signals. The IPMT may not send a signal to any level of the organization that conflicts with

IPMT

Integrated Program Management Team
- Oversee execution of program
- Share collective knowledge
- Act as single customer interface
- Ensure compliance to customer requirements
- Develop program strategies
- Communicate across and throughout value stream
- Ensure program-level knowledge capability
- Ensure program-level cost performance
- Ensure program-level quality performance
- Ensure resources throughout value stream
- Monitor reliability of products and services
- Monitor lower-level design/process changes
- Ensure systems integration

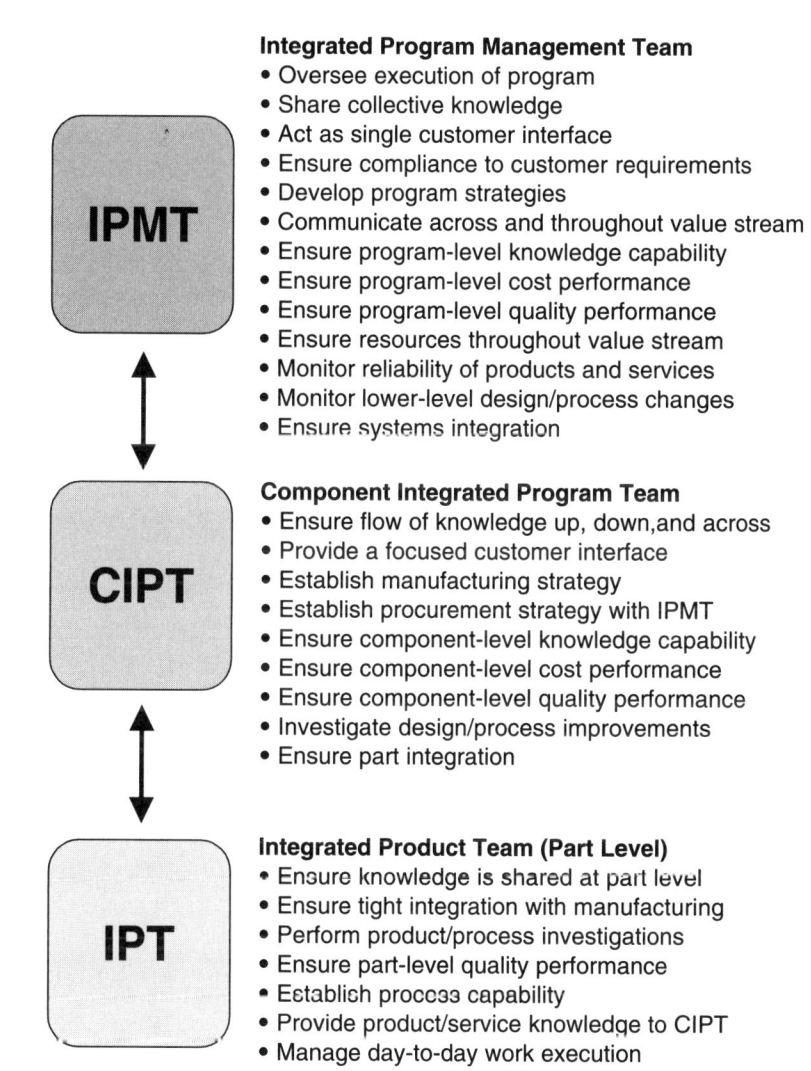

CIPT

Component Integrated Program Team
- Ensure flow of knowledge up, down, and across
- Provide a focused customer interface
- Establish manufacturing strategy
- Establish procurement strategy with IPMT
- Ensure component-level knowledge capability
- Ensure component-level cost performance
- Ensure component-level quality performance
- Investigate design/process improvements
- Ensure part integration

IPT

Integrated Product Team (Part Level)
- Ensure knowledge is shared at part level
- Ensure tight integration with manufacturing
- Perform product/process investigations
- Ensure part-level quality performance
- Establish process capability
- Provide product/service knowledge to CIPT
- Manage day-to-day work execution

Figure 2.12 Sample of IPMT roles and responsibilities (not all inclusive).

existing policies and procedures of the organization. This can severely upset the balance of the organization (homeostasis) and undermine the desired culture. Where there is a need for system change, such must be coordinated prior to execution. Defined expectations for action, also known as policies and procedures, are addressed later in this chapter. However, they are absolutely critical to ensure one pulse beat for action in the organization and throughout the value stream.

As for smaller, single-site organizations, the structure is similar to that of the multisite organization, except for of course the number of layers needed to serve the functions previously described. The IPMT may not need to comprise full-time positions, but rather the organization identifies team members who execute the responsibilities of an IPMT. But remember, if we feel something is important enough to do, we must either allocate sufficient resources to do it properly or not do it at all. Thus, if someone is filling many other roles in addition to their IPMT duties, their focus and performance obviously will be diluted across all of their responsibilities. In other words, "you get what you pay for." Regardless of the size or geographical separation of the organization, there must also be a test applied in establishing a structure.

Alignment of Functional Leadership

In the functional leadership model the functional disciplines are enablers, not executors, of process. One way of providing such leadership is through homerooms. A *homeroom* is little more than a structured focus on a process or functional discipline; it can be either a physical location or established through virtual means to manage a distributed organization. The key in structuring homerooms is to clearly identify leadership, expectations, and the value that is to be created.

The functional disciplines or process owners provide homeroom-type leadership value by ensuring that skills (knowledge capability) are at required levels, processes are executed as defined and standardized across the businesses, technology development is fostered and standardized, and capital equipment is standardized and capacity leveraged across the business. With the functional disciplines and process executors aligned throughout the processes, their primary focus is consistency in action, integration throughout the system, and sustainability of performance.

Functional discipline homerooms may also provide a level of work as a shared service throughout the organization. For example, in a manufacturing environment, the *quality* discipline may recognize an opportunity for providing a centralized service of nondestructive testing. This may be based on the expense of the equipment, volume of work, or any other rationale that makes sense. But in doing so, that discipline should consider itself in two roles—as a homeroom for standardization and capability development and as a cost center that must maintain focus on execution of work. Though a centralized function frequently fulfills this role of a homeroom, in practice it can be located anywhere in the organization where capability and capacity exist. Homerooms can be scattered throughout a large organization and integrated through process and systems.

To facilitate synergy within a function across a larger business, the concept of a *council* can be applied. Councils are different from homerooms in that councils are formed at a higher level of the organizational leadership and may have a number of homerooms under their leadership. For example, the quality council may have a quality engineering homeroom, special processing homeroom, and regulatory affairs homeroom, as well as others, and it will provide high-level guidance and direction.

There are two types of councils: one focuses on the leadership and functional level and the other on process and technology. The latter is discussed along with the structural model for communities of practice. A functional leadership council, such as a manufacturing council, would focus its efforts primarily in the direction of leadership within the function and across the business. It has a membership of functional discipline leaders who drive the process of the discipline throughout the business. A functional discipline leadership council also provides the structure for interaction among other functional leadership councils in and outside of the organization.

Cost Centers and the Supply Chain

An organization that has multiple sites or business units may be best organized where the functional disciplines such as quality, finance, engineering, facilities, and human resources are aligned throughout the process of value creation with the lines of business (P&L) on top of a matrix. Cost centers, or elements of the value stream, become the horizontal steps that execute work for the P&Ls. Because each cost center or sub value stream may support multiple P&Ls, it is important that balance be maintained among the P&Ls as to priorities and investment. The financial and performance aspects of the structure are addressed in the following chapter; however, it is important to recognize that there is a connection between organizational design and performance expectations (see Figure 2.13).

Communities of Practice (Councils)

Communities of practice should be created as needed to ensure that across the lines of P&Ls there are means for sharing knowledge that is process or

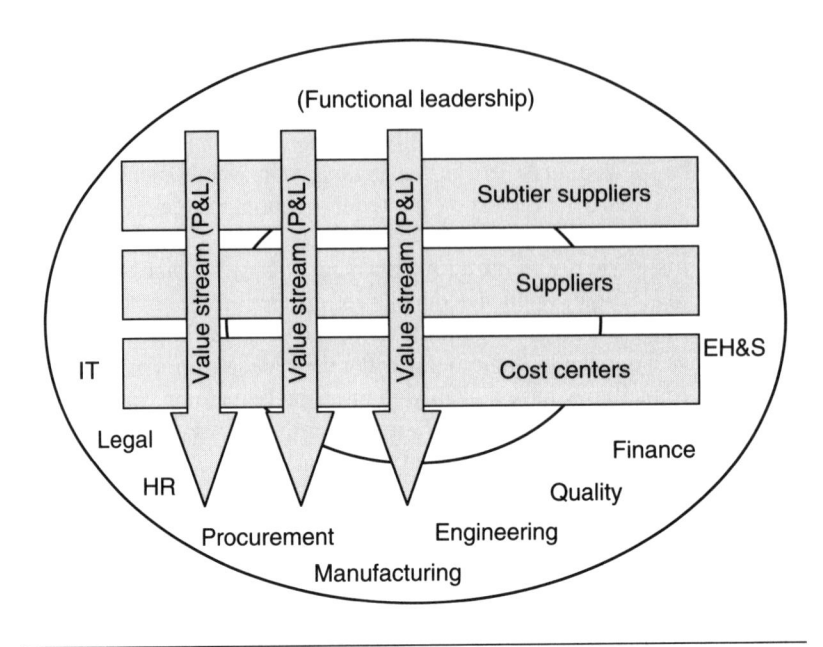

Figure 2.13 Example of an integrated organizational structure.

technology based or of special interest. These are much like the functional discipline councils discussed previously, but they will have great functional diversity in membership. Consider the concept of a community of practice when we speak about the processes of an organization. If an organization divides a process into the traditional responsibilities of functional disciplines, the process is rarely perceived as a whole but rather in its functional parts. Engineering will look at a process from one perspective, production from another, quality from another, and so on. A community of practice addresses the process in its entirety, ensuring that perspectives from all areas are brought together across the business to come up with a total solution and promoting integration into the larger social system. It allows for dialogue and fosters a higher level of understanding, as well as challenging assumptions. Structurally, communities of practice could be considered technical- or process-based councils and are either permanent aspects of the structure or temporary, based on need.

An example of a community of practice that focuses on providing leadership for a technology or process is a weld council. The weld council's charter could be to ensure that the organization understands the latest technological advancements, integrates weld technology into new designs, and develops training for persons interacting with weld processes, and to ensure that executed weld processes in the organization or at a supplier are capable. To succeed in this charter, the weld council would require a diverse representation to address all aspects of the scope from various perspectives. The council would structure itself with identified members, link itself internally and externally to other related groups and councils, create measures of performance, and advance the practice and process of welding. It would keep in the forefront the expectation that its actions are creating value, and it would continuously challenge its activities to ensure that. For example, this could apply to a government agency as follows. If there is an expectation for a certain proficiency of a skill within a large body of knowledge, the agency could establish a council to focus specifically on that skill. Specialists from various government agencies could pool their resources to focus on that skill and could solicit integration with industry to make the perspective more complete (for example, fingerprinting, radio communications, computer information, education, manufacturing processes, and so on).

DECIDING ON THE STRUCTURAL DESIGN

Here is the test question for structural design (see Table 2.1): Does this aspect of the organizational structure provide value by reducing variation, increasing productivity, enhancing compliance, increasing commitment, increasing customer satisfaction, or ensuring sustainability, or is it required by contract or regulatory requirements? If the answer is no to all of the elements of the question, you must still do significant work to achieve integration and value without adding fat. The more *yes* responses, the higher the efficiency and integration. But please keep in mind the needs of the people who create the value in the organization when developing a structure. In Chapter 4, "Leadership," I will discuss *visionary leadership* principles that are critical in developing a sustainable, integrated organization. In short, visionary leadership is made up of aspects of transformational and transactional leadership. It also deals with how a leader perceives time. A visionary leader considers not only the transactional aspects of value but also the transformational aspects of value. For example, the transactional leader focuses predominantly on the numbers. The transformational leader looks at employee engagement and learning. Relative to temporal vision, a leader looks for value that will foster the cultural norms desired, which take significant time spans to achieve. There must be a balance in organizational design—making the immediate numbers while growing and engaging the membership while planting cultural seeds for future benefit.

Table 2.1 Questions to ask when determining organizational structure and process value

Structural/Process Value Questions Must be able to respond "Yes" at least once.	Yes √	No √
Does this aspect of the organizational system provide value by reducing variation?		
Does this aspect of the organizational system provide value by increasing productivity?		
Does this aspect of the organizational system provide value by enhancing compliance?		
Does this aspect of the organizational system provide value by increasing commitment?		
Does this aspect of the organizational system provide value by increasing customer satisfaction?		
Does this aspect of the organizational system provide value by meeting regulatory or contract requirements?		

THE NOTION OF DECENTRALIZATION

The relationship between the functional disciplines or homerooms and the lines of business is a critical one. The functional disciplines need to hold the system together by focusing on culture, process, and tools, as well as leadership. Losing the integration of functional expertise throughout the organizational life cycle will cause excessive decentralization and will create waste. As in all things, a balance must be maintained between centralized activities and decentralized execution. The U.S. banking system is a good example of simultaneous centralization and decentralization. There is typically one central system for managing data that ensures that the organization is utilizing one source for its core organizational memory. The same is true for its processes that control loans and personal accounts. However, at the local level, organizational members typically attempt to provide a local flavor to their customers. For example, the appearance and location of a building will typically complement the culture and architectural style of the community. The local bank may sponsor a neighborhood baseball or soccer team or participate in other community activities. The local management typically exercises discretion over loan approvals and the operating hours of the facility. All of these actions are localized and decentralized, yet they must be consistent with the expectations of the centralized organization and process controls.

Back in the 1970s, U.S. companies jumped feverishly on the bandwagon of decentralization. They did so because they were taught that by having many little companies within the larger company, innovation would flourish, as would a sense of internal competition. Unfortunately, most companies who followed this direction of structural chaos did not follow the road map very well; nor was the road map to decentralization well defined. At the core of much of the decentralization frenzy was a professor by the name of Karl Weick. In his early writings (Weick 1976, 1977, 1979) on decentralization (he referred to it as *coupling*—tight or loose), Weick focused mostly on only the concept and its benefits and rarely on its limitations. As with many new ideas, consultants latched onto the concept without really understanding the theory behind it and went full force prophesizing about the benefits of a decentralized organization. The result: many companies went too far and lost organizational balance. Some organizations underwent a series of restructuring efforts, and others went completely out of business. The amount of energy it takes to move an organization from one form of structure to another is immense. To do so multiple times is irresponsible. In the 1990s, Weick (1993a, 1993b) refined his concept of decentralization, to include its limitations. In essence, centralization in systemic performance needs to be balanced by decentralization in innovation and limited discretion. To decentralize an entire organization and expect predictable performance is madness. It results in duplication of effort and little learning occurring across the organization. To maintain a completely centralized organization rarely makes sense either. Organizations must be balanced to be as efficient and effective as possible and to focus on the elimination of waste. Purely centralized organizations lose sensitivity to the processes, services, and products they provide to customers.

As previously discussed, organizations that are structured with multiple sites or business units, or both, usually are done so to focus on core competencies in design, production, or service execution. Examples of such a specific focus are machining, composites, or assembly in manufacturing settings. Marketing, customer support, and billing are examples in service settings. To be efficient, it is important that such units be self-contained with the physical and human resources necessary to accomplish their objectives. They should be allowed significant discretion in the innovation of their core competencies but none in the systemic processes of the organization that may affect someone upstream or downstream in the process. When a product crosses multiple lines of business, it is imperative that there be accountability in the system for the overall execution of all the processes that bring the product to market. This is an example of decentralizing and organizing for action while maintaining a central function to define the boundaries for action to occur. In so doing, we have bounded discretion, which will foster local innovation, which will result in performance that conforms to the expectations of the stakeholders, regulatory agencies, and top leadership.

AUTHORITY THROUGH REPORTING LINES

How many times have you heard that it does not matter who someone reports to because we all work for the same company? I'd say in a perfect world that is true, but we don't live in a perfect world. Human nature always intervenes in organizational structures, especially during the stress of a market downturn or when leadership is faced with poor performance. In the discussion about organizational structure and matrix organizations we need to ensure that the lines of business, as well as the IPMTs, are appropriately staffed with the functional expertise needed to do the work. But there must also be strong reporting responsibility to the functional leadership of the disciplines. This is the tightrope that is challenging to transverse.

So, do we tell general managers of a line of business that they will be held accountable for the performance of their business, yet the functions within their organization are to report outside of their organization? Absolutely not. But according to the concept of integration, we must ensure that both the skills and staffing levels of the disciplines within the lines of business are adequately addressed as well as throughout the entire value chain. The organizational structural design must ensure that human nature does not undermine the long-term success of the organization. Two ways to address the reporting structure are through direct lines to the functional executives and through a system design that has checks and balances. A third way combines the two. The right one for your company is the one that works; however, the design that provides the greatest integration is the combined system. We'll address each, but first we should define the difference between solid-line reporting and dotted-line reporting structures.

A *solid-line* reporting structure ensures a well-defined relationship between a leader and a subordinate. The leader maintains financial resources to staff the subordinate, and performs performance reviews with the subordinate; at the end of the day, it is clear that the solid-line boss is the boss. On paper and to anyone on the outside looking in, the solid-line leader maintains authority over the subordinate. It's a simple rule of economics.

A *dotted-line* reporting structure is leadership through association (see Figure 2.14). The relationship is typically that of a leader in a supporting role or overseeing a field of practice. In dotted-line relationships, there is always a solid-line relationship as well, meaning a subordinate may be serving two or more leaders. The intent of a dotted-line relationship is to ensure that the dotted-line leader has the authority to exert some level of influence

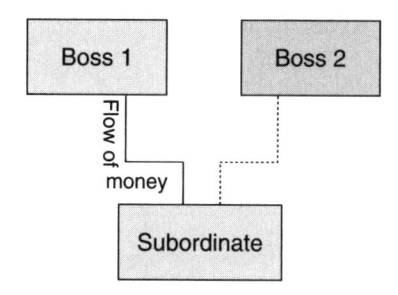

Figure 2.14 Dotted-line versus solid-line reporting.

and leadership over the subordinate. This leadership may be in the application of skills specific to a field of practice or in the execution of day-to-day work of the organization. But when there is conflict in direction between a solid-line leader and dotted-line leader to a subordinate the solid-line leader will almost always prevail. That's because the solid-line leader typically has final authority over compensation and retention, and a subordinate's desire for self-preservation usually kicks in. As will be discussed later, individuals' needs drive their behavior, and the need to survive (Maslow 1943) is a strong motivator. Don't misunderstand the message here. Organizations need both solid-line and dotted-line reporting structures. The important aspect of this method of defining leadership accountability is to ensure that the solid-line exists between the two people who require the most integrity in execution (Jaques 1986). Always remember that in any process the greatest source of variation is always human. If there is more than one boss, the organization owes it to the employee that the signals sent to the employee are synchronized.

Direct (solid-line) functional reporting

As implied, solid-line reporting means that the entire organization of the functional discipline reports to the functional discipline executive, even those in the distributed lines of business. For example, all the inspectors, quality engineers, and quality managers report up to the executive quality position. This provides a sense of community in the discipline, but it may disconnect it from the line of business. As noted earlier, the higher in the hierarchical chain a leader is, the more insulated the leader becomes from the day-to-day issues of the organization's work. Business sensitivity can be managed; however, this design fosters a perception of the organization as being "stovepiped" into functional disciplines and fosters the creation of bureaucracy. The organization's objective is to provide value, and the functional disciplines are purely enablers to that end.

System (matrix) accountability

Accountability for skills and staffing levels can be designed into system processes so as to prevent, or at least catch, human intervention. For example, a general manager could have the entire organization solid-line reporting to them. As such, the manager can rate performance of the various disciplines under them and adjust headcount appropriately. However, a system design that has checks and balances would require significant changes to be first coordinated, and possibly approved, by functional discipline executives prior to implementation. This might slow the organization's ability to change, but it will ensure synergy. The performance appraisal process also would require a "sign off" by the functional discipline executive to ensure that the appraisal represents the roles and responsibilities of the discipline and is not solely weighted by the expectations of the line-of-business owner. Skills of the functional disciplines would be routinely assessed by the homeroom functional discipline to ensure that levels are maintained and gaps identified. Balanced expectations and good methods of communication and measurement are essential for this process to work (see Figure 2.15).

Figure 2.15 Integrated organizational structures don't think in terms of reporting lines; they pull together for success.

Combined direct reporting and system design

In a structure that combines functional leadership responsibility with solid-line reporting, the general manager of the cost center or top facility leader has complete accountability for all resources at his/her disposal, and the central functional leadership maintains responsibility for deployed functional resources. As described under the system accountability, the organization should have methods installed that will continuously measure and update skills within the functional disciplines. For example, if personnel are moved within the line of business, a method must be in place that makes sure that the skills meet the tasks and that the magnitude of the task is matched with resources. This is predominately the responsibility of the top leader in the line of business. Unskilled workers are clearly a significant source of waste. In each line of business, there will be functional heads such as procurement, engineering, quality, production, and human resources directors. It is recommended that these top functional positions within each line of business report hard-line fashion to the functional discipline leadership and dotted-line fashion to the line of business leader.

Solid-lining the reporting structure directly to the functional leadership establishes functional accountability and community within the discipline. Synergy within the specific discipline is better ensured, and learning flows faster through the organization. The risk of not hard-lining is the potential for creating a conflict of interest within the line of business. When people are given a choice between following the direction of a solid-line or a dotted-line reporting structure, the solid line will normally win. This is particularly true in organizations that struggle with the concept of integration and with executing a common vision with synergy. However, there must be assurances that the sensitivity to business needs is not lost by disconnecting the functional resources from the reality of business. The functions below the line-of-business functional heads could report to the functional head, but the resources below them should be allocated to the line-of-business leader. The exception would be for temporary resources that float among the various lines of business—often referred to as *water spider* resources. These should be allocated to the central functional discipline for ease of movement and synergy in companywide action.

The topic of organizational structures can be an emotional one for many organizations and leaders. Regardless of the manner in which an organization chooses to structure its reporting lines, consideration must be given to responsibility, accountability, and communication. The more lines there are from leadership to an individual, the greater the potential for variation in expectations. Organizational leadership must give this serious consideration to ensure consistency in messages and to address the members' need for certainty. It is important that whatever the final design of the structure, it must be congruent with the culture of the organization and the needs of the customer.

The Informal Organization

An additional aspect of organizational structure that leaders frequently do not plan for is the informal organization. An *informal organization* is one that exists naturally within a social structure. As individuals find common interests or purposes, they tend to operate more closely with one another than with others they have little in common with. These relationships can be and frequently are more influential than actual formal organizations. They don't have any documented accountability requirements or procedures that drive their performance and behavior. Rather, they function through discretion and personal choice. An example of an informal organization is a group of individuals who decide to share experience and solutions around a new software application in an office. Office secretaries frequently establish their own informal organizations while planning schedules and travel itineraries. Some informal organizations develop according to length of service time in an organization—the "old-timers" who stick together, sharing experience and history, or the "new generation" who are trying to figure out the ropes of the business.

Informal organizations can be a very positive aspect of an organization. The challenge for leaders is not to ignore their existence and to leverage their effectiveness. Leaders who have been in the organization for some time will more than likely have a good idea of where some informal organizations reside, but it is doubtful that they will know about all of them. New leaders of an organization will need to depend on those who have "lived" in the organization for guidance. As with any aspect of the organizing process, informal organizations should be treated as a process. This will not be an exact science, but with the assistance of the organizational membership, the key informal organizations can be identified. Variables such as membership, purpose, and methods of communication can be identified. Once the informal organization networks are made visible and understood, they can be leveraged to achieve greater consistency in organizational action.

DEFINING A COMMON DIRECTION

Because an organization's culture drives sustained behavior, which affects performance, organizations should focus resources and action on those attributes that influence organizational culture. According to many researchers

(Schein 1986; Smircich and Calas 1987; Senge 1990), culture is built on a system of shared beliefs. So let's look at how we can build a belief system. First off, we need to have something to believe in. Organizational integration begins with a vision. The vision must be consistent with the overall environment in which the organization finds itself. The vision must be crisp and easy for the entire organization to understand. If a vision is understood only at the top, we have just disabled many of the components of our organizational system, and it will not perform in the way we intend it to perform.

There are many books and journal articles about how to create a vision statement. So, if you want to become an expert in writing one, go ahead and read a couple. The short of it is a *vision statement* needs to be brief, contain meaning, lack ambiguity, and provide the organization with a focused direction for future success. A vision statement must give the organization something to hold onto and believe in. Moreover, if we truly want to strive for a lean enterprise the vision must focus on the customer.

On the other hand, a *mission statement* must bring action to the vision in terms that the organization can understands so that they can see how to achieve it. However, mission statements have a tendency to get a bit lengthy and often are so complex that only few in the organization ever spend time to try and understand them. The mission statement should provide the organization with a purpose and expectations for performance. The mission can be helpful when the organization is confronted with trying to understand its own identity in times of chaos or uncertainty. For example, if an organization is designed to be a service organization within a very specific niche market and an opportunity exists to expand into another segment, its existing mission statement may need to be modified to address the new market expansion. If done right, the company's existing mission statement should clearly define the markets in which it performs and crisply identify the value created. The new opportunity should require a change not only to the mission statement but also to organizational design and performance metrics.

Neither a vision statement nor a mission statement is absolutely required, but what is required is some means of communicating to the organizational membership what the organization is all about and where it is going. The people in the organization need something to hang onto and to help them focus their energies. Otherwise, the organization has no hope of ever establishing synergy in its actions and achieving balance (see Figure 2.16).

Strategic plans are also important tools for communicating direction. The important aspect of developing a strategic plan for an organization is to develop one for the entire organization throughout the value stream for as far out as the vision can be projected. While we recognize the need for an entrepreneurial spirit within an organization, unless the resources of an organization are harmonized, they are competing, and gains realized in one area can

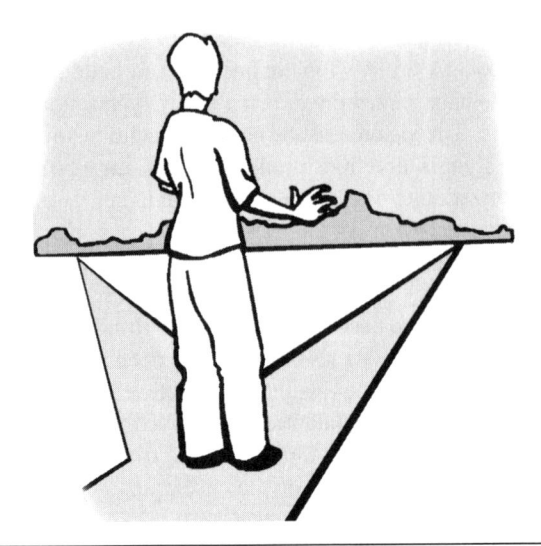

Figure 2.16 Organizational members must have the requisite knowledge and a clear understanding of the vision in order to make thoughtful decisions.

be at the expense of another. The idea of business is to compete with your competition, not yourself. Business planning needs to be balanced in the organization, including allocation of financial energies—budgets. Though we'll talk more about the need to align the organizational budget in the following chapter, for an organization to realize its greatest efficiency, the efforts of one should contribute to the success of all. To accomplish this, the top-level strategic planning should flow into the lower-level deployment plans of the organization. If lower-level plans are not in congruence with the overall strategic plan, leadership must address that by changing the top-level plan, changing the lower-level plan, or acknowledging that the incongruent aspects exist, are at the expense of organizational integration, and potentially create waste. The liability of losing integration is obvious on the efficiency side of the equation, but the greatest impact is on organizational culture. People will perceive the incongruence as managerial lies with regard to the intent of integration.

However an organization finds its balance in business planning, it must always consider the influence on organizational culture. By allowing part of the organization to behave in one manner and another part in a different manner, leaders establish competing belief systems. With competing belief systems, we have divergent organizational cultures and, again, the creation of waste. With divergent cultures, we have no chance at integration, but rather at best only linkages.

INTEGRATING INITIATIVES

A practical example of nonintegration is the total quality management (TQM) movement of the 1970s and 1980s. The potential value to organizations implementing TQM was obvious. The concept was one of empowerment and process control, which meant greater efficiency and effectiveness. By definition, TQM means that the organization's culture is defined by and supports the constant attainment of customer satisfaction through an integrated system of tools, techniques, and training. This involves the continuous improvement of organizational processes, resulting in high-quality products and services (Sashkin and Kiser 1993).

However, where most organizations failed in the implementation of TQM was in integration. We should look at the management system of the organization as a system of interrelated processes and routines that are defined to ensure consistent execution. TQM rarely found itself as an integral aspect of the defined system. Namely, the organizations that implemented TQM rarely modified the procedures and policies to make TQM part of their normal routines. TQM became something in addition to the normal work of the organization rather than an integral part of everything an organization does. In addition, while the concept of TQM lends itself well to the idea of managing an entire value stream, that rarely occurred. In a review of history, I would venture to guess that most, if not all, quality and/or performance initiatives such as TQM that have failed have done so because of their lack of integration into the organization's everyday management system. Companies failed to make it part of their organizational DNA (see Figure 2.17).

The performance improvement tool currently in vogue in many companies around the world is *Six Sigma*. Six Sigma is a statistical process control methodology that measures and controls variation in processes. In many organizations in both manufacturing and service settings, the application of Six Sigma methods has significantly improved quality and cost performance. However, sustaining that improvement will be a problem if organizations don't make the practice of variation control an integral part of their management system. More specifically, most organizations that have implemented Six Sigma methods have done so at the hands of experts and at the direction of their top leadership. These experts are typically called *Black Belts*.

Black Belts select, or have selected for them, "projects." Projects typically consist of a manufacturing or service process that contains significant variance that needs to be controlled and reduced. The objective of a project is improved performance. Sounds good, right? Well, it is, for the short term. But if the organizational membership in its totality is not an active participant in

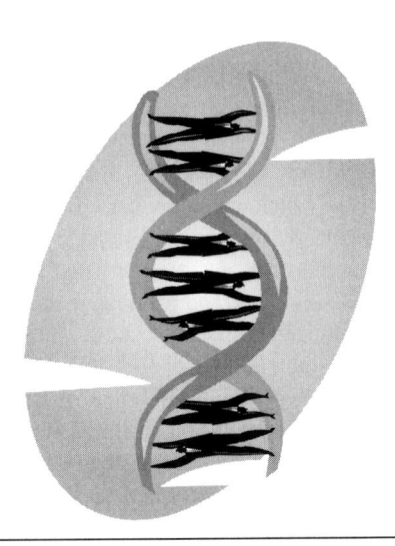

Figure 2.17 Initiatives and performance expectations must be integrated into the organizational DNA to ensure sustainability.

the execution of the Six Sigma process, the process cannot become an integral part of the organizational culture. Through heavy internal and external marketing, the company creates awareness, but unless people themselves are engaged and can actually contribute to the organization's performance, Six Sigma is only a nonintegrated tool that is used when someone determines it is desired. The risk here is that it is leader dependent and subject to a huge amount of variation in sustainability. Let's say a CEO is a strong advocate of Six Sigma methods and requires the organization to apply them. A huge investment in implementation will be made, and some returns will be realized. But now let's say the CEO leaves the organization, and, though committed, the next CEO is not as vocal about Six Sigma. Since Six Sigma has not been integrated into the overall organizational management system and has excluded the majority of the organization, it will likely not continue with the same level of energy and organizational commitment. It may even go away, as did TQM.

Please don't take this to imply that Six Sigma or any other statistical tool is not of long-term value. Removing variance from processes is of key value to an organization and must be a fundamental responsibility of everyone in the organization. However, there is a smarter way to go about implementation—through total integration and making Six Sigma, or any other tool, a routine of the business. Keep in mind that at its core, Six Sigma is a well-packaged statistical process control methodology and is not a philosophy in itself or something totally new to the world. Deming (1980) wrote of the benefits of statistical process control years ago to include the value of variation reduction in business processes. Variation in process, whether in human interaction or in work processes, is waste in its purest form. It is important to allow the system to drive performance and to engage employers to use the appropriate tools for the situation—consistently and predictably and with a focus on the entire life cycle. To accomplish this, the membership must understand how they interrelate with the systems of the organization and with the value streams. People need to understand how they provide value and how applying tools in a certain way will aid them in creating value. Only when variation is removed from the entire value stream is *leanness* achieved.

Since we have discussed Six Sigma in some detail, let's look at a number of other initiatives currently in use today. *Integrated process and program development/deployment* (IPPD) grew out of concurrent (or simultaneous) engineering in the 1980s. The objective of IPPD is to engage multifunctional teams of design and manufacturing engineers to develop the manufacturing process concurrently in the product life cycle. Ideally, IPPD expands on the technical integration employed in a disciplined, systems engineering approach to integrate business functions as well as technical functions. Integrated performance leadership provides a structured approach to developing organizational systems and processes that will enable an organization to perform as integrated program/product teams with assignable accountability throughout the value stream.

Capability and maturity model integration (CMMI) is a structured measurement method for measuring the maturity of organizational processes. Developed by the U.S. government and Carnegie Mellon University, its initial focus was on measuring the maturity of software, but it has expanded to include an organization's business processes. When combined with IPL, CMMI provides an excellent measurement framework by which the organization can understand its journey to, or status with respect to, integration.

Lean manufacturing is a means of reducing waste through value-stream alignment and process improvement. Though lean manufacturing has its origins in the business of manufacturing, the concept has expanded to include the notion of a *lean enterprise*, which includes all business processes including those of service industries and government agencies. The primary focus is the elimination of wasteful action and the creation of value for the customer (Womack and Jones 1996). The concept of IPL integrates well with the lean thought process, in that the focus of both lean and IPL is the elimination of waste and the creation of value for the customer. However, IPL applies additional emphasis on the elements of organizational sustainability, such as learning, culture, leadership, and managing the environment. There is an important caveat regarding the deployment of lean process: an organization can only be as lean as its customers allow it to be. In other words, if a customer does not have the characteristics that allow its suppliers to interact with it in lean processes, the supplier can only deploy lean processes so far because it depends on cues from its customers for action.

Quick response manufacturing (QRM) (Suri 1998) is a tool for improving organizational performance by structuring capacity so as to have inherent surge elasticity to address market changes. Like lean manufacturing, QRM focuses on the reduction of queue time between work time (touch time) and can be applied to business processes as well.

The challenge to the organization is not to treat each of the initiatives as separate from each other and separate from the organizational processes and procedures, but rather to seek their complete integration into the routines of the business. When the tools for performance improvement are integrated into the business processes of the organization, and leadership behaves in such a way as to unconditionally support and lead the organizational processes, the initiatives become more integrated into the organization's culture. It becomes the *way* of the organization as opposed to something *in addition to* the organizational work.

SYSTEMS OF ROUTINES AND CHAOS

Most formal organizations are governed by a structured series of policies and procedures commonly referred to as an organization's *management system*. The objective of a documented management system is to provide a means of communicating performance expectations to the organization and to establish a system of predictability. That is, if I do this in accordance with this procedure, my partner in the process is sure to receive the output in a predefined fashion. Predictability in an organization is absolutely mandatory in order to control chaos. One should view a management system as any other process. If we allow too much variance to exist, we must inject excess energy into the process to sustain performance. The by-product of putting too much energy into a process is waste. If a system is designed with the entire value stream in mind, the documented management system can be analogous to a blueprint for a lean enterprise.

A major source of management system variance comes from aligning the policies and procedures of an organization by functional owner and not by process. For example, in new product introduction it is not uncommon for an organization's engineering, procurement, manufacturing, and quality departments all to have individual procedures to govern the process. Guess what? None of the departments reads the others' procedures. And why? Because the system does not drive them to do it, and there is no time for it. Frequently organizations allow their departments to create procedures to address their slice of the pie and ignore the fact that there is a total pie in front of them—resulting in more waste. An obvious risk of having a management system defined by disciplines is the creation of gaps in process control. Because there are too many documents of too many functional owners controlling the process, frequently something is forgotten and ultimately nobody controls the complete process. And since one department is concerned with executing its own slice, it's not concerned with another's slice. It often takes an auditor or a customer to point out such disconnects.

Now here is where organizations can significantly reduce cost and increase their ability to turn on a dime. Stop writing procedures around functional disciplines. Define the management system around the processes of the organization, and integrate the functions of each department that engages with a process into one controlled system. This way the right hand knows what the left is doing. Picture yourself as the product or service being created, and allow yourself to go through the entire value stream. You won't care about the functional disciplines, but rather about the actual actions. What is transpiring as the product or service is having value added to it, and are there excessive handoffs in the processes? How long do you wait between actions of value creation? How long does it take for someone to notice that the process is not in control and mistakes are occurring? Also, keep the focus on what the customer is willing to pay for. Womack and Jones (1996) talk about three levels of waste in the value stream (see Figure 2.18). The first level is not necessarily waste but rather what is required to provide value to the customer. The second level is essential to the delivery of the product or service but may have undefined opportunities for waste reduction. The third level provides no value to the customer whatsoever and can be

Level 3: No value to customer and can be eliminated without integrity of system or product.

Level 2: Essential for delivery of product or service but has opportunities for waste reduction.

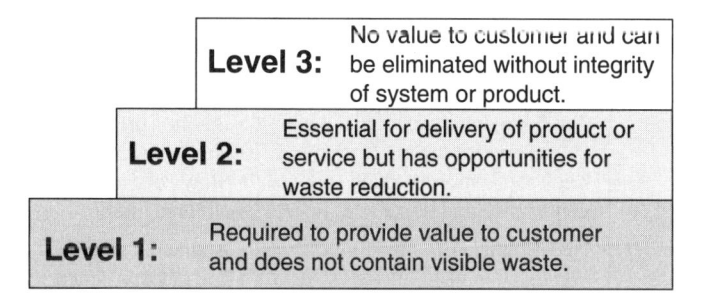

Level 1: Required to provide value to customer and does not contain visible waste.

Figure 2.18 Three levels of waste (adapted from Womack and Jones 1996).

immediately eliminated without affecting the integrity of the system. However, if we were to consider the life cycle of the organizational processes, we may want to perceive the processes in relation to the value they create.

In IPL we identify the processes of the organization within four orders of value (see Table 2.2). The first order is the most valuable to the customer and is that which the customer is willing to pay for. This may be in the form of product enhancements, enhanced reliability, more bells and whistles, or anything else the customer may identify or agree with. The bottom line on first-order value is that the customer recognizes it, wants it, and will pay for it. Most of the time, this is what is being directly supplied to the customer in the form of the final product or service.

Second-order value is that which is not immediately perceived as value by the customer but fosters the environment in which services and products are created and without which first-order value would not be created. For example, second-order value can be training in environmental health and safety practices, a robust calibration system that ensures reliable measurement, team-building activities that strengthen trust and understanding, training on managing customer satisfaction or customer interaction in a service environment, or advanced computer systems for engineers to create faster and more reliable designs. Second-order value is an enabling factor for the creation of first-order value. Second-order value can also be considered the

Table 2.2 The four orders of value.

Value	Definition	What it may look like
First-order	Customer recognizes value and is willing to pay directly for it	• End-item product • Product enhancements • More features • Quicker service
Second-order	Not immediately recognized by customer as value but is required to create first-order value and contains no visible waste	• Employee training • Computer systems (ERP) • Calibration systems • EH&S program
Third-order	Not immediately recognized by customer as value but is required to create first-order value and contains visible waste	• Batched processes • Nonfocused training • Slow computers • Nonintegration
Fourth-order	No recognizable value to the organization or to the customer and can be eliminated without any impact to system or product	• Nonaction meetings • Unread newsletters • Unread reports • Conflicting signals

cost of doing business. For some industries this will be higher than for others. Consider, for example, a pharmaceutical manufacturer; we would expect it to have stronger controls in place, such as checks and balances and additional testing, than what we would find at a textile manufacturer. Although both manufacturers require second-order value processes, the challenge is not to allow them to become third- or fourth-order value—which are more wasteful. Another example of second-order value is the reservations system of an airline. Some reservations systems are extremely user friendly and promote customer satisfaction, whereas others are cumbersome and may drive customers away. The reservations system is not first-order value because the customer is paying to travel, not to book a reservation, although without the reservations system, first-order value is not possible.

Third-order value is that which contributes to customer value but is not necessarily delivered in the most efficient or effective manner. Examples are batched training as opposed to training deployed as and when needed and nonintegrated production flows. Third-order value is inefficient second-order value. Most likely, the third-order value began its existence as second-order value but over time lost its alignment with the needs of the organization. Additionally, it is not uncommon to see third-order value processes in organizations as a response to an earlier noncompliance finding. In the rush to take corrective action, the organization may put a superficial or third-order value process in place to satisfy an immediate need. This may be warranted at the time; however, it should be revisited later to realign it and integrate it with the business as second- or first-order value.

Fourth-order value is that which in reality is no value to either the customer or the organization. Examples are newsletters that no one reads or meetings without action or results. These must be eliminated immediately.

To define an organization using a value-stream or life-cycle method, a company has some very big decisions to make, such as who will develop and define the processes and control the content and release of procedures and how they will do that. Under a traditional method, each functional discipline owner would be responsible for approving the procedures. Procedure ownership can be a huge challenge for those organizations that operate in regulated fields, such as nuclear, pharmaceutical, and aerospace. Compliance to external rules is an obvious expectation, which sometimes defines who in an organization should control certain procedural documents or functional processes. Even for organizations that do not operate under external regulation, who should own the procedure process? Some would say the process owner. However, you risk losing integration when too many process owners are involved in defining the management system of a value stream. Besides, who owns the process of new part introduction? Some would say engineering because it designs it. Others may say manufacturing because it produces it. And still others may say quality because it verifies and certifies. But at the end of the day, it's the organization in total that is responsible for the introduction of new parts or anything else it provides as an output.

To achieve an integrated management system, the system's design and documentation should be under one hat of responsibility. That does not mean the functional discipline leaders lose their ability to contribute. That can be maintained through a ballot process and through participation in development. But placing all the system documentation responsibilities under one central point ensures synergy around processes, not politics. Imagine the positive impact on the organizational membership when they can simply go to one procedure to understand a process rather than several disjointed procedures. I suggest the overall impact would be an exponential improvement in process execution and reduction in waste. In my experience, the most common cause of product nonconformance or system noncompliance is people not following procedures, and that is not industry specific. Because procedures are outdated, hard to understand, not effective, difficult to revise, or not easily accessible, people frequently ignore them. The result is a loss of system predictability due to variability and a degradation of organizational performance; moreover, the company's ability to consistently execute processes will be seriously questioned by its stakeholders, members, and government agencies. As a matter of fact, most companies experience this condition today, and if they allow it to go on too long, they will more than likely go out of business. The organizations that focus on making their systems easy to understand by their membership will find enormous competitive advantages. Reducing the complexity of the management system and reducing the number of redundant actions reduces waste. Making processes easy to understand reduces the amount of energy required to make sense and act, which again, reduces waste.

However, we are still left with the question of system (procedural) ownership which for many companies may not be an easy question to answer. Those who understand the "power of the pen" understand why. Someone who controls the requirements for action for an entire company has significant organizational power. The challenge for organizations is to make that power neutral in bias and positive in performance. In ultrasmall companies the answer can be simply the Office of the President. This method requires the president or an assigned delegate to approve each procedure. But such a practice is not feasible in larger organizations, and it is even questionable in smaller ones. The president or chief executive would be in a constant state of system review and would never get any other executive work done. I recommend creating a new organization or evolving an existing one. The decision should be influenced by the organizational environment and culture. For example, if an organization has not had one predominant department that has significant system ownership responsibilities, then it makes sense to create a new department that would manage such. It could be titled the Office of Management Systems or the Office of Business Processes. On the other hand, a department such as the quality department typically has much experience in management systems and business processes. However, there is a caution here: I'm speaking of the big "Q," not the little "q." By that I mean some organizations have evolved their quality organizations into being proactive and driving performance improvements through system enhancements to include the business processes of the organization requiring abilities in industrial psychology and sociology. Others may still be stuck in an inspection mentality, which is the little "q," also referred to as quality control.

When we think about leadership in the area of quality, we can draw an analogy to the position of chief financial officer (CFO) of an organization. Where a CFO is responsible for ensuring that appropriate accounting practices are maintained and that the organization is making sound financial business investments, the individual responsible for quality and performance outcomes must also ensure that expectations are met. We could call this person the chief quality officer (CQO) or, more broadly, the chief organizational performance officer (COPO). It depends on the breadth of responsibility the organization assigns to them. If it is only the quality of performance, then CQO suffices; however, if the individual is assigned the broader responsibilities of business process performance, then COPO is appropriate. Where the CFO may deploy auditing processes to ensure compliance with accounting rules, the COPO or CQO would do the same to ensure compliance with organizational business processes. The COPO or CQO would also continuously monitor other business process measures such as knowledge capability, capacity alignment, customer feedback, and any other measure that provides meaningful insight about organizational performance. They would also be responsible for ensuring that the organization is in appropriate alignment with its external environment, such as, for example, ensuring the organization has membership on government or industry committees, or that its scanning activities of the external environment are capable and encompassing (see Figure 2.19).

Even for the most advanced quality organizations, taking on responsibility for the entire system is an evolutionary step that must be undertaken carefully. The concepts of organizational development, and human resources management, and fiscal management need to be integrated into the design concepts of an organizational system. The organization must understand of the concepts and theories around organizational learning and organizational behavior, as well as the methods of performance motivation and professional cognition. And the ability to comprehend the relationships throughout the

Figure 2.19 Organizations must leverage the power of the pen in government and industry groups, and minimize external threats of control.

entire value stream is an absolute requisite. The best way to create a department that possesses such abilities is to merge many into one. For example, using the quality organization as a core, one could align the functional aspects (verification and validation of product) of quality assurance under one arm and systems management (business processes) under another. Under the systems management arm, one could align the departments of organizational development, continuous improvement, and any other that manages the system actions of the organization or has performance enhancement responsibilities, including training. The result should be a department that understands organizational system design and the interrelatedness of organizational performance and that can define expected actions and convert them into organizational learning. There is no one best design for all organizations—doing what makes sense and is consistent with the organization's culture is the best advice that can be given. But don't allow fragments of the organization to reside outside the whole and send conflicting messages into the organization. Consistency in communication is essential. Also, beware of consultants who don't clearly understand the concepts of organizational learning, systems theory, professional cognition, and leadership. Without the entire package, important attributes in the formula will be missing.

The next step is the alignment of procedures and policies. This is no easy task, but it is one that will pay huge dividends in organizational performance. One must sort the organization's procedures around common processes—ideally using the life-cycle model as a template. Once sorted, one of two things can be done—either throw the existing procedures and policies all out and start over using a new process design review or capture the contents of the existing by merging into one. Preference should be given to the latter—redefining the objective of the process, walking it through, capturing the required actions, and rewriting the procedures. This may actually be the fastest method and provide the best return on your effort. It also allows tools such as the *kaizen* (incremental improvement) and *kaikaku* (radical improvement) methods and benchmarking to be applied to possibly fine-tune or even reinvent process execution. The greatest potential of IPL is to provide a framework in which *kaikaku* can occur. A *kaikaku* change results in exponential improvement in performance and always requires a hard wire change in the way people think about a process; whereas a *kaizen* change results in incremental performance improvement and requires only slight modifications in the way people understand and interact with their processes. But in the zeal to reinvent an organization, don't forget the lessons of the past. Existing procedures should always be reviewed to ensure that regulatory and contract requirements and other required actions are not forgotten. Also, keep in mind that procedures are archives of organizational memory and may contain lessons learned that should not be relearned the hard way. The inverse is also true—eradicating memory is frequently the fastest way to change organizational behavior and performance (Hedberg 1981). Just do so smartly. The other method of alignment, merging many procedures, can be accomplished remotely and simply requires alignment of steps. However, there is a risk of merging nonvalue action that reduces organizational effectiveness and may undermine organizational buy-in to the entire process. Either method will result in a greater alignment of organizational energy and a better method of communicating to the organization the interrelatedness of members' actions. The objective is to have a defined system of action that allows only first- and second-order value to exist in the value stream.

Technology can be applied to make this process even more manageable. Using electronic media to communicate to the organization has the potential to mistakeproof many of the organization's process. Some electronic systems will allow the organization to perform its processes only within certain preestablished definitions and parameters. The result is greater predictability in the execution of processes. From a learning perspective, the procedures actually become transparent to the process executor because his or her actions can be prompted. Still, the organization needs to have overarching definitions of its business processes so that the membership understands their individual roles and interrelatedness. Using process flowcharts to either augment the procedures, or as the procedures themselves, will facilitate the understanding of process flow.

As with procedures, organizational memory is archived in the minds of the organizational membership (Hedberg 1981). When the system changes, so must the understanding of the organization. This may be the hardest part of all of executing change. We can use conventional methods of training and, as discussed earlier, electronic real-time media that mistakeproof action. Whatever method the organization chooses to communicate system changes, it must be effective for its individual environment and culture. But almost without exception, there will be that 5 percent of the organization who we can refer to as "loggerheads." The loggerheads are those folks who are overly resistant to change and will never really accept it as the new way of being. My recommendation is not to waste any time and get rid of them. A company's membership is one of its most valuable resources; however, value is based on the membership's ability and willingness to execute the organization's business. Loggerheads slow the organization in everything it does and actually undermine its capability for integration. They are catalysts of waste. Act swiftly and fairly and change will occur more quickly and as intended. Please don't mistake a loggerhead for the sole voice of reason, even though sometimes wisdom resides in isolation and is not recognized immediately. As leaders, we must use wisdom and actively listen to others' perspectives. Otherwise we risk instilling fear in the organization, and nobody will dare speak up.

The concept of membership engagement is paramount. As previously discussed, a workforce that is not engaged in an organization's processes may become complacent and disengage from the organization. Ample research supports the need for organizational engagement. So if an organization attempts to make the work so easy for the workforce that people actually have little need to think, it runs the risk of undermining many of its performance metrics, including quality and throughput. People become bored and disinterested in their work. Design the processes of the organization to elicit maximum engagement, permit minimum discretion in process execution, and supply the greatest opportunity for learning, and employees will concentrate and the process will suffer from little waste.

SYSTEM VALIDATION

Once the system has been redesigned into integrated process-driven procedures and documented, it should be deployed within a validation process. Deploying the newly defined processes at select locations can limit the impact of errors in design to those locations and not affect the entire organization. The validation process should consist of releasing the new processes and monitoring their execution. A formal validation protocol should be established that measures each delivered process against the predefined requirements. This protocol should not be confused with an internal audit process; an internal audit process is for recurring validation, whereas the initial validation protocol should determine initial adequacy, efficiency, and appropriateness. The validation protocol could be a simple checklist prompting a review of the deliverables. For example, are only first- and second-order actions defined in the process? In addition to reviewing the process flow for the elimination of waste and the creation of value, you should also review it for robustness. For example: "Is the design review process mistakeproofed so as to prevent violations of standard work?" Points in the process where discretion is required should be adequately defined to ensure consistent results. People who exercise discretion in execution need to be aligned with the level of ability required by the process. Any points of process vulnerability need to be pointed out as presenting risk as early in the process as possible.

Additionally, you need to resolve process ownership issues so that you can design measurements of accountability. There is little more damaging than for an organization to allow processes to exist without clear accountability. This is very tricky with regard to IPL. As discussed under organizational structure, the ideal IPL structure is constructed around accountability. Each line-of-business leader has their own perspective on performance, but they must see through the lens of the IMPT or value steam and ultimately the customer. From the perspective of metrics and ownership of the documented management system, measures of compliance, effectiveness, and efficiency work best. Are the integrated organizations doing what they say they are going to do? Are they performing their functions without excessive waste? Organizational processes must be measured throughout the value stream (IPMT level) and across value streams (across IMPTs). This provides the big picture, identifying opportunities for improvement.

The validation process should be a formal, documented process that allows the organization to later understand what has occurred. As processes mature, they inevitably need to be revised or modified, and it is very helpful to understand past actions, including issues encountered during validation. Companies that have implemented management systems in compliance with ISO 9000, or any of the industry-specific standards such as QS-9000 (automotive) or AS9100 (aerospace), have some experience in these methods. But what is being suggested here is more the retention of organizational memory than objective evidence of compliance. The more organized an organization's memory is, the better it can understand its actions. This is an area where private industry can learn from the public sector. In the rule-making processes of government, almost every rule begins with a foreword document. This foreword is referred to as a *preamble*. It captures much of the intent and provides background as to why the rule is created in a certain way. This is a form of organizational memory. Private-sector organizations should also consider a similar process in creating definitions of their business processes. The more an organization knows why a process is defined in a certain way, the more it can make sense of how to improve upon it.

Only after an organization is confident that the new processes are performing as desired should it release them into the greater organization. There are two camps with regard to deployment of mass system change. One camp says that incremental (phased) deployment is less intrusive and allows an organization to gradually learn its new systems. Organizations frequently use this method when they implement new electronic enterprise resource management systems. On the one hand, shortcomings are identified as elements of the system are released and can be managed without the organization's becoming overly inundated. Organizational membership can also be trained gradually as the system deploys. On the other hand, the organization may have an overlap in system deployment—the new and the old may coexist for a time, sometimes a year or more. Maintaining two systems in operation concurrently is costly and can create gaps in the system and compliance.

The other camp is for mass deployment all at once. This typically means one system is turned off when people go home at night, and the new one is turned on when they arrive the next workday. This method reduces the need to maintain two systems and significantly shortens the duration of deployment. The complete deployment method requires that the organizational membership have training in all of the new processes prior to execution. This can be facilitated somewhat through the use of *power users*. Power users are organizational members who have extensive training in and knowledge of the new electronic systems being deployed within the functional discipline they represent. Understanding that organizational members don't typically engage with the entire system or value stream at once, training of the majority of employees need only be done initially to the degree to which individuals interact with and are accountable for work processes. Follow-on training in greater depth can be delivered in other areas identified as creating first- or second-order value. The major risk here is that if the validation processes have not been done thoroughly, the entire organizational system could collapse and actually put the organization out of business until the old system can be reestablished or the new one fixed.

Validation before deployment is a critical part of system execution. If the validation process is not designed adequately, deployment failure is imminent. In this area, the science of a quality discipline becomes very useful. Don't cut corners on this very important process or you will pay dearly in loss of capability.

FEEDBACK AND SYSTEM DESIGN

One thing is guaranteed about this process: the system design will always have the opportunity for fine-tuning, further reduction of waste, and realignment according to the changing environment. For many reasons, it is critical to have the ability to modify the organizational system design quickly. Poorly defined processes undermine the credibility of the system as well as that of the organization's leadership. To be responsive, the system requires quick and accurate feedback about performance. The membership must be encouraged to speak up in the event of shortcomings and must understand how to provide such input. It must be clearly understood by members of the organization that they are not to tolerate inferior processes—they must speak up. And in advance of the membership's speaking up, the organization needs to develop mechanisms for capturing feedback as well as for integrating it into the system—quickly. Resources need to be allocated in the deployment processes for adjustments and fine-tuning.

Again, organizations that have implemented management systems consistent with ISO 9000 have experience in the process of internal auditing. The internal audit can be a powerful tool in system design if it assesses not only compliance but also adequacy and value creation. For this reason, it makes sense to structure the organization so that the resources that are responsible for system design are closely linked with those that evaluate it. As I noted earlier while discussing Parsons's theory of action (Parsons 1959; Bluth 1982), the internal audit process fulfills an environmental scanning role. The scanning process should look both internally and externally. As the external environment of an organization evolves, the internal systems need to change as well. Additionally, changes within the value stream need to be recognized quickly; otherwise, entropy takes over and the extinction process begins.

SUMMARY

Because the concept of integration is very broad, this chapter is one of the largest in the book and represents some of the complexities in developing a synergetic organization. Organizations must consider integration in all of its system design activities, especially those that influence behavior and decision making, and understand that no one part of the organization operates in isolation. People must think and act holistically—in terms of the whole organization and not its suboptimal pieces—and understand how they personally relate to the value stream. To understand the models of integrated social systems is to consider integration as a manageable and measurable business process.

As with everything in nature, our organizations must be adaptable and respond to the needs of the environment in which they exist. The term that describes these adaptive characteristics is *requisite variety*. Which means that the organization has the characteristics to adapt when necessary. When leaders understand how to plan for a changing environment, they can develop systems and people that can predict change and stay ahead of it in a cost-effective manner. And when an organization masters this process, it finds that it can actually influence the environment and encourage it to change. Participation in academic, industry, and government forums can provide the organization with the power of the pen.

The structures of leadership in an organization play a significant role in the actions of its members. Despite the well-intended theoretical ambitions of multiple report structures, when a person receives too many directions from too many leaders, they become confused or muddled or even paralyzed. The organization must understand why it is structured in the fashion it is and truly comprehend the lines of communication connecting its people. This chapter discusses a number of structural forms and the influences each has on the organization. An organization deploying IPL must understand the implications of each structure and find the appropriate mix for its business processes and people. The processes of communication and organizational sense making should be central in this consideration.

As the organization engages in understanding its business processes, it should apply a life-cycle perspective—by looking not only at what happens inside its four walls but also at suppliers and customers. Applying mapping processes to make the business process visible enhances one's understanding of what's going on in the business. A macro-level map will provide high-level visibility, whereas a micro-level map shows the processes at the level of execution. These maps highlight the actions of the business and may disclose gaps and overlaps in performance. Existing processes should be questioned for value, and those that provide none should be eliminated. Processes that have gaps or possible overlaps represent levels of waste and must be addressed quickly.

As the organization redesigns its business processes, it should integrate all its existing initiatives, such as lean manufacturing, Six Sigma, CMMI, ACE (achieving competitive excellence), JIT (just-in-time production), QRM, TQM, and others, so that they become an integral part of doing business and not add-ons. Integrated performance leadership does not replace any of these good tools, but rather provides a framework for integration so that the tools are interwoven into the organization's DNA structure.

As with any product or process, the organizational system must be validated to ensure that it is delivering as intended. The validation process should be a planned part of the rollout and must include the organization's people.

The membership must understand the new processes and feel free to engage in dialogue to enhance understanding. The validation process must be measurable and visible. Senior leadership must play an active role in implementation and may opt to form standing reviews of the implementation process.

As the system matures, leaders must ensure that it is still applicable to the needs of the organization and its customers. Feedback mechanisms that facilitate quick-time measurements of performance need to be embedded in the processes. In addition, formal review processes that assess not only compliance but also organizational commitment to the designed business processes are a must. Such measures of commitment provide an indication to leadership of the culture of the organization. The integrated business processes of the organization and its membership should be the primary responsibilities of the senior leadership. They must accept that leading the organization is critical to sustainability and that managing the business of day-to-day transactions is a function of management. Both are necessary and must be balanced.

3
Performance

This is the "so what?" chapter. Organizations exist for the specific reason of creating value. Governmental organizations exist to provide social services that ensure the form of government a nation desires and to provide safety and a commerce system for citizens. Not-for-profit organizations exist to provide services to communities, either professional or social, and their focus for revenue is based primarily on maintaining the ability to provide services. And for-profit organizations are simply in existence to provide financial returns for their stakeholders, and they do so by providing value that customers are willing to pay for. Those who have admirable ideas about for-profit organizations existing to provide services to humanity as their primary objective are not being totally honest with themselves. For-profit organizations exist primarily to make money, or they would be not-for-profit organizations or part of the government.

We can measure the health of an organization using many performance metrics that are relevant to its stakeholders. Regardless of whether an organization is governmental, not for profit, or for profit, the performance measures most important to ensure sustainable existence must be identified and then made tangible throughout the organization. This is easier said than done. Many executives of for-profit organizations would claim that the most important measure of success is an organization's stock price. However, a stock price is a temporal measure influenced by many attributes that cannot be controlled, including very subjective brokers. Though critically important to a company's existence, if stock price alone were used as the sole measure of an organization's health it would lull an organization into a false sense of security—or insecurity. Organizations that have low revenue growth but high bottom-line performance are very profitable businesses, possibly with good stock performance, that may be highly susceptible to acquisition—possibly through hostile means.

It's important for organizations to step back and take an accurate reading of their overall health—continuously. For example, organizations that have significant margins on existing product lines may be doing well today, but if they do not invest in new products, they may find themselves without anything to offer their customers in the near future. From an employee satisfaction perspective, employees who are afforded little opportunity for growth or who feel unfairly treated may decide to strike for a long duration, putting an economic strain on the organization, or may contribute to high turnover rates that undermine the internal learning curves.

There is growing evidence in research that the long-term survival of the organization is strongly dependent on its ability to provide services or products that meet its customers' expectations, and that meeting such expectations is a measure of quality performance. Though this seems obvious, customer satisfaction metrics are rarely the priority in an organization's business plan. From a lean enterprise perspective, this relates to creating value for the customer, especially that which they are willing to pay for. One aspect of performance measurement is certain: there is no one measurement that provides a complete assessment of organizational health. Each organization must establish its own set of success measures that address the whole of the organization, not just the parts. A word of caution that will be discussed shortly—never focus solely on end-output metrics. Input and throughput measures are equally important in the measure of value creation. This includes measures of attainment of employee needs and of organizational culture.

In regard to integrated performance leadership, performance measures must be balanced in the organization and must not compete. That means that in the pursuit of managing one metric, another should not be compromised. For example, cost-reduction metrics should not be allowed to drive quality in the wrong direction or compromise employee satisfaction. In so doing, the organization may meet short-term goals at the expense of its long-term objectives. It would also be selling itself short in its efforts to become a lean enterprise because waste would be generated to meet the nonintegrated metric. There are two major aspects of performance that the organization must address in its journey to integration. The first is to develop a set of performance measures that accurately and comprehensively measure the organization's health. The second is to align the organization's internal budget allocations so that internal competition is reduced and collaboration enhanced. The first is easier to do than the second. But before we talk about alignment of performance metrics and budget, let's first understand the concept of performance in greater depth.

DEFINING ORGANIZATIONAL PERFORMANCE

What is organizational performance? In their research, Lewin and Minton (1986) traced the philosophy of organizational performance from Taylor in 1911 to Peters and Waterman in 1983. They concluded that empirical research has been noncumulative and has not contributed to the development of a unified theory of organizational performance. This means that from an academic perspective there is no consensus, and performance metrics are what you want them to be. Adding to the confusion, the term *organizational performance* is frequently used interchangeably with *organizational effectiveness* (Yuchtman and Seashore 1967; Steers 1976a, 1976b; Scott 1977; Seashore 1979; Bedian 1980; Miles 1980; Daft 1983; Quinn and Rohrbaugh 1983; Faerman and Quinn 1985; Lewin and Minton 1986). In a review of the literature, Campbell, et al. (1974) identified 30 criteria of organizational performance (effectiveness), summarized in Table 3.1. This table is helpful because it provides a basis from which a vocabulary can be established and from which measures of relative performance can be created. For the purposes of IPL, review the list from a waste-generation and cultural perspective. For example, how does employee morale relate to the generation of waste? How do accidents in the workplace relate to waste? In the creation of organizational metrics, we need to use a perspective that takes into account the entire value stream and how individual metrics contribute to the creation of first- or second-order value. The more third- or fourth-order value present in a process, the more waste will be imbedded in the value stream.

Not surprisingly, most performance measures found in business and academic research take a financial approach (Denison 1990; Kotter and Heskett 1992; Chung 1996) or take into account employee satisfaction and motivation (Bennis 1979; Lorsch and Morse 1982; Yukl 1994). Yet each of these research measures frequently suffers from its own form of variance. Many human resources approaches (for example, employee satisfaction and motivation) suffer from common method variance (Podsakoff and Organ 1986) in which measures of two or more constructs or variables are collected from the same respondents and correlated—which speaks to the accuracy of the assessment. For example, subordinates or supervisors may provide both the focal leader's leadership and performance criteria ratings. The problem with this is too much subjectivity. The best way to resolve such issues of variance or subjectivity is simply to qualify the measures with others' perspectives—frequently referred to as 360-degree assessments. An organization should never allow single-source surveys to serve as stand-alone measures of organizational performance. Opinions and subjective perspectives can often lead

Table 3.1 Campell's list of effectiveness criteria (Campbell et al.1974) provides a framework for establishing performance measures that have meaning to different communities.

• Overall effectiveness	• Productivity
• Efficiency	• Profit
• Quality	• Accidents
• Growth	• Absenteeism
• Turnover	• Job satisfaction
• Motivation	• Morale
• Control	• Conflict/cohesion
• Flexibility	• Planning and goal setting
• Goal consensus	• Internalization of organizational goals
• Role and norm congruence	• Readiness
• Managerial interpersonal skills	• Stability
• Managerial task skills	• Utilization of environment
• Information management and communications	• Value of human resources
	• Achievement emphasis
• Evaluations by external entities	• Participation and shared influence
• Training and development emphasis	

you down the wrong path. The assessment will provide a qualitative measure of the leader's perceived performance and a measure of style. As will be discussed in the next chapter, it is not advisable to have leaders who make their numbers at the expense of the organizational culture. They have to perform in both measures, being transformational in developing the capability and capacity of their organization, which includes developing peer-based relations, as well as being able to make the business plans that will ensure success.

Many studies of financial measurement approaches find that the attribute of customer service is frequently ignored, although it is a major external constituency theorized to affect an organization's long-term survival (Buzzell and Gale 1987; Zeithaml, et al. 1990; Berry and Zeithaml 1994). By looking only at the numbers without qualifying them with sustainability measures, the financial measure is truly only a snapshot in time that is very susceptible to change and can that be achieved at the expense of other measures.

Recently a variety of new approaches centering on quality, service, and organizational learning have caught the attention of both organizational managers and researchers in search of answers to help organizations increase their long-run adaptive capacity and performance. At the core of these approaches is a relentless commitment to adapting to the environment (Weick and Daft 1984; Lawrence and Lorsch 1986) and especially to meeting the needs of the customer (Colyer 1996). While financial measures such as profitability are still viewed as indicators of an organization's performance, customer service is beginning to be recognized as a means to financial ends (Dwyer 1993; Berry and Zeithaml 1994). However, the reality of business has kept these quality measures mostly in the domain of research and rarely in practice. This area of research offers a direct application to the concept of a lean enterprise and to the creation of value for the customer as it relates to organizational success. Although the *strategic constituencies* model (Miles 1980; Daft 1983) was not developed with IPL or the lean enterprise in mind, it provides some definition of organizational performance as related to the organization's ability to satisfy the expectations of those stakeholders throughout the value stream upon whom the organization is critically dependent, as shown in Table 3.2.

In their strategic constituencies model, Daft and Weick (1984) suggest that customers' expectations are mostly directed toward the quality of goods and services provided. This suggestion is supported by Campbell's effectiveness criteria (Campbell et al. 1974), which include quality and many of its associated features as criteria. Deming (1986), Ishikawa (1985), and Juran (1969), all leaders in the field of quality, share the view that an organization's primary purpose is to stay in business, so that it can promote the stability of community, generate products and services that are useful to customers, and provide a setting for satisfaction and growth of organization members. Implicit in Juran and Ishikawa, but explicit and prominent in Deming's (1993) writing, is that producing quality products and services is not merely

Table 3.2 Strategic constituencies (adapted from Daft and Weick 1984).

Constituency	Performance criteria
1. Owners	Financial return
2. Employees	Work satisfaction, pay, supervision
3. Customers	Quality of goods and services
4. Creditors	Creditworthiness
5. Community	Contribution to community affairs
6. Suppliers	Satisfactory transactions
7. Government	Obedience to laws, regulations

less costly but, in fact, absolutely essential to long-term organizational survival. However, such must be balanced. In the zeal to provide the highest quality of products and services, organizations should not give customers more than what they are willing to pay for or more than what they want. It is important to truly understand the needs and wants of the customers, because if we assume the customer wants something and the change or addition we make to the product fails to add value, that is another form of waste.

The *performance* aspect of IPL is about the balanced value proposition to customers, to internal membership, and to the value stream. It is also about the elimination of waste throughout the value stream. We need to consider the four orders of value in any established metric of the organization. If we design our processes correctly and ensure alignment according to the environment, the creation of value for shareholders will occur automatically.

In defining performance metrics relative to value creation for the customer, organizations frequently look to measures of service or product quality. Unfortunately, organizations typically focus on tangible outputs of their processes and systems. Those often include the number of problem parts per million, scrap rates, warranty costs, process capability, and the frequency of defective products sent to customers (*escapes*), as well as numerous others. Don't misunderstand—all these measures are important, especially escapes to the customer, but they don't accurately reflect the performance of the complete business. Organizations rarely measure the intangible costs of poor quality, which include loss of reputation, loss of potential sales, engineering changes, excess inventory, expediting costs, long cycle times, employee frustration, and many other expenses that are difficult to measure. All of these contribute to the creation of waste in the value stream.

An indication of how poor quality can erode the performance of an organization was found by Reichheld and Sasser (1990). Their research reported that for the various service organizations they studied, which included banks, auto repair shops, insurance companies, laundries, and shipping and distribution firms, a 5 percent decrease in customer "defections" would represent an increase in profit of 25 to 85 percent.

In most cases, keeping customers is much cheaper than finding new ones. And one way to keep customers is to satisfy them by meeting their expectations—for example, with quality products. If an organization allows customers to be continuously disappointed, then it should be obvious to the leadership that the customer is looking for other options. Given the opportunity, a dissatisfied customer will gladly jump to another provider of goods or services even if it only promises better quality without having demonstrated such. So, it is critically important for the organization to establish and maintain a relationship with its customers. For the organization that interacts directly with its customers, this could be through relatively personal means, whereas a more commercial product organization will need to be creative in ensuring that customer's voices are heard and that customers perceive that they are being heard.

Ideally, customers should feel a connection to the organization through some sort of affiliation. For example, as a consumer I would buy a television only from manufacturer X because I can relate to the quality of its products and I know it will always be there for me. As a service example, when Hurricane Andrew hit Florida in 1992, some insurance companies gained customers for life, whereas others lost customers for life. The discriminating difference between the two was the sense of caring for the customer and being responsive. While some insurance companies were quick to respond and went to extreme efforts to ensure their customers were cared for, others did not. This is the difference between establishing relationships with customers and establishing business opportunities.

A real example of how an organization can realize a return on quality improvement and investment is that of a major manufacturing organization that we will refer to as Aircraft, Inc. In its endeavor to reduce escapes throughout its value stream, Aircraft established as an objective reducing escapes by 45 percent in one year. That objective became a major part of the organizational road map; an integrated leadership team named the Escapes Elimination Board was established, as was a routine of deployed leadership. The board was populated by the business leaders who had all the resources necessary to fix whatever needed to be fixed in their respective value streams. These were the general managers of each line of business. The quality leader of the organization (VP-level) organized and facilitated the process. Recognizing the short-term expectations for improvement, immediate actions were sought. The board worked from the historical escape data of the organization and identified the top three systemic issues in the company. Although these were not going to be the only things to be worked on, they were the three areas that the entire company would concentrate on in an integrated manner to ensure that the root causes were identified and eliminated.

Because many opportunities for improvement were found between groups, some low-hanging fruit could be picked for quick results. As an example, parts were being rejected by the assembly organization because of visual defects such as nicks, dents, and scratches. Simply by bringing those who produced the parts together with those who installed them, solutions were developed to protect the parts in transport and change handling methods in both locations. As a by-product of integration, this subteam shared what it learned throughout the organization to eliminate other like causes of escapes.

Identification markings on parts also presented the company with a significant challenge by contributing to a high percentage of overall escapes.

Parts could be mismarked in a number of ways. Employees who "engraved" the parts by hand could easily transpose letters and numbers of a 20-digit identifier, not to mention the artistic license that could be taken in handwriting. The Escapes Elimination Board wanted to prevent marking escapes from ever occurring again and sought a technological intervention. The solution was an automated two-dimensional vibropen marking process. This marking method is an automated process that applies both a man- and machine-readable marking technique directly to the part. No human touches the part in a marking process—which eliminated numerous inspection stamps, resulting in a cleaner product. Traceablitiy of each individual work operation applied to the part was documented within the company's computer system and provided to users downstream in the value stream. Service information could now be collected for the life of an individual part, controlled by a virtual means, and networked to return value to the customer.

To deploy this new technology was not difficult at all—because it was an integrated decision. Funding was provided by the program office to change drawings (where necessary); the leadership of the lines of business deployed the capital investments based on the greatest needs; the manufacturing engineering and quality assurance organizations teamed to ensure standardization of equipment and repeatability of readability; and engineering was engaged in application analysis (where necessary) and in providing a global change to the engineering standards that allowed the marking method as an option. The procurement organization was key in bringing the supply base on board with the new technology. Another important player in the intervention was the customer. Customers were informed (read, *educated*) of the new marking methods, mostly to ensure that parts would not be rejected upon receipt because their own folks did not recognize the two-dimensional method.

Aircraft, Inc. is a large company and some would speculate that such an intervention would take years to deploy, and they would be partially correct. To go back and redo all of the mature products could take years—however, the need to do so did not match customer needs nor was it required by performance measures. To eliminate the sources of known marking escapes (repeat offenders) took only months. As a two-dimensional marking process was deployed in a production cell, marking escapes became pains of the past.

These remedies could have been deployed with local leadership in a nonintegrated fashion a year earlier. But because the organization had failed to perceive its performance in the way the customer perceived it, as one entity, past efforts were localized and minimally successful. It was after a collective leadership decision to perform as one that the organization took a great step forward in satisfying its customers. At the end of the year, the company realized its 45 percent reduction in escapes, and the cost avoidance was estimated roughly at $140 million.

The challenge for organizational leaders is to establish an environment that fosters the desired organizational performance and behavior and to think and act as one. Such an environment espouses collaboration and minimizes internal competition. For the leader, the task is to focus behavior and action on the desired culture for the organization. It's also to design the work of the organization so that variance is minimized. And because organizational culture is one of the more complex and challenging parts of an organization to influence and maintain, it must be in the forefront of leadership's actions—including performance measurements. Deming (1986) and Ishikawa (1985) suggest that an organization must remove all organizational systems that create fear—such as punishment for poor performance, appraisal systems that involve the comparative evaluation of employees, and merit pay. Though I may not totally agree with doing away with holding individuals accountable as individuals and rewarding them as well for individual contribution, I would agree that fairness must be practiced. Removing fear from an organization is inherent in the role of leadership (Deming 1986); that removal can be supported by the systems of the organization and the communication signals sent throughout the organization.

Although leadership is discussed in the following chapter, I will say here that the challenge for organizations is to develop measures that accurately assess those attributes that only leadership can influence—such as the level of fear in an organization. Take, for example, an organization that is highly transactional and in which leadership drives through intimidation by speaking only in terms of immediate numbers and rarely in terms of organizational growth and culture. How willing would the organizational membership be to engage in transformational endeavors that may have short term cost implications but promise the transformation of the organization in terms of culture and employee engagement? Well, it depends on how many times the functional or line of business leadership has been to the transactional whipping pole. The more often they have been there, the lower the likelihood of transformational behavior. Accountability must be holistic, balanced, and fair. Short term business performance measures must be balanced by long-term organizational success factors such as culture and membership growth.

ALIGNING PERFORMANCE METRICS

So how should we measure organizational performance? It depends entirely on the specific organization, its environment, and the design of its value stream. It also depends, most importantly, on the needs and desires of its customers and its members. As illustrated in the strategic constituencies model (Table 3.2) performance measures depend on your vantage point, that is, where you are in the value stream. If you are an employee, you are concerned about work satisfaction, pay, and supervision, as well as other attributes such as job security and growth—you are concerned with having personal needs met. A customer is interested in quality goods and services provided with convenience, dependability, reliability, expected cost, and on time—again, with having their needs met. One method for aligning the performance metrics of an organization is to establish a top-level road map with assignable performance measures at all levels of the organization.

A *road map* is a simple communications tool that defines the vision, ethics, culture, and tactical direction of the organization. It is purely a vehicle of communication. But it can provide the lightning rod around which the organization rallies to focus its energies. But the road map must be balanced, exacting in the critical few things the organization will do, and funded.

IPL focuses on balance throughout the organization and value stream—creating a homeostatic environment. To achieve a performance metric balance, one must view the organization from all perspectives that matter. For this reason, we will focus on the strategic constituencies model for our road map framework to measure organizational performance. The top level of the organization's road map should assign overall targets for performance for each of the strategic constituency attributes, and each must be balanced among the other attributes. For example, the stakeholders will demand a certain financial performance metric such as a specific revenue and EBIT (earnings before interest and taxes). To achieve this, the organization typically flows specific sales numbers down to the marketing group and cost reduction numbers to the production organization. If the organization has focused on integration, it will have also established collaborative teams, such as integrated program management teams that will look for opportunities to integrate engineering, production, procurement, sales and marketing, and quality into developing business solutions for achieving the specified financial numbers. However, it is essential that one does not ignore the other attributes of the strategic constituencies. For example, let's say the organization makes its financial numbers, but does so through major reductions in its membership, also known as head count reductions. The liability of lost memory and productivity can significantly overshadow the immediate financial returns, not to mention its impact on organizational culture and trust. Granted, head count reductions may be needed to make an organization more profitable, but they should not be the default response. Preferably, the organization should look for opportunities to improve performance through waste reductions in both its white-collar and blue-collar work processes. Get rid of third- and fourth-order value; get rid of waste! For example, the alignment of design and production capability frequently brings organizations capacity improvements because product is flowing faster with little to no scrap and with higher turns of inventory. To achieve this, all aspects of the organization must collaborate to make technical and business decisions about what gets changed. More accurately stated, the organization must be integrated in its action. The most significant metric that gets improved through integration is that of employee satisfaction. The mere fact that the membership can see how it contributes to organizational success can provide a feeling of engagement and pride.

The top-level road map must ensure that balance is designed into the business model and that it can be understood from all perspectives of the organization—inside and out. To achieve this, the leadership must challenge the metric for each strategic constituency in comparison with the others. For example, if we establish a performance metric for *owners* in financial terms, what metric should we establish to ensure balance with *community*? Obviously, every company wants to be a good neighbor. So in terms of providing a performance metric for this attribute, the organization could establish measures of waste reduction that protect the local area's environment or could provide stable and safe jobs that provide security for the local community. These metrics speak to terms of costs to the system, but also interrelatedness with employee satisfaction. So as an organization develops its top-level metrics, it must balance goals and measures to ensure consistency in the signals its sends to its membership, customers, suppliers, community, and government.

The next step in aligning performance metrics is to flow the performance expectations to the functional leaders and to the various lines of business throughout the value stream. Herein lies the highest probability for the metrics to become disconnected and possibly even to conflict. Ideally, the process of performance metric alignment in the organization is undertaken as a collective body with senior leadership representation from each of the functional disciplines and lines of business. These leaders must have sufficient knowledge of the overall business and of the unique and specific needs of the part of the organization they represent. They must also fully understand the vision of the organization and how organizational performance is interrelated with a lean enterprise. The size of the group is contingent upon the size of the overall organization, but it must be manageable.

The top-level performance expectations are the foundation upon which the next tiers are developed. This should not be a process of solving world hunger, but rather of identifying the few important and systemic issues the company is going to rally around. As a matter of fact, the greater the number of different and unique performance metrics used in the organization, the higher the probability the organization will have disconnected strategies for action. Let's take one measure as an example. Let's say the organization desires certain financial performance that requires increased sales and reduced costs. In qualifying this metric, the organization finds a need to improve employee satisfaction and determines that greater engagement is an appropriate strategy. From a customer perspective, quality of delivered product needs to be improved. There are also regulatory and community demands to reduce hazardous wastes. All of these strategic constituency attributes can be aligned through one integrated action throughout the organization by funneling the causes of waste through one investigative process. If the organization analyzes its internal quality performance metrics, it will typically find that the data fall into groupings such as a cause, department, or part number. If cost data such as scrap, rework, inventory turns, warranty, and escapes are shown for each of the groupings, the organization will quickly find where it can get the greatest return on its quality improvement efforts through surgical integrated action.

Again, the recommendation would be to align design and production capability for each of the product lines or part families. Here we can align our strategy for customer and owner through one focused direction for action on improvement of delivered quality and internal performance enhancement. We can address community and government needs by looking for opportunities for improvement within these focused areas to reduce hazardous waste material while also looking for opportunities to improve safety. The next step is to align the employee satisfaction strategies.

Research (Cartwright and Zander 1960; Likert 1961, 1967; Weick 1979; Podsakoff and Organ 1986) has shown that employees who feel they can contribute to an organization's success have higher levels of satisfaction. So, the greater the employee's engagement with the business, the greater their satisfaction. If the organization designs methods by which employees can contribute to the reduction of variation in business processes and does so on those groupings that drive cost (waste) and customer satisfaction, reduce hazardous waste, and improve safety, then integration in action begins to materialize. I'll discuss this further when we talk about human psychological needs and how leaders have a responsibility to understand how those relate to organizational performance.

IPL is about integrated and focused action, but action that is realizable. It is a typical practice of leadership in the United States to establish *stretch goals* that are frequently far in excess of aligned resources—also known as BHAGs (big hairy audacious goals). This is not necessarily a detrimental practice because it provides the organization with a vision of what could be. However, it is important that the organization understand the definition of a stretch goal; otherwise it runs the risk of becoming a lie. If a stretch is a stretch, it should be communicated as such. Otherwise, the organization risks driving the wrong behavior and risks creating waste through nonintegrated action, also known as heroism, and driving up the level of fear. It does little good to bite off all the performance issues of the organization one only has the resources to fix nibbles of the drivers. Focus on what can be accomplished effectively and quickly, and have a plan to do the rest. It is imperative for the credibility of leadership not to fail in action. Once creditability is lost, it is difficult if not impossible to regain. The same is true in the eyes of the customer. If the organization fails to deliver on what it promised, customers will begin to look for other options.

To drive consistent action, the process of creating performance road maps should be replicated as far into the organization as makes sense. This means specifically making sense to organizational members at various organizational levels who must enact the strategy. As the process is replicated, the test of integration must be conducted upwards and sideways—viewing the entire value stream. The measures must make sense to the membership and must be realizable. As the road maps become more concrete, the final litmus test is the "So what?". If we do this at this level of the organization, how does it affect the top-level performance expectations and how does it influence the value stream? This is a critical test because this is where the membership can understand its interrelatedness in the overall business and can measure its own engagement through contribution. The concept of sustainability also needs to be part of every thought process. Are the decisions that are made in the interest of short-term results made at the expense of long-term performance? If so, that should be recognized and not covered up.

Now, honestly speaking, this entire endeavor is not one that will fill the organization with joy or one that you will accomplish in a matter of hours. Depending on the size of the organization, it can be a laborious task involving days of leadership commitment and possibly a large number of revisions. It's also a practice that needs to be repeated every year in alignment of organizational resources and action. It may need to be revised even sooner if significant events or market turns occur. The process should also be performed in the development of five-year (or longer) business plans. Long-term implications for culture may require much longer plans. For example, some Japanese firms have 100-year plans. Though these may be lofty objectives, they do provide a long-term direction for leadership and performance and set the tone for the desired culture.

Actions that significantly influence organizational culture always take numerous years of consistent action and behavior (Schein 1985). The benefit of a multiyear and multilayered road map is a vehicle that communicates strategy and vision to the organization and provides a foundation to take the next step—alignment of organizational resources and a level of certainty.

ALIGNING OF ORGANIZATIONAL RESOURCES

The alignment of organizational resources may be the biggest challenge for most organizations. The larger an organization, the greater its potential for being sliced and diced into bits and pieces of manageable, but suboptimal, segments. Frequently, such slices are by programs, profit and loss (P&L) centers, or by functional disciplines. Each slice is typically funded and held accountable for its area of assigned responsibility. The problem with this financial model is that it provides little incentive for the organizational slices to collaborate for the good of the whole when each is held accountable for its individual performance. To illustrate, envision the value stream of a manufactured product in a traditional manufacturing environment.

Assume we already have a designed product and we want just to focus on the fabrication processes. In fabricating the product, we need to consider the raw materials and components that are typically procured by a procurement organization. The procurement organization typically has its functional head that manages buyers and may or may not have quality personnel assigned to it. The buyers should be trying to get the best deal for the organization. This best deal would include not only a good price but also a dependable level of quality and a dependable delivery schedule. The internal production organization would focus on the integration of raw materials and components into the finished product. It would be looking to decrease the time it takes for its internal labor as well as to ensure that the organization meets its cost and quality objectives. The design organization may or may not play an active role in the production processes. But if it does, it may be limited to a liaison role in dispositioning nonconforming material. Each silo of the process is focused on managing the budget within its own segment, and its decision making is influenced by the ability it has to change things within its realm of control and responsibility.

For example, if the procurement organization's financial performance is influenced only up to the point that materials are delivered to the door of production, it is possible for the real financial performance of procurement to be understated. A decision may be made to select a supplier of castings based solely on price and delivery. If during one of the production processes, such as machining, subsurface defects are detected, the castings may need to be scraped—adding additional cost to the organization. If these costs are allowed to be carried by production, the real price (better stated as cost) of the castings is not captured. The result is flawed decision making by procurement because the financial performance measures are not linked. Now, if we take this one step further into the design process, it should also be asked whether the grade of the castings is appropriately identified in the initial design by engineering. If, for example, the yield rate on castings is low because of a design error, then the costs associated with the initial design need to be adjusted, and those responsible for that process need to be held accountable. The same should also be true if the design complexity of the casting causes high scrap because of producibility issues. Each aspect of the value stream must be integrated through financial accountability; otherwise, functional contributors may have the ability to snorkel behind someone else who may be limited in their ability to fix the root cause of the cost driver.

An example from personal experience involves an attempt to secure engineering resources to solve quality issues in production—internal and external. In most organizations, the engineering personnel are *direct charging*, meaning that the time they spend on work is assigned directly back to a program or product. *Indirect-charging* personnel are typically carried in the overhead of the organization that employs them. Frequently, quality and procurement professionals are indirect charging. Because they are not required to account for their time specifically tied to a product, it is typically easier to move indirect people around as you need to or as the situation dictates. Indirect-charging methods provide for great flexibility but little cost accountability. However, for a leader to solicit help from direct-charging personnel, it is not uncommon for a series of negotiations to transpire within leadership to acquire a charge number for direct-charging personnel to work to. The folks who have P&L or program responsibility typically control engineering budgets and may not be sensitive to the issues affecting another part of the business.

Negotiations for resources, then, include an educational aspect to help the solicited leader understand the urgency or need. Sometimes the case must be escalated to gain the support of leadership at a point in the hierarchy at which the budgets converge. It is not uncommon for such negotiations to be unsuccessful and result in costly waste for the product and organization—and ultimately increased customer frustration. After awhile, some leaders may become fatigued with the pursuit for support resources and give up the fight. This is a terrible situation for leadership to allow to exist because it represents the death spiral of waste. Once a leader stops trying to get the root cause fixed and allows others to drive his cost up, he gives up his power to be the best he can be. Waste begets waste, meaning, it becomes contagious. If allowed to exist, it becomes the norm, and the people accept the suboptimal process and behavior as the rule. They also discount the sincerity of leadership when the vision speaks of continuous improvement and waste reduction, and the opposite is the case.

When an organization's financial accountability processes are not integrated throughout the entire life cycle of its products or services, substantial waste will always be generated by its business processes. Those who have lived through the frustration of not being able to get the support they need to fix a problem because of competing financial accountabilities may immediately recognize and appreciate the concept of integrating financial accountability in a life cycle. In those cases where support is needed from the cost generator and it cannot be obtained, the financial accountability processes of the organization should provide relief for those bearing the cost and redirect the accountability to those who cause it. The battle cry of the organization should be "Those who cause the cost will bear it." However, we must keep that mantra balanced with the understanding that poor quality equals high cost and that investment in improving processes should be viewed as reducing costs.

It is common for a cost center, such as a manufacturing organization, to sign up for a target cost for a specific product at the beginning of a budget process. This acknowledgment of the target cost is based on a number of assumptions. At the time of initial design release, the assumption is that the design is stable enough, or mature enough, to project a cost based on a learning curve for production. It is also assumed that projected production volumes will absorb overhead expenses, such as those of core departments like finance and legal. Further assumptions include the costs of raw materials and value-stream capability. As the assumptions change in the life of the product, especially in the early life, so should the assignable cost responsibilities. Let's say the marketing organization was mistaken in its projections for the volume of units to be sold. This requires the production organization to absorb the general and administrative (G&A) costs of the enabler organizations into the cost of producing products. Because there are now fewer units to absorb the cost, the overall cost of producing products will in turn increase and the production organization may miss its own targets due to little fault of its own. Granted, the production organization must scale the capacity to the demands of the market, but if the data it receives from another part of the organization are flawed, the causal leader should bear the accountability for the poor projections—or better stated, poor performance—of their organization.

This same argument can go in any direction. For example, if the sales group is able to increase volume through increased sales, it should be afforded a less expensive product from the production organization because of the increased capacity to absorb cost—which could also make it possible to sell more product for a lower price or increase the organization's profit margin. Regardless, the argument must be made that process owners are to be held accountable for the piece of organizational performance they are capable of influencing.

One important aspect of this thought that businesses frequently ignore is that subtle changes in design may disrupt projected learning curves and productivity. Take, for example, an aircraft manufacturer. Frequently, it projects a unit cost based on the number of units produced since initial design release (at unit 50 the aircraft will cost $$x$ and at unit 100 it will cost $$y$). This allows the production organization to "learn out" the processes required to produce the product. For example, a change to product geometry may require tooling to be produced or to be modified to ensure producibility or productivity. Employees then need to become familiar with the new tooling. The change requires work instructions to be modified, requiring the expense of a planner in addition to the time lost as employees familiarize themselves with the new documentation. Some cases may call for the training of personnel in new special processes or production techniques, albeit on-the-job training in many cases.

The affects of the change become magnified as the implementation of the change is pushed deeper into the value stream. Suppliers typically require more time to make sense of a customer's changes to technical data than does the customer's own organization. Costs will be incurred by various organizations in the clarification of expectations and in the validation of the implementation. Regardless of their perceived significance, as design changes creep into the production of a product or service, it affects the learning curve or productivity measures to some degree. This thought process is not limited to manufacturing organizations; it should also be applied to service organizations—in both the private and public sector.

By establishing financial systems that incorporate waste accountability, we support an environment of fairness, and those who influence resource requirements will continue to maintain a measure of sensitivity and understanding of their actions. IPL requires all leaders to be accountable for their actions, including the influences on the value stream. This sense of fairness should go in both directions—added value and increased cost. If actions are taken upstream in the value stream that have a positive influence on the cost of those downstream, then the downstream organizations should be challenged to improve on their cost performance.

As in the earlier example of volume fluctuations, if the sales volume increases, then the absorption rate for corporate overhead expenses for the production organization is improved. Its unit cost should come down. If castings are designed to be closer to their final dimension (near net), then less machining efforts are required and unit cost should come down. If the insurance company simplifies claim actions by moving the labor to the customer over the Internet, then the claim-processing department should reduce its cost structure. These are all simple examples, but they only occur consistently when the organizational processes are hard-wired to require such reviews and adjustments.

The final financial dilemma I will discuss is that of any organization-wide process improvement effort such as just-in-time (JIT) production or lean manufacturing. These two tools, especially, require integration of financial accounting in order to ensure success. JIT and lean manufacturing are closely related in that they require systems that pull product and processes through the life cycle. That is, as a process is ready to consume a material, the material is there waiting for it, and such is true throughout the life cycle. The trick is not to accumulate inventory or to have weak points in the pull process. As one can envision, every aspect of the process must be aligned, including all of the supporting or enabling processes. The perspectives an organization must have are a complete understanding of customer needs and wants and the capability of the entire value stream to deliver. Those that play in this arena frequently understand the need to think more broadly than just making sure materials are where they need to be when they are needed; they employ the concept of sustainability—keeping the process capable for the long term.

For example, the tooling and machines that support the production processes need to be maintained at a frequency that supports the production rate. The people in the process also periodically require training to ensure that their personal capabilities match the needs of the business. The contract reviews and purchase orders need to be released to match the rate of customer demand. As well, the enabling processes of procedural revisions and internal auditing need to anticipate and be responsive to the pace of business. Supplier capability must be continuously monitored to guard against surprises. Environmental changes such as revisions in regulations or industry standards must be predicted and, I would suggest, influenced. In addition, the behavior of the customer must be understood and integrated as the pull element of the organization's value stream. If any of these aspects of the business is treated as though it is not linked to the rate of customer demand, the organization is in denial about the connectedness of the business.

Additionally, customers may need to become an active participant in your planning. Your internal performance can become only as choreographed as your customers allow. If their demands fluctuate a lot, that will trickle down the entire value stream. I suggest you engage your customers in managing the processes that influence demand requirements, which will in turn require them to assess their broader internal business processes and organizational structures. In doing so, you may distinguish yourself to your customers as a greater value provider than just of products or services. In short, if there is value in performing the process, then it should be accomplished well, and they must be resourced appropriately to do so. Otherwise, stop doing the process because it provides no value.

An organization needs to think and act in terms of integrated performance and accountability. To expect that leaders will work together on their own and offset each other with performance expectation adjustments is delusional. Even if an organization has a great leadership team that works closely together, it is unreasonable to think that individuals will miss their performance goals to support another aspect of the organization if no process of fairness exists in the performance accountability process. Even if some individuals are willing to take the risk of doing the "right thing" for the organization, it is not sustainable. Normal attrition and environmental factors such as pressure (for example, tight delivery schedules, labor actions, budget reductions) will inject variance into human behavior. People will perform according to the method by which they are measured.

This claim is pretty much aligned with Darwin's theory of evolution. Creatures adapt to the environments they inhabit, (their real environment, not an espoused environment), or they cease to exist—also referred to as having the capabilities of requisite variety. The environment of an IPL organization must have hard-wired performance accountability processes throughout the value streams, or the desired collaboration and teaming will not exist. This hard-wiring must require performance accountability reviews of changes as they occur. Creating a process that rolls up changes for block accounting is a good first step for organizations that want to start with IPL accountability. However, it should be understood that the greater the interval between the change and the accounting, the greater the distance to the recognition of accountability and the greater the potential for an undesired costly change to be implemented.

IPL contains no magic process or formula for alignment of financial accountability. Each organization is influenced by its own environmental factors, particularly those that perform within government accounting structures. But IPL does demand that organizations create standard work processes that project accountable performance (for example, cost per unit, number of claims processed, time to delivery), that they validate the target cost at the points at which the projections are set (for example, unit number 100, two weeks on the job); and that they frequently review this performance to ensure sustainability. IPL also demands that as anything changes in the assumptions, regardless of how minor, the accountable performance measures be revisited for the entire value stream in all applicable directions to evaluate potential impact. There is no such thing as a minor change that won't make any difference in cost. As mentioned earlier, the sum of many minor changes can exceed what would be considered a major change.

A preferred method for performance accountability is, as mentioned earlier, hard-wiring such into the change process. When a change is proposed, as a standard step in the change process, an analysis of performance impact should be done for the entire value stream. So far our focus has been on financial accountability, but the performance influence evaluation should also consider variables of quality, delivery, safety, employee satisfaction/human factors, and anything else that can be converted to a measure of value delivered to the customer or cost to the organization.

SUMMARY

The concept of integration is a broad one. It includes organizational processes, structures, leadership behavior, and financial accountability. To create sustainable synergy in the organization, leadership must treat the organization as an interrelated organism. Organizational structures must ensure that the membership is hard-wired for collaboration and for learning. Leadership influence through and across lines of authority must be understood and variance reduced.

For an organization to have the incentive to perform as one, its members must be fairly measured and held accountable for a collective level of performance. When individuals are allowed to make their numbers at the expense of others in the organization, there is little likelihood of leveraging synergies in the organization. This is a huge challenge for organizations to overcome, because traditional accounting practices have driven organizations to suboptimize their financial management processes. Organizations need to rethink their accounting structures so that resources are allocated fairly throughout the organization and that when cost changes occur during the financial year, those who caused the cost are held accountable for it.

The existing tools of the organization need to be integrated into its DNA. These may include Six Sigma, CMMI, TQM, JIT, lean manufacturing, and others. The tools should create value not only by reducing costs that are simple to quantify but also by their application to business processes leading to intangible benefits for the organization, which will frequently provide greater value to the customer. To ensure that both ends of the organization's life cycles are included in the improvement processes, both suppliers and customers should be included in planning activities. An organization can become only as efficient or lean as its suppliers and customers allow it to be.

When it comes to rethinking the financial accountability structures of the organization, the most significant senior leadership challenge is to break the reporting and management practices that serve solely Wall

Street. It is not suggested that leadership ignore the creation of value for stockholders, but rather, that the value creation should be real and not just reside on paper. For long-term sustainable success, leaders must have vision and plant the seeds for future capability. In many cases, the returns of such planting may not materialize until well after the leader who did the planting has moved on to new opportunities or has retired. That is the responsibility of leadership, not only to their customers and stakeholders, but also to the people they employ.

4
Leadership

It is the "L" in IPL that enables the organization to perform and that exercises the greatest influence on success. Leadership in an organization has the ability to influence culture, systems, and resources so that the actions of an organization respond accordingly. Leadership also can influence misbehavior. For example, the top leaders of an organization determine whether people comply with established processes and procedures. They do so through their own actions and messages—also known as "leading by the actions of their feet." The way leaders behave in organizations is probably the most critical characteristic of an organization's potential for success, especially in the collaborative actions that are required for integration. Take, for example, the leader who is faced with a delivery challenge at the end of a quarter. If they send a signal to the organization to increase production deliveries to meet accounting targets and that message is understood as "just make it happen—regardless of everything else," employees may understand that ignoring the established systems of defined processes and procedures is acceptable. They may even believe that becoming a hero in spite of the established processes and procedures will provide them personal rewards and perceive that to be the desired behavior. If such a practice is permitted, the culture is influenced in such a manner that defined processes and procedures provide no sense of value and are to be ignored. Furthermore, in hero cultures there is typically little collaboration and excessive parochial leadership. For a hero to share their glory is to diminish their personal significance.

Leaders must always be conscious of their actions and the signals they send. Even the slightest hint of misbehavior by leaders can influence organizational culture and performance. The eyes of the organization are always watching. If a leader, even without meaning to, carries him/her as a very transactional person, the values that leader enacts may become those of the organization. An organization that is too transactional becomes so at the expense of transformation and employee growth. In a transactional environment, the focus is on the here and now, and long-term sustainability is not typically a core element of the plan. There is also a significant debit to collaboration within the value stream as well as to the attribute of trust. If those outside the organization who support the value stream perceive that the organization's leadership is not committed to a long-term, collaborative relationship that has the predictability of process performance, then why would the organization assume that the value stream would behave any differently? A balance must always be maintained between the application of transactional and transformational leadership—between managing the business and growing the people.

VISIONARY LEADERSHIP

Part of IPL is understanding the need for leadership balance and for growing visionary leaders. Sashkin (1996) defines *visionary leadership* as this:

> "The leader is able to develop long-range visions of what his or her organization can and should become. The leader understands the key elements of a vision to direct the organization into the future. The leader can communicate his or her vision in ways that are compelling and make people want to buy into the vision and help make it happen."

Visionary leaders can balance both transactional and transformational leadership behavior so that the organization performs to its stated objectives as well as grows its membership in terms of beliefs and abilities. IPL introduces an additional dimension to applied visionary leadership. Leaders must be able to see the holistic interrelationships of the organization—horizontally across functions as well as vertically throughout the value stream. The horizontal relationships are those among the functional peer groups and across multiple value streams and throughout the value stream, from the raw material to well into servicing of the delivered product. This requires leaders to be able to perceive the organization as an interrelated system of action and to understand how performance is interdependent throughout the value stream. Leaders who are purely transactional focus their behavior on making the numbers that are assigned directly to them. Their focus is typically on immediate performance and doing what it takes to get the job done—for now. Their vision typically is short—possibly the financial quarter or maybe the year. This may not be the result of their personal abilities or desires but rather of environmental influences—namely, expectations from institutions such as Wall Street.

Granted, there is a time and place for transactional leaders, but it is not where the long-term survival of the organization is the issue. Transactional leaders perform well where their behavior is not witnessed by the organization and their actions won't have an impact on its culture. It is also important that such transactional behavior does not adversely affect the synchronized motion of the value stream. If transactional behavior were allowed to be witnessed by the organization or to affect the balance of the value stream, that would most definitely be a spike in the heart of organizational culture and would disrupt the established trust in flow and process. In turn, that undermining of trust lessens system predictability and compromises value-stream capability. As a result, inventory levels and cycle times increase, and profitability decreases. Don't misunderstand the point here. Every leader must perform transactionally to some degree to ensure a balance of accountability and to execute work. However, transactional leadership by itself pulls more energy from the organization than it contributes.

Transformational leaders focus their efforts on the empowerment and growth of the organization. They are mindful of culture and of the factors that influence culture. This mindfulness may grow out of learning or training, but it is richest when it comes from the heart. When caring and concern for people and the organization are real and not because it's a requirement of the position, the transformational leader is most effective. This is when passion and convictions are manifested and become themselves a contagious virus. Burns and Stalker (1978) first described transformational leadership as occurring

> "when one or more persons engage with others in such a way that leaders and followers raise one another to higher levels of motivation and morality. . . . Their purposes . . . become fused. Power bases are linked not as counterweights but as mutual support for common purpose. . . . It raises the level of human conduct and ethical aspiration of both leader and led, and thus it has a transforming effect on both."

Burns and Stalker's definition speaks to the development of trust between the leader and those that are led. When this type of leadership behavior is operationalized with suppliers and customers in the value stream, the obvious benefits of fair and trustful relationships become visible and begin to build. In addition their definition refers to an obvious symbiotic element. Two are typically stronger than one and a trustful value stream that is bound by integrity and characterized by sustained, predictable performance is stronger than a traditional supplier-producer or provider-customer relationship.

There is another component of the theory of visionary leadership—the time span of vision. The further into the future a leader can conceptualize issues and solutions, the more of an asset the leader is to the organization and the more visionary they are. The notion of time-span capability comes from the research of Elliott Jaques and Kathryn Cason (1994), who investigated human capability. Let's say an effective leader who can move product through the processes with little to no waste, and at the same time grow the organization into a talented customer-minded team, is clearly a valuable asset to the organization. However, if the same leader does not think in terms of years down the road but focuses predominantly on the here and now, namely, on the next couple of months, their vision span is limited. Until the ability to see further into the future is developed, this leader should be kept from migrating to the higher levels of the organization. The higher leaders are in the organization, the longer their vision must be. For example, as an organization's targeted market shifts, such shifts must be perceived—or better stated, anticipated—as early as possible. Long vision will ensure that product development continues even in down years, that capital investments are maintained in the value stream, and that equipment and material have a useful life that meets the business needs of the organization and generates long-term value for the customer. Decision makers with short vision spans frequently find themselves throwing away equipment or investing in skills that are no longer needed because they misread a technology or market shift—they made the wrong choice (a failure of leadership). Short-sighted leaders also find themselves in the situation of labor-load fluctuations that require frequent "right-sizing." Long-visioned leaders predict market needs and technology shifts and adjust their systems and organizations early enough so that impacts are rarely negative. The longer the time-span vision of a leader, the greater the possibilities they can perceive of what the organization can be and what it can accomplish.

As a rule of thumb, Jaques and Cason suggest that the time-span vision of leaders should be aligned as displayed in Table 4.1. A leader whose vision span does not align with the responsibility of their position will most certainly make poor decisions for the organization. Such decisions affect not only the business but also the people. As organizational members witness the misalignment of vision capability and position, they develop a perception of acceptability in the organization. If it is acceptable for the leader to think in such terms, then it must be acceptable for me to do the same.

Being able to perceive the interrelatedness of an organization is as important as having a perspective of what lays far ahead. A lean enterprise is led by a leader with long-range vision and a broad, interrelated perspective, who balances the characteristics of transformational and transactional leadership to create systems of sustained capability (see Figure 4.1). An interrelated perspective and long vision span are essential for making wise

Table 4.1 The vision-span structure for leadership.

Time-span	Industry	Military	Government
50 years	Super corporate CEO	5 star	Extraordinary president
20 years	Corporate CEO	Army (4 star)	Administrator/ secretary/SES-1
10 years	Corporate EVP	Corps (3 star)	SES-2
5 years	Business unit president	Division (2 star)	ES-3
2 years	General manager	Brigade (1 star/col)	GS-15
1 year	Unit manager	Battalion (LTC/major)	GS-14
3 months	First-line manager	Company (cpt/lt. E8-E9)	GS-11-13
	Operator	Private and NCO (E1-E7)	GS8-GS10

and informed decisions for the organization—for making the right choices. Understanding how synergies can be maximized through interaction is a capability that must be nurtured in those leaders who possess the willingness and "wiring" to collaborate. In my opinion, not everyone has the ability to be visionary and perceive interrelatedness to gain possible synergies. This is the age-old nature or nurture question, and I believe both are a factor. If we as human beings have not been exposed to the environment of collaboration early in our upbringing, it is unlikely that we will be wired to collaborate as leaders. This does not mean that it cannot be learned, but rather that it will not come naturally, which speaks to actions of the heart. Organizations that are looking to reduce waste through synergy should seek out those leaders who have a natural capability for pulling people together and creating a vision of what can be. But that capability must, and I repeat must, be balanced with expertise in the functions they lead. It does little good to put a good leader in a function they know nothing about, especially if it requires unique knowledge and informed decisions to be made.

94 Chapter Four

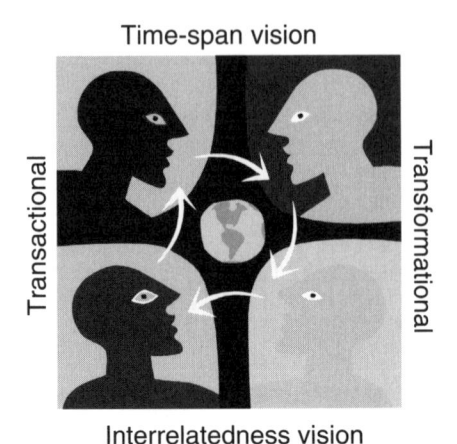

Figure 4.1 The four characteristics of leadership in IPL.

CONTEXTUALIZED LEADERSHIP (UNDERSTANDING)

Making the right choices is not always an easy task. It depends on thoroughly understanding the environment and the specific situations at hand as they apply to the individual value stream and the total organization. Where many leaders fail in the decision-making process is by not adequately understanding the total environment. Some may say that many leaders lack the experience to comprehend the total environment. This in itself should be characterized as a failure of leadership. Leaders place leaders in positions of influence and accountability. If a leader is placed in a position beyond his/her abilities, the leadership above has failed the organization, value stream, and its customers.

It is critical to the success of an integrated organization that the embedded leadership has the ability to see the big picture accurately so as to anticipate environmental changes. Too much to ask for? Absolutely not! All that is required is a conscious effort on the part of the organization to grow and place people in the right positions. Organizations should treat the knowledge capability of their people as a process and a critical attribute for success. I don't know how many times I have seen a new manager enter an organization with little or no understanding of the organization, value stream, or market. Frequently, these newcomers are from disciplines other than the one they will exercise management discretion over. It is not uncommon for leaders who have no contextual understanding of their position to immediately make uninformed decisions. The result almost always disrupts synergy in the organization and in the value stream. If the organization performs in a regulated environment, the poor decision making of a leader may have serious outcomes—usually in terms of penalties. The same can be true in regard to products that can cause harm to customers. Shame on organizations that fail to indoctrinate their leaders as to the environment and their responsibilities prior to placing them in control of organizational resources.

For organizations to do a good job at placing leaders in the right positions and levels, they should ensure that the leader has a good understanding of the environment they are entering. Later in this book, the concept of integrated knowledge management is introduced as a process that can ensure that peoples knowledge is aligned with their responsibilities. In short, integrated knowledge management requires that the organization be thoughtful in its assignments of people. The process is data driven and provides the organization with visual tools that can minimize risk associated with gaps in knowledge capability. The term *knowledge capability* encompasses more than the cognitive process; it includes the ability to apply what is known. However, when leaders are inserted for developmental reasons, it is essential that they are "sandwiched" between technical experts charged with the responsibility of making sure that decisions do not have a negative impact on the organization. This can be a daunting task because you want the person to consider new approaches and "stretch" the organization and its processes. Yet it is critical that personnel development does not occur at the expense of customer satisfaction.

That a leader should possess a general understanding of the business sounds logical. But because we frequently place growing leaders in developmental positions, we may forget that the development of the individual may be at the expense of others in the value stream. Leaders should be prepared when entering a new leadership role. This means they should have a good understanding of how the position relates to the value stream, of the controls of the processes, of the culture of the organization, and of the external requirements and expectations. It does little good to place a procurement professional into a production leadership role without first indoctrinating the individual into the fundamentals of manufacturing.

In many industries, leadership positions in quality are frequently used as "developmental opportunities" for upcoming leaders of other disciplines. As a result, the quality profession has significantly suffered in the development of new professionals and in the advancement of the science. I would even go so far as to say that in some cases product quality has suffered as a result of *novice* leadership in quality roles. My advice to senior executives is to stop putting novices into quality leadership roles immediately and start looking for those with a depth of knowledge in the field and develop them to transform your business. I would add that this is not an avowal of more of the same, but rather I'm saying that the discipline must be led by those who know the discipline and have the ability to project vision into organizational processes. Find these experts within the disciplines, and grow them into the visionary leaders that will eliminate waste and create greater value.

GLAUBWÜRDIGKEIT (BELIEVABILITY)

The contextualized understanding of the leader must include organizational vision. It is only when vision is shared with and believed by the entire organization that organizational culture can move closer to being that which is desired. The German word *Glaubwürdigkeit* comes to mind (well at least to mine) when we talk about leaders sharing the vision of the organization. *Glaubwürdigkeit* translates to believability. If the words that come out of a leader's mouth lack the attribute of accuracy, those who should be following the leader become skeptical and may cease following together. Why would anybody follow a leader they don't believe? A leader without followers becomes very lonely indeed, and eventually become powerless to create wide-scale change or even to perform. Leaders must be believable—Glaubwürdig.

Another aspect of *Glaubwürdigkeit* is the leader's ability to communicate effectively the direction and vision of the organization to the people. This is particularly challenging if the vision contains ambiguity and uncertainty. As with any learning activity, abstractions must be applied to practice. Abstractions detached from practice distort or obscure intricacies of that practice. Without a clear understanding of those intricacies and the roles they play, the practice itself cannot be well understood, engendered, or enhanced (Brown and Duguid 1991). It is the leader's responsibility to fulfill the role of teacher in ensuring that the organization learns and understands (Senge 1990b). As a teacher, the leader educates the organization by means of what Dewey (1916) characterizes as a fostering, nurturing, and cultivating process. This can be accomplished only when the leader is perceived by the followers as credible. And credibility is very much related to action. According to Huber (1996), learning need not be conscious or intentional. The leader establishes the conditions and environment in which the organization can learn (Schwandt 1994). Through personal engagement with the people and by relating to their and the organization's needs, the leader creates a sense of openness and learning.

One way leaders facilitate organizational learning is by reducing equivocality (Daft and Weick 1984). *Equivocality* is the extent to which data are unclear and suggest multiple interpretations about the environment. Daft and Weick (1984) suggest that equivocality be reduced through shared observations and discussion until a common grammar and course of action can be agreed upon. The greater the equivocality, the more times data may be cycled among members of the organization before common interpretation is reached. The great threat of equivocality is that wasted time and energy will degrade organizational performance and that greater variance will be introduced into the processes of the organization (Womack and Jones 1996). Herein is a significant opportunity for waste reduction in an organization. By facilitating a common vocabulary and interpretive schema, the amount of energy it takes to cause action can be greatly reduced. This is the value of contextualized leadership in IPL and underscores the need for organizations to treat knowledge capability as a critical business process.

MANAGING LEADERSHIP ABILITIES

IPL requires organizations to treat leadership as a critical characteristic of their business planning and regard it as a process that needs to be controlled and capable. Without the right leadership, organizations will never be able to see the holistic nature of value streams and the interrelatedness of action. In turn, they won't be able to reduce waste and increase value to the levels that could be possible. Consideration must be given to how leaders are developing their broad, interrelated perspectives, knowledge capabilities, balance of transaction and transformation, and lengthening their vision. These abilities don't develop on their own. The organization must plan for leadership growth and capability. The organization's internal environment must encourage such leadership characteristics for these capabilities to emerge and be sustained. The internal environment is that which the organization creates through its processes, procedures, actions, behavior, and culture. Again, these are all choices made by leadership.

Organizations need to establish methods for developing transactional, transformational, time-span vision, and interrelatedness capabilities. The first of these, transactional leadership capability, is probably the easiest for most organizations because it has been the primary focus of business for years. An example is the MBA programs that companies send their people to so that they can develop business acumen. Not to speak ill of MBA programs, but few provide for significant leadership balance in their curriculum. Typically, an MBA readies the graduate to conduct business primarily from a financial perspective, not necessarily to grow people and organizational capability, and the true understanding of ethical behavior and its importance in establishing the underlying fabric of the organization is frequently not integrated into the business cases of study. Ideally, MBA programs would evolve to teach that there is a need for robust organizational systems and human balance and to recognize that the traditional business capabilities are the honing of only part of the formula. Value creation must be understood in broader terms than the immediate measures of finance. Though difficult to calculate, the value created by an engaged and committed organization is much greater than that created by one that is not. There are other aspects of transactional leadership that are not typically taught in MBA programs that need to be developed.

The concepts of a lean enterprise are only now finding their way into traditional university settings and curricula. The ability to measure waste throughout the entire value stream requires the destruction of parochial financial accounting systems and the development of collaborative processes that leverage synergy and ensure accountability. Tools such as process mapping need to be incorporated into a leader's cognitive thought process as well as the ability to think in terms of boundless geography. To see the wholeness of the value stream, in as broad a sense as possible, provides the leader with a better understanding upon which to make better choices. Thinking in terms of a global economy provides the leader the ability to develop creative solutions in terms of logistics and resources and potentially to create greater business opportunities through new perspectives. An additional area of cognizance is that of environmental impact. Greater understanding of how the business affects the environment will facilitate better decision making for long-term sustainability. Given that resources typically are limited, it's important to understand where the balances reside. The same is true with pollution. The expense of later cleanup can far exceed the short-term financial gains of the present when less-than-appropriate controls are in place. So how does an organization go about developing such cognitive transactional abilities in its leaders? It depends. It depends on the value proposition of the business. The objective is to create an understanding of the global value stream that is specific to the organization. From the transactional perspective, the leader must have intimate knowledge of the value of their effort, whether it be within an engineering, procurement, production, or quality discipline.

For example, an engineering leader should have sufficient breadth of knowledge to know what other organizations in the world are doing in the field of engineering. Such a leader should also know where global investments are being made in science and in products and what the various timelines are for deployment. This is basic Darwinism—understanding the competition and survival of the fittest. In addition, a general understanding of what's going on in governmental agencies is valuable, so that the organization will not be surprised by new regulatory actions—again, a Darwinian idea of predicting environmental changes for adaptation. I would even suggest that leaders do their best to control the environment. One effective method of developing this capability is through participation in industry groups. The higher an organizational leader is in the organization, the more active they should be leading industry groups. An excellent example of executive leadership's choosing to influence its environment is within the quality discipline of the aerospace manufacturing industry.

The aerospace manufacturing industry represents companies that provide services and products (value) to commercial and freight airlines, general aviation, military aviation, buyers of commercial and military spacecraft, and buyers of missiles and rockets. There is also some crossover into other industrial segments, such as with the industrial gas turbines built for power generation and marine uses as well as electronics and sensors made for other commercial uses. Though the technical requirements of the various organizations that interact in the aerospace industry may vary greatly, conceptually the expectations for quality are the same. Recognizing a need to reduce variance in quality requirements throughout the aerospace value stream, the top quality leaders of the largest U.S. aerospace manufacturers agreed to collaborate in a leadership forum to drive standardization in the industry. This group quickly expanded to include companies from around the world and became the International Aerospace Quality Group (IAQG). A few times a year, the top quality executives of the world's aerospace organizations meet at different locations around the globe to control their collective environment. Their presence represents approximately 80 percent of the global financial spend on aerospace products—mostly prime manufacturers. So when they jointly agree to take a certain action within the global value stream, that action is quick and effective.

The IAQG has three components, which represent the Americas, Europe, and Asia, each with its own internal leadership structure. As projects are defined and worked, lower-level subteams are established to work the details. From a transactional leadership perspective, meaning to get work done, leaders are represented at each echelon of the IAQG hierarchy. By design, their respective positions in their companies define their participation within the IAQG hierarchy. For example, vice presidents serve at the IAQG council level, senior managers at the global sector level, and midlevel and senior practitioners at the subteam level. The greater the participation, the greater the return to the organization. One needs only to reflect on the phrase of "the power of the pen" to realize the validity of this concept. Additionally, through their industry participation, leaders develop an understanding of their global value stream and environment and develop unique abilities to influence it. This group's effectiveness has been widely recognized by both regulatory bodies and other industry groups and has taken the point position for industry leadership in the aerospace quality field.

Participating in such industry forums creates awareness outside the organization's four walls. However, that is possible only through contextualized leadership—leaders who have knowledge capability within the discipline. If companies sent leaders to participate in such a forum who had no contextual wisdom of the discipline, the effectiveness and value of such a global group would be greatly minimized. Recognizing the ability of a group such as the IAQG, private industry should consider its collective ability to influence its environment. Most government agencies lack the ability to move swiftly, primarily because they are designed to ensure a democratic process. The last thing an industry wants is a regulated environment that has the ability to change without due process of review and comment. However, what is important to recognize is that those in private industry have the power of leadership and deployment of capital. If they chose to do something and collectively commit themselves to making it happen, then there is a very great likelihood of success.

In addition to industry forums, periodicals can be a valuable source of information and growth. The challenge is finding time to read them as a leader. The only advice that can be given here is to find periodicals that provide the richest source of information about your value stream and schedule time to review them. But this is a must-do. If leaders are not informed of recent advances in their field, they quickly become a follower of the competition. At all levels of the organization, members who scan the trade periodicals should be expected to share important information with their colleagues. By doing so, we start to bridge transaction with transformation and broaden the definition of leadership. Leaders should consider developing internal structures for such information sharing. Don't make it a costly endeavor, but do make it conscious and visible. It's when leaders transform information into knowledge by contextualizing it for the organization that they act as transformational leaders. When these same leaders transform this knowledge into action and value, the value stream benefits.

The use of a tool such as the integrated knowledge management matrix, which is discussed in a later chapter, takes much of the subjectivity out of the assessment of knowledge capability. It is suggested that organizations adopt a process like integrated knowledge management to treat the development and sustainability of knowledge capability as a process. Once knowledge capability is managed as a process, the aspects of leadership can be included in the process for development.

LEADING FOR AN ENVIRONMENT OF DIALOGUE

Just as leaders' knowledge capability must be aligned with their organizational responsibilities, they should be capable of creating a work environment where people feel comfortable engaging in dialogue with each other. This speaks to the qualities of transformational leadership. As leaders facilitate dialogue in the workplace, they strengthen the processes of sense making and knowledge capability building in the organization. Dixon (1994) recognizes that it is not realistic to talk about individuals in isolation because we exist in a social environment. Thus, "individual learning is dependent upon the collective," and the converse is also true: "collective learning is dependent on the individual." Fiol (1994) adds that organized action is a requirement for organizational learning, which is accomplished by developing consensus around interpretations embedded in the content as well as by framing communications and forms that people use to construct a framework for organized action. That essentially means that the organization makes meaning by its members communicating with each other. Sackmann (1992) talks about sense-making mechanisms that organizational members use to attribute meaning to events. These mechanisms "include the standards and rules for perceiving, interpreting, believing, and acting that are typically used in a given cultural setting." They can include the definitions that organizations apply to situations and terms and that frequently are influenced by the systems leaders deploy into organizations. For example, if an organization deploys standard tools for identifying projects and applies investigative tools, the organization will interpret its environment and work in specific routines. As is discussed in a later chapter, organizational mechanisms such as VISION centers can facilitate structured dialogue to promote the application of consistent interpretations and action. However, organizations must be careful not to overcontrol the ability of members to engage freely in dialogue in a process of discovery; otherwise innovation and creativity may be stifled.

Through dialogue we learn to become self-directed in our ability to spell out the specifics of our experiences (Mezirow 1985). Organizational members must feel comfortable and safe enough to openly discuss things with leadership and other organizational members. This speaks to the spirit and heart of the organization. If the organization is tense and uncomfortable when discussing challenges and opportunities, it is unlikely the organization will perform to expectations. On the contrary, it will require additional resources to overcome the internal friction and will lose much of its competitive edge.

Deming (1972) suggests that removing fear from the organization is the greatest challenge and responsibility of leadership. This includes the removal of fear about speaking up when there is a need. Dialogue is not based on finding the right answer; it is about inventing or making meaning from a situation. Partners in dialogue are challenged to find a coherent interpretation of their multiple perspectives (Bennett and Brown 1995) and make sense of what's going on. Sense making is greater than an individual or collective understanding, interpretation, or attribution. Sense making is the individual and collective process of making meaning of an organization's actions (Daft and Weick 1984); it involves the process of reflection (Schön 1987). At the social level, dialogue recognizes and clears up the incoherence of our thought (Bennett and Brown 1995). We sometimes refer to this as thinking out loud, but with others to support the process. By challenging our own perspective or understanding with that of others, assumptions are validated or refuted and broader learning or sense making occurs in the organization. One of the dangers of not having open dialogue is the potential development of groupthink.

Groupthink is a paradox that frequently occurs because organizations take action contradicting the data they have for dealing with the problem, compounding the problem rather than solving it (Harvey 1988). When deeply involved in a group, members striving for unanimity or acceptance may fail to realistically evaluate alternative courses of action. Independent critical thinking about the problem and the potential solutions put forth may appear foreign to the group. Members of a cohesive group are less willing to risk social rejection by questioning the majority point of view or presenting a dissenting view (Yukl 1994); this in itself is a source of fear. The adverse effect of groupthink can be minimized by making people aware of the phenomenon and using a definitive process to increase the critical evaluation of alternatives. Essentially, by centering the discussion on facts and using a process for inquiry, the group is forced to challenge assumptions. An example of such a process is *problem resolution*.

Problem resolution in an organization generally precedes an organizational change. Problem formulation and resolution is key to successful change. Clearly defining the problem, understanding the solutions previously tried, defining the planned change, and implementing the plan are the steps recommended for successful change (Yukl 1994). Throughout the process, the dialogue focuses crisply on the problem and when it is effectively led, there is no fear of retribution for sharing an honest perspective. There is also an added value when data are presented in a constructive manner; decisions can be more informed. While first-order change appears to be based on common sense, second-order change usually appears weird and unexpected, with a puzzling, paradoxical element (Watzlawick, et al. 1974). Second-order change lifts the problem out of the current circumstance and deals with effects rather than presumed causes. To minimize groupthink, the crucial question regarding the problem is *what*, not *why* (Watzlawick, et al. 1974). Concrete change and successful implementation of change cannot take place where "Lindbloom's variant"—gradual change or muddling through—is sanctioned (Janis 1982). Failure in the implementation of change is likely when the change is unrealistic, inappropriate, or improperly framed (Watzlawick, et al. 1974). This frequently occurs when the perceived "right" answer is brought to the table without allowing dialogue about the facts or others' perspectives.

Smith and Berg (1987) investigated internal group processes and group dynamics. They suggested that to gain insight about the paralyzing conflict that seems to be a natural phenomenon in group life, one should study group dynamics associated with the paralysis. They presented their information by focusing their discussion on common areas of group paralysis but filtered their argument through a lens of paradoxical perspectives on the causes of the group's paralysis. Some of the paradoxical perspectives included belonging, engaging, and speaking. They also discussed problems associated with communicating frames of reference (schema) and paradoxes of scarcity, perception, and power. Dewey (1967) wrote: "Men are guided by internalized meanings, habits, and values. Changes in the pattern of actions or practice are, therefore, changes at the personal level in the habits and values and, at the sociocultural level, in normative structure and in institutionalized roles and relationships."

Related to the concept of organizational paralysis is that the difference in status or position of organizational members can result in obstructive stalemates precluding open dialogue (Watzlawick, et al. 1974). Again, this relates to a fearfulness to speak up, possibly due the anticipated response of the boss. Stalemates are indicative of the intrinsically competitive and political nature of organizational life (Culbert and McDonough 1985). An approach to problem solving that is built on trust and respect is strategic, providing a long-term solution with the interests of all the players taken into consideration. As we consider the social dynamics of integrated program teams, the ability for team members to contribute their abilities through dialogue becomes obvious. If we can agree that dialogue is a critical element for organizational learning that contributes to long-term success, then understanding the social dynamics and psychology of dialogue is a key requirement for successful leaders.

THE PSYCHOLOGY AND MOTIVATION OF DIALOGUE

The term *engaged* implies that an individual becomes psychologically connected to an action. To engage in dialogue, a person must have a sense that they will be heard. This speaks to the credibility and commitment of leadership in the process of open and honest dialogue. Leaders must be sincere in their request for their people to share perspectives and concerns. Otherwise, their people will become psychologically disengaged and cease sharing their knowledge and perspective. Vroom (1960) defined the amount of psychological participation as the amount of influence that an individual feels they have in decision making. Just consider some of the business meetings in which you may have participated in the past that did not allow open dialogue and reflect on your personal feelings at the time. If the environment was such that you may have been criticized for speaking up, how psychologically willing were you to contribute? Now consider this in the context of an organization that seeks integration. If the leaders allow disengagement as a practice, then what is achieved is dysfunction and not integration.

For group sense making to occur, there must be openness, that is, a willingness to enter into a process of dialogue about meaning with others over a period of time and to recognize that, so far, "no one has found the once-and-for-all answer" (Vaill 1996). The psychological investment of the individual is based on as many variables as there are individuals. Coleman (1969) suggests that individuals can experience "being" by increasing their self-awareness, self-direction, true communication with others, concern with values, and acceptance of the responsibility for making choices and directing their own destiny. These ideas of self-directedness and controlling one's own destiny are consistent with the internal locus of control tenets. Employees who feel empowered and generally good about what they are doing will most likely be more productive than those who do not. The same holds true for teams that sincerely believe they can influence the processes for which they are responsible.

Consistent with Vroom's (1960) perspective, Ackoff (1981), as did Rogers (1959) and Maslow (1943, 1954, 1970), argued that individuals' degree of motivation is determined by their emotions, desires, and ability to express their self-determination. Further, Ackoff acknowledged that people feel a sense of purpose and meaning when they are progressing toward an ideal, which converts mere existence into significant living by making choices meaningful. This speaks to commitment and conviction. He believed that when individuals do not perceive that they are in control of their futures, they see the choices they make as meaningless. The work organization may provide a place where individuals make choices and create meaning in a confused world, where identification and commitment to the management and organizational values provide purpose and meaning (Bowles 1989). Ackoff (1981) viewed individuals' sense of purpose and meaning as being especially important to a highly educated workforce that is positively motivated through self-determination. Otherwise, people can decrease the quality and quantity of their output significantly. This is especially significant for organizations that employ people for outcomes that require complex intellectual abilities and skills and whose output is difficult to measure. However, if their work is rewarding in itself, those individuals will be highly motivated without a lot of supervisory intervention. This is especially true in industries like software programming and consulting, where individuals have an immediate sense of personal contribution and significance.

The *involvement trait* is one of the four traits of culture identified in Denison's theory of organizational culture (Denison and Neale 1996). The involvement trait helps the organization address the challenge of internal integration of resources through building human capability, ownership, and responsibility. The involvement trait is one of the oldest and most researched of the cultural traits and stems from human relations theory (McGregor 1960). The central notion of this theory is that involvement and participation on the part of organizational members leads to higher effectiveness. Historically, involvement has served organizations as an effective management method for better performance and as a strategy to create a better work environment (Walton 1977). It has also been suggested that involvement has been an alternate strategy to bureaucracy (Ouchi 1981), which implies less need for management—but not leadership. Transaction costs are minimized when members of an organization act from value consensus rather than from bureaucratic rules and regulations (Ouchi 1981). This is because organizational members are committed to performance as opposed to just being compliant. Commitment comes only after understanding has been established and people understand why the work they are performing is important. Cooke (1992) found through investigation that the involvement of members in key decisions has a direct link with return on investment and results in higher product and service quality and, subsequently, improved organizational performance.

High levels of involvement and participation create a sense of ownership and responsibility, resulting in increased commitment to the organization. The benefit to the organization is a reduced dependence on an overt, explicit control system. An implicit system of control, reinforced by cultural norms, ensures coordination of behavior (Denison 1990). Because the organization receives multiple viewpoints when employees are involved, there is a richer understanding of situations and more likelihood of implementation of decisions. Better decisions will result in better performance (Denison 1984), and possibly greater innovation. Bennett and Brown (1995) suggest that strategic innovation is more likely to occur in an organization when its members are able to articulate, such as through open dialogue, the mental models that shape key decisions as well as the deeper beliefs and core assumptions underlying both thinking and action. This is when members share the "why" of their understanding.

The link between cultural norms and values, employee involvement, and organizational performance can be further understood through the psychology of inclusion (Denison 1990). Harris (1994) explains that there are two basic dimensions along which an individual can be psychologically attached to an organization: normative or attitudinal, and compliant or calculative. Normative commitment refers to attachment based on an internalization of the values and beliefs characterizing the organization and valued affiliation with the organization (Harris 1994). This converts to terms of loyalty and belonging. Based on this perspective, involvement of employees in defining the values and beliefs results in internalization of those values and beliefs and, hence, attachment and commitment to the organization. Organizations that routinely create a context that is high in visibility, volition, and irrevocability should generate stronger commitments and richer justifications and should make more sense to their members (Weick 1995). The value of commitment versus compliance is that the personal investment an individual is prepared to make is founded on personal belief. If one is committed to something, they believe in it and will do everything they can to ensure that it is successful. If one is compliant with something, they undertake actions because they have to, not because they want to. Creating a work environment where employees' shared values and vision become a part of the way business is conducted may be an alternative strategy by which organizations can better retain valuable employees.

The challenge for leaders is to create an environment wherein people feel they can be engaged, be empowered, and have an influence on the actions of the organization. This requires the leader to listen, facilitate, and act. Leaders must be able to suspend their personal bias and allow for others' perspective and contributions. As noted earlier in this chapter, not all leaders are wired for this kind of leadership interaction. Some leaders will find it impossible to sustain the behaviors that are required for transformational leadership and environments of open dialogue. That fact must be recognized by organizations that are seeking the engagement of their people for integration, and it holds true at all levels of the organization, including the top. If the top executive does not have the ability to encourage open dialogue through their own actions, the organization's integration and improvement efforts are doomed because learning will not take place at a competitive rate.

Leaders must not only understand the processes and value of dialogue in the organization but also recognize the psychological implications attached to it. We intuitively know that if a situation lacks clarity, we need to either go get more information or process the information we have. Dialogue is a powerful tool for reducing ambiguity and uncertainty if organizations plan for it, make it happen, and reward it.

REWARDING PERFORMANCE AND BEHAVIOR

Humans are creatures like any other—we value pleasure over pain and acceptance over rejection. By recognizing the influence of satisfying a person's needs, leaders can improve their own ability to influence individual and group performance. Traditionally, organizations use reward systems to address those needs. Throughout this discussion of IPL, aspects of both extrinsic and intrinsic rewards have been at work in all of the motivational theories. Extrinsic rewards are typically described as hygiene factors (Herzberg and Mausner 1959) and material rewards, such as money (Maslow 1943, Porter and Lawler 1968, McClelland 1970), compared with intrinsic rewards, which are associated with a sense of craftsmanship, successful completion of a difficult project, acquisition of a new skill, and performance up to capacity (Costello and Zalkind 1963). Maslow (1943) believed that extrinsic rewards motivate persons who have unsatisfied lower-level needs (physiological, safety, and affiliation), while intrinsic rewards are desired by persons seeking higher-order needs (esteem and self-actualization). However, Herzberg saw extrinsic reinforcement as a maintenance function, serving to maintain employees' satisfaction levels (Herzberg and Mausner 1959). The achievement motivation theory's basic tenet was that intrinsic rewards, in relationship to the task on hand, motivated individuals who have a high need to affiliate with others (McClelland 1970). Vroom's (1964) expectancy theory was expanded by Porter and Lawler (1968) to include extrinsic and intrinsic rewards as key variables in their model. Specifically, individuals' perceptions of such rewards, following performance, determine their sense of satisfaction and in turn affect their motivation to exert effort, with intrinsic rewards providing higher levels of satisfaction. Given that rewards have been demonstrated as motivators, the challenge of the leader is to determine what rewards will enhance open dialogue within the organization, enhance individual engagement, and promote personal commitment to performance.

Skinner (1986) claimed that to reinforce management expectations, behavior and performance should be aligned with the appropriate responses. For good behavior and performance people should be rewarded, while for inappropriate behavior and performance a counterresponse should be provided. This would apply to dialogue. Assuming the environment fosters open dialogue, if people are unwilling to share perspectives or speak up when they recognize issues that should be shared, leaders should apply a stimulus to change such behavior. On the other hand, individuals and groups should be rewarded for engaging in meaningful dialogue and especially for pointing out problems in advance of organizational impact. But this also goes back to how we measure performance. Leaders need to recognize the value of avoiding cost as well as of actual cost reductions. The process of speaking up and taking action is probably the easiest way for an organization to avoid unnecessary costs.

Leaders should take into account the resident culture of the organization when applying incentive actions. Incentives may vary greatly based on what part of the world you find yourself in. For example, although individuals are expected to perform as part of a greater team for organizational success, American managers must realize that American culture requires that individuals be rewarded for their achievements (Sashkin and Kiser 1993). Thus the leader must reward both the individual and the group, but in such a way that they are mutually reinforcing. That is, an individual should not be rewarded in such a way that they become concerned only with their own performance as an individual contributor. That would end up undermining the cohesiveness of the team. However, rewarding only a team, without any individual recognition, potentially allows individuals on the team to perform at lower levels and "free-ride." Recognition and rewards must be fair and deserved. To facilitate a sense of fairness, the reward system should be tied to the performance-feedback system (Sashkin and Kiser 1993). According to Sashkin,

> "When the reward system, especially at the individual level, is separate from the performance feedback system, then individual rewards for individual performance will not conflict with the use of information for quality improvement. Individual rewards can be based on skill improvement, on the development of new skills, on quality improvement ideas and actions, or on a variety of other performance-relevant factors. The only limit is the imagination of managers and employees."

By establishing transparent reward systems, you give members an incentive for even greater performance; however, don't let this become a system of entitlement. People are compensated with their salary and benefits for doing their job. Rewards are to be used primarily to recognize a special effort or an extraordinary performance above baseline performance. In some cases, a reward may be used as a tool of encouragement when morale is low or times are tough. But make sure it's not classified as a reward, but rather as a pep-up or other encouraging term.

In addition to the formal reward system an organization may develop, leaders should understand their members' day-to-day needs for feedback and psychological energy. Consistent with Maslow's (1943) theory of human needs, Tony Robbins (2001) suggests that in order to focus on performance and improvement, we should focus on the fundamental psychological needs of people. Robbins posits six fundamental needs: (1) certainty in life; (2) uncertainty for discovery; (3) significance; (4) conviction and love; (5) growth; and (6) contribution (see Table 4.2). He makes these observations as a global notion, noting that these are basic human psychological needs regardless of one's cultural background. If leaders focus on addressing members' psychological needs on an ongoing basis and recognize the value of increased stimulus for anyone or a combination of factors as a reward mechanism, then leaders are focusing on the core of the person, which can convert purpose to belief and conviction. This also supports the sustainability of the organization by significantly reducing the amount of energy required to function. The more committed and enthusiastic a person is to their work, the less motivation they require to perform it. Additionally, the amount of creativity and innovation one finds in a committed organization is much greater than in one that is merely compliant.

For example, the psychological need for *certainty in life* speaks to security and predictability. One becomes comfortable with one's environment, and self-esteem is high. Leaders can reinforce this need through various means, extrinsic as well as intrinsic. People want to remove as much uncertainty from their lives as possible; this lessens anxiety and fear of the unknown. By providing clarity about an organizational member's future and present position, leaders can reduce uncertainty in their performance. Financial stimulus can do this, but it should never be provided without the associated verbal feedback explaining why they are receiving money, which supports other needs such as significance, connection, and contribution.

On the other hand, to remove all uncertainty from the organization is not desired because it means that people are no longer in a mode of discovery. People will cease to grow, the organization will lose touch with its customers and environment, and it will eventually cease to exist. So the need for *certainty* must be balanced with the need for *uncertainty*. For leaders to trust their people to engage with each other to understand an environment of uncertainty guards against boredom and static performance. People develop a sense of value and contribution, and they grow. Leaders can use uncertainty as an effective reward mechanism by communicating how they trust their people to make sense of the environment. Putting people on teams or projects that require them to apply their own discretion provides them the

Table 4.2 Leaders need to understand the psychological needs of their people (adapted from Robbins 2000).

Psychological need	What it looks like
Certainty in life (sense of safety)	• Job security • Understanding of business health • Trust in leadership • Feelings of empowerment
Uncertainty for discovery (need for variety)	• Part of problem-solving teams • Environment to learn
Significance (self-esteem)	• Positive public feedback • Membership on highly-visible teams • Empowerment for decisions • Empowerment for change
Conviction and love (spirit and heart)	• Engagement on teams • Inclusion in communication • Positive mentorship • Nonconflict environment
Growth (alive)	• Participation in industry forums • Professional development • Assignment to new projects • Ability to move in organization
Contribution (giving back— meaning of effort)	• Feelings of value • Making a difference • Measurable progress • Recognition for effort

opportunity to work through uncertainty, as well as providing them a sense of significance.

To address an individual's need for feeling significant means to make them feel like they are important. A leader can praise the person for their contributions and share with them how they have contributed to the overall success of the business. Again, you can reinforce this with monetary rewards, as well as with public recognition. However, I advise you not to allow the recognition to get out of control. If individuals begin to value their own significance more than that of the team, potential exists for a hero culture. You should never reward an individual for performance that was achieved at the expense of others in the organization.

As a leader, when your people are recognized for their significance, you also may feel a sense of accomplishment. One of my proudest professional days was when one of my subordinates was honored with a very public professional recognition. It was the first time that a professional in our functional discipline had ever been recognized in that way, and it was a big deal for the whole organization. Vicariously, I felt pride because I knew that I had supported this person through the nomination process and been his most public champion. So, being a leader can have other benefits than just pay; again, this speaks to the heart and spirit of leadership.

The need for *conviction and love* is powerful in that if an individual feels that they don't fit in or belong, they are less likely to perform as part of the team. As we have discussed, the leader is responsible for ensuring that members perform and engage as a team and for ensuring that information is not provided to some on the team and not others. Members should not be treated with special considerations, especially if those are visible and public and others in the team observe them as unfair. Leaders must emphasize the importance of the team's performing as one and must reward them as one. Leaders must also strive to help members understand how they are connected to the overall scheme of value creation and share with members appreciation for their contributions. This relates to feelings of being wanted, desired, and valued.

The next two of Robbins's needs are absolutely critical to address when rewarding behavior and performance. We must recognize that if people don't feel like they are *growing* and *contributing,* then they are most likely unhappy and bored with their work. Even the best performers will not sustain their performance if they become disengaged. These are basic tenets of Darwin's thought on evolution. Everyone must grow and give back, or they will cease to evolve and their value will be lessened, potentially to the point of extinction for the company or for themselves. Leaders must recognize the need to provide an environment in which opportunities for growth continue to exist and people have a sense of belonging. It is not unheard of for people to leave a stable job for one that pays less but offers opportunities for growth and personal fulfillment. This speaks to the need for excitement of the human spirit. People must feel alive and must believe that what they do is important. If these needs are not met, a void grows in the individual and his/her performance will not be up to its fullest potential. This does not mean that leaders must always provide promotions or even financial rewards; just giving individual's an opportunity to expand themselves can be reward enough. Lateral movement and leading special assignments or project teams allows the person to gain breadth. However, caution must be exercised with such moves so that they don't result in the member's being left "stranded" in a foreign discipline because of a downturn in business or a significant change in leadership.

An additional step leaders need to take when addressing peoples' performance and behavior is to establish their own sense of awareness. That is, understand what drives your people. Understand the current psychological state of the organization. How do people feel? Are their needs being addressed? Recognize that if needs are not met that regardless of beliefs or vision, people will do what is necessary to address their needs. By addressing the needs of their people, leaders strengthen the commitment to the beliefs and values of the organization. One role of a leader is to be a designer of the patterns for employee fulfillment, and to ensure that action and performance are aligned to sustain the business.

SUMMARY

In review of our expectations for leaders, it could be perceived that we are asking a lot from them. The response to such a perception is that we *should* expect a lot from leaders. We should expect organizational leaders to be transactional in understanding how to get work done and sustain the business. To do so, they need contextual knowledge of the value they exercise discretion over. Leaders should understand the interrelated nature of their business and value stream, as well as the interplay of the environment with the business. The ability to envision the business's future should weigh heavily in how high in organizational authority they ascend. They must also recognize the need to grow their organization through transformational means. This means understanding the psychology and sociology of their organization and how to motivate the people they are responsible for.

Organizations need to recognize that if they are ever to achieve the goal of performing as one, leadership needs to be treated as a process and the assignment of leadership positions should not be at the expense of the membership. By using tools for mapping the contextual expectations of leaders within the organization, leaders who choose leaders will make more informed decisions. As is discussed in a later chapter, the integrated knowledge management tool can provide such clarity.

5
Making IPL Work

In previous chapters, we discussed the three major constructs of IPL: integration of systems and structures, alignment of performance expectations and measures, and contextualized visionary leadership. As the term suggests, the objective of integrated performance leadership is to design the organization to perform as one. Waste is to be eliminated and people valued. The challenge is for organizations to implement it—completely and successfully. The challenge will be greater for some organizations than for others. For example, if an organization is just being formed, there may be fewer cultural issues and resident memory to contend with. Essentially, the organization would be starting off with a clean sheet. On the other end of the spectrum is the organization that has been around a while and may have undertaken a number of organizational initiatives such as JIT, TQM, or lean manufacturing. Depending on their successes in these past initiatives, there may be a resident antibody that will automatically attempt to reject anything new and unfamiliar like IPL. Clearly, if there is a will to undertake implementation of anything that makes sense, then it will happen. However, sometimes an organization needs more than just will. I would suggest a well-thought-out plan for integrated and sustained action.

To structure the deployment of any widespread change I offer the following 10 steps for consideration. Keep in mind, you might also need other steps based on your specific environment, but these 10 will pretty much cover most organizations:

- Completely understand any new initiative prior to deciding its implementation.

- Be decisive.

- Create a sense of urgency.

- Create a new mental model throughout the organization of what will be.

- Create a real plan for action.

- Design for incremental and frequent successes.

- Take massive action.

- Continuously measure engagement.

- Communicate frequently.

- Stay true to the plan.

UNDERSTAND IT

Many companies engage in various initiatives because the other guys are doing it or because the idea sounds good and they think they should be doing something. Organizations should completely understand any new initiative prior to deciding on implementation. For example, many companies embraced the TQM wave but never truly implemented the philosophies throughout their business. Many held the team meetings and created the charts but did little to improve the abilities of their people, interaction of their people, or the behavior of their leaders. To implement IPL, the organization must truly understand what it means to do so. For those who are currently functionally structured, as many traditional companies are, it will mean a significant culture change for the organization as well as a reconstruction of the mental models in the organization. They need to be recognize that such change does not occur overnight, nor does it come without growing pains. To truly integrate an organization in systems and behavior, it takes the sustained commitment of the entire organization—especially that of leadership.

The organization needs to understand that implementing IPL means to integrate all of its business processes and its financial accounting structures—no simple task for any organization. Existing leadership needs to be assessed for their abilities to perform as visionary leaders; some leaders must be reassigned and others mentored. Organizational structures may need to be altered, and most definitely people must be educated, not just once but throughout the implementation process. Plus, after the systems have been integrated, the organization must pay attention to sustainability. People and processes will need to be continuously updated to ensure their relevance to the environment. As new people enter the organization, they will need to be indoctrinated in the way of the organization. Moreover, these must not be assumed processes but rather very visible, measured, and with clear accountability.

The organization must understand that time and resources will need to be allocated to the integration process; otherwise the day-to-day work will override the change process. In reality, the integration activities must become part of the day-to-day activities. The integration becomes effective when the organization stops treating the integration process as something that is "in addition to" but rather as how they perform and behave.

Leadership must really understand what it is they are committing themselves to, why they are doing it, and how long it may take. This is why it is important that leaders understand the three major constructs of IPL—integration, performance, and leadership—that they know what is required and understand why it is important and essential for all in the organization who will be leading the charge for change. Leaders must be able to articulate the change to others and lead by their example of appropriate behavior. When leaders understand what they are attempting to lead, they come across to the organization as believable (*Glaubwürdig*), and members are more prone to follow the lead. However, if leaders come across as confused or their message conflicts with the messages of other leaders in the organization, the organization will either muddle through the process or possibly enter into a state of paralysis.

In this first phase of implementation, I recommend that considerable time be spent with the senior leadership of the organization to ensure that this is the path they all buy into. Once they have accepted the path as their own, bringing in various levels of organizational leadership in open dialogue will flush out ambiguity prior to public announcement of the change process. Leadership throughout the organization must be as one in understanding the concept of IPL, the benefits it will provide, and the challenges along the way; and they must be believable in communicating commitment to the organization.

BE DECISIVE

Once the organization has decided that it wants to perform as one and implement IPL, make that decision as public as possible and clearly state that all alternative paths are ruled out. Once the organization understands that this is the one direction, it will waste no time on other options. The concept of decisiveness is pretty much the same as any other variation control process. The more options that exist, the more time that is required to process them. Take alternatives off the table, and reduce organizational variation. Set one direction and go for it. This direction must be articulated by the most senior people in the organization, and they must continuously reinforce the direction to their people. No dissension can be tolerated.

Be clear and specific in the direction to be taken and crisply identify the scope of the integration. All ambiguity should be removed as to the intent and objective of integrating IPL. There should be no one in the organization who thinks participation is discretionary. Turn the decision into action quickly. Make things happen by appointing leadership to implementation roles, and engage the people immediately. But be careful. Don't take action for the sake of movement. Take mindful action that results in value. Otherwise, if nonvalueable action is undertaken, leadership and project creditability is put at risk.

CREATE A SENSE OF URGENCY

If people don't recognize an urgent need for action, they typically establish mental priorities that place improvement activities far down the list for action. It's human nature to respond to the most urgent stimulus we sense. For example, if someone is starving, they place the acquisition of nourishment high on their priority list. This may be despite the fact that their real need is shelter. Or, when someone feels that the business is fat and secure, they may not be as aggressive in removing waste and improving performance. Their actions are geared more toward sustaining the status quo than toward radical improvement. People need to understand that even if an organization seems fat and secure, that is only for the moment. Things change. Markets fluctuate, government may change regulations, and competitors may improve their value to customers, or new competitors may emerge from unanticipated sources. Even more alarming should be the concept of disruptive technologies that can make an entire product line obsolete.

Regardless of whether the organization implements IPL, leadership must create an understanding of the dynamic nature of business. What was good today may be substandard tomorrow. Someone is always out there trying to steal your market share, and the organization must take every action to secure and grow its own. The same is true in public settings.

Public agencies have the responsibility of ensuring safety and a strong commerce model for their citizens. As threats to both evolve, so must the business processes of public agencies. For these reasons, the organization must create an appreciation of the urgency for change in the mind of every employee in the organization. To get people moving, they need a reason. Give them a compelling reason. And no, don't make it "Because I said so" or some bureaucratic gibberish that few people will comprehend. The reason should be simple and become personal so that people can believe it. The organization knows why it is in business; make that the reason. For example, a developer and manufacturer of pharmaceutical products develops products to help people who are sick. If the organization can't stay in business, people may have to go without the important drugs the company provides. That is not to mention the safety and security the company provides to its employees through continued employment. The reason should speak to the heart of the people, and if not to the heart, then to one of the other psychological needs such as certainty.

In responding to the sense of urgency, the organization must be able to link why it is engaging in the implementation of IPL to that of the threat. Because IPL offers the opportunity for the organization to perform as one and to possibly increase the level of innovation from integrated teams, it has great potential for improving performance. People need to understand that waiting for change is not an option and that the strategy of going forward will help get them to where they need to be.

CREATE A NEW MENTAL MODEL THROUGHOUT THE ORGANIZATION OF WHAT WILL BE

Granted, it can't be expected that everyone in the organization will immediately grasp the entire concept of an integrated organization or even that of the desired leadership behaviors. The organization must consider what mental models people have regarding integrated systems and routines. In other words, when people think about integration and a collaborative work environment, what do they envision? The organization must recognize that the mental models will be as diverse as the people themselves and that, if left unaddressed, they may evolve into inconsistencies with the desired objectives. Leaders should consider the mental models, which are essentially the formulas people have in their mind and apply to interpret the concept, as a process that must be planned for so that variation can be controlled. This is very important to manage, especially if we recognize how of belief structures affect action. If a mental model is how one understands something, then it will be strongly related to what they believe about it. Belief will strongly relate to commitment. If people do not believe that what they are doing is important or that it will make a difference, their type of engagement will be one of compliance at best.

The members must come to understand the interrelatedness of the business and how they fit into the value stream. By using analogies, examples of familiar terms or activities put to the unfamiliar, and applying these examples to the current situation and through brief storytelling show how success can be realized and facilitate understanding for organizations within their own settings. The abstract must become understandable. The value of performing as an integrated organization must be made obvious and visible. The organization cannot overcommunicate when it comes to developing these mental models of integration. Focusing not only on systems change but also on how people think about integration must be part of the plan.

Educational processes can be deployed to increase understanding; however, I have found that the most effective learning occurs while doing the actual work of the business. Leaders and peers must learn to be effective facilitators of learning in their business and accept that it is everyone's responsibility to help people progress in their understanding of the benefits and practices of integration.

Because the life cycle is essential to IPL, it is also important to include your critical suppliers and customers in this process. If suppliers and customers are left in an ambiguous condition as to what the organization is doing, human nature dictates that they will become nervous and establish their own perceptions of what you are doing—good or bad. Apprising suppliers of what will be may provide opportunities and solutions not thought of before. The same is true of customers, and it may actually result in increased commitment on their part. If nothing else, keeping your customers informed of what the organization is engaged in is critical to prevent their sending negative signals to the process. Customers should be your greatest market supporter.

CREATE A REAL PLAN FOR ACTION

Frequently good ideas lose steam shortly after they are shared because they are not accompanied by any real planning for implementation. The organization can't just talk about doing something; it really needs to consider all the known challenges and develop strategy and tactics for deployment. The natural desire for most leaders is to get it done quickly. It's not uncommon for leaders to establish the vision and then let others work the details. For something such as IPL to be successfully implemented, leaders must take an active part in the detailed plans for deployment. They need to clearly understand the challenges of deployment and link the current needs of the business to the resources available for change to happen. Challenges should not be allowed to sit on the table long without being effectively addressed.

But when we speak in terms of developing an integrated business, we are also speaking in terms of cultural change. Some have suggested (Schein 1985) that organizations should consider five years as the norm for any real cultural change to take root, although it has also been suggested (Huber and Glick 1993) that this can be accelerated by dramatically changing out organizational memory—which means changing out people. The reality is that it does take time for cultural change to take root, so plans should reflect such. The cultural change process will be directly related to the language and behavior of leadership. The more visible leadership's commitment is, the more serious people will take the implementation of IPL.

It doesn't take as long to change the systems of the organization. Systems drive the desired actions of the organization, while the culture drives the behavior. Together they can considerably influence performance. The quicker the organization moves on aligning its structures and business processes, the more visible change will be to members. As a result, cultural change will be accelerated, and the desired synergy will occur.

In planning the change, consider the behavioral aspects of the organization in system design. If it is suspected that members will reject collaboration and teamwork—and yes, that does happen—force it to occur in process design. Through the routines of the organization, people will become conditioned to work together. Violation of the defined processes cannot be tolerated, and the new systems and plans for deployment will need to address this as well. This includes the very top leadership of the organization. If the top executives of the organization are not committed in language, behavior, and action, that must be addressed by the top boss.

There should be one global implementation plan that has well-defined milestones with assigned dates for completion. The plan should be realistic. The saying "You get what you paid for" applies to any wide-scale change effort—including IPL. Cutting corners or rushing a process before it is ready almost always will result in poor execution. Treat the IPL implementation plan as you would any program plan. Plan for steps of validation along the way to ensure that the organization is getting what it intended. Make the plan visible to the entire organization and frequently communicate successes and next steps. Ensure that those who have deployment roles to play thoroughly understand what is expected of them, and when.

For those organizations that have embraced Six Sigma, lean enterprise, and/or CMMI, the deployment plan could be a series of interrelated projects. There should be one global integration project and a series of subprojects that are neatly aligned for purposeful action. By doing that, the IPL initiative does not compete with any other existing initiatives but rather complements them by providing an integrated framework for coordinated action.

To manage and lead the deployment effort, it is suggested that you appoint a strong leader with that as their full-time responsibility. As recommended in Chapter 2 "Integration," you can establish a single office for business processes to develop the synergy in defined (business process procedures) action. The future leader of that office would be a logical candidate for the deployment role. The individual must be able to see the organization in its entirety and be familiar with the products and services the organization provides. They should have excellent leadership and communication capabilities and cannot be bashful in pointing out leadership roadblocks. What is needed is a change agent who understands the true interrelatedness of the organization—inside and outside its four walls. If the organization operates in a regulated environment, the leader should understand well the rules that govern the business and have an established relationship with those who oversee the organization. Additionally, this integration leader must have a thorough understanding of the human dynamics of the organization to ensure that organizational learning and knowledge become considerations of the new organizational design.

To measure this leader's performance, both short- and long-term measures need to be established. Short-term measures should reflect the execution of the plan, whereas, longer-term measures will address the visionary aspects of leadership. This leader must have a clear vision of future business process challenges and must plan for them early. The IPL deployment leader should be planting seeds with long germination times so that future leaders are being developed and that processes are proactive in improving performance before significant investments are made.

To support the integration leader, you'll need to organize a deployment team. The team should have cross-functional representation and should comprise some of the most visionary leaders of the organization. These folks will need to not only coordinate the deployment processes across the organization but also perform in the role of mentor for the rest of the organization. They must to facilitate understanding of not only the plan but also its importance. Select these people wisely. Putting someone in this role that either does not get it or is not committed will inject a virus into the implementation process. These people must be enthusiastic and naturally espouse the leadership culture that is desired. They should also have established relationships throughout the organization to facilitate quick action.

At a minimum, the plan should contain the following considerations:

1. *Definition of integration scope.* Clearly define how broadly the integration is to occur within the organization and/or value stream.

2. *Expectations of performance* (time, cost, and so on). Be specific about funding for the integration project and in setting timelines for milestones. Results will come only after successful integration is realized, and these too must be quantifiable.

3. *Definition of team members and their specific roles and responsibilities.* Ensure that the integration project does not become the responsibility of a single department in the organization. Carefully select the right talent to ensure that the team has capable cross-functional representation to get the job done successfully.

4. *Macroprocess mapping.* Thoroughly understand the current state of the business processes in the organization by aligning the existing procedures with the macro business processes. This will expose overlap, redundancies, and gaps. Then redesign the system to remove all sources of waste.

5. *Alignment of performance measures with macroprocess.* Develop performance measures that will provide an indication of health and performance. Consider more than output measures. Input and throughput measures provide early indicators so that timely action can be taken to avoid cost.

6. *Development of a financial accounting process that fosters collaboration and holds sources of costs accountable.* In most cases this requires a complete rethinking of an organization's financial accounting processes. The cause of a cost must be held accountable, and parts of the organization should have an incentive to perform as one.

7. *Assessment of leadership capabilities.* The organization must ensure that the leaders have not only the business and technical skills to do the job but also the visionary leadership characteristics to transform the organization. Applying a tool such as the integrated knowledge management matrix can expose strengths and weaknesses.

8. *Engagement/inclusion of the value stream (suppliers).* Ensure that the voices in your value stream can be heard while redesigning your system. Sometimes your suppliers know more about your organizational performance than you do.

9. *Engagement/Inclusion of customers.* An organization can only become as lean as its customers will allow it to. Include the voices of your customers in your planning process to ensure that they are integrated with the changes.

10. *Training/education of organization and value stream.* People need to understand the new processes before they are rolled out. As part of every plan, organizational know-how must be considered, measured, and controlled.

11. *Communication processes.* People need to be kept aware of the progress, challenges, opportunities, and successes of the integration project. The plan must make frequent communication part of the deployment.

12. *Measures of success.* Establish common metrics across the organization relative to business process performance so that progress can be measured and seen.

13. *Measure of engagement.* This measure is important to ensure that people don't opt out of the integration process or simply delegate down. Leadership must hold leaders accountable for leading integration, and a measure of engagement needs to be developed. This may end up being a subjective assessment of engagement, but it must be a conscious one.

DESIGN FOR INCREMENTAL AND FREQUENT SUCCESSES

We all know that change is difficult and can become fatiguing if we don't receive energy back from our actions. The organization needs to be periodically refueled to continue its drive for change and improvement. As the plan is laid out, it should recognize logical steps that can be acknowledged as successful milestones. After all, how do you eat an elephant? One bite at a time. As each manageable bite is consumed, the organization should publicly recognize the accomplishment and celebrate it. Recognizing people for their effort lets them knows they are valued, strengthens their belief that what they are doing is important, and solidifies their commitment. If the organization tries to make the steps between recognizable successes too far apart, it may run out of fuel before it reaches its destination. Besides, the greater the size of the project steps, the higher the probability that variation will creep in and compromise project execution.

Design the deployment process for quick and frequent wins, and make it enjoyable along the way so that people prefer the new way of doing business. Make the deployment process fun by speaking to the need for personal growth and discovery. By doing so, the successes will also speak to the psychological need for certainty—you know that you can succeed.

If the organization is using other measurement tools, make their incremental improvements very public. For example, if variation or cost is being reduced and the organization speaks in the vocabulary of Six Sigma, share these improvements in those terms using the language that people are familiar with. The same is true for lean manufacturing or CMMI, where measures of waste reduction or process maturity can be displayed. IPL should not be something that replaces all of the other good work of the organization; rather it should bring it together in a unifying process of structure, process, and thought.

TAKE MASSIVE ACTION

Good comprehensive planning will make all the difference in success, but unless it is put into action it might as well be art hanging on the wall. Once the decision has been made to implement IPL, then get to it. Momentum can be gained only through action, but once it takes root things can happen quickly. The time between action steps should be as short as possible to minimize disruption to momentum. Don't allow other disruptive factors to upset the momentum. One of the biggest killers of projects such as this is to be overtaken by events, such as a change in market conditions that limits investment capabilities. Once momentum is disrupted, it takes much more energy to regain it. Establish capital resources that are somewhat immune to external influences. Stay true to the plan, and plan for external influences that will attempt to disrupt momentum. Keep the train of change on track, and it will arrive at its desired station.

A word of caution: be careful not to overload the organization. Everyone in it must be committed and engaged in the change process. But to simply add the project to the existing work of leadership may result in the transactional side of the business slipping. Leaders must be empowered with the appropriate talent and resources to accomplish both the transactional aspects of the day-to-day business as well as the transformation to IPL synergy.

CONTINUOUSLY MEASURE ENGAGEMENT

If the organization is truly to become an integrated entity with all of its members contributing to a common objective, then everyone in it must be engaged in IPL. No one can be allowed to opt out, or you will have variance in integration. For some organizations this might be acceptable for the short term to address urgent business needs, but when such variance exists in leadership, it is important to recognize it and manage for it. It cannot be assumed that those elements of the organization that are not integrated will perform in a predictable manner with the integrated aspects of the organization. They may be very capable elements, but if not integrated they will have greater variance in organizational linkage and will generate waste. Know where the variance resides, manage for it, and most desirably, eliminate it.

There are a couple of factors that need to be considered when thinking in terms of engagement. One I just mentioned—system integration and leadership engagement in the deployment process. The other is cognition. Without exception, everyone in the organization must understand what the integration process is and why it is so important. This must be treated as a visible process. As part of the deployment process, awareness sessions should occur throughout the organization. They don't need to be time consuming, but they do need to be applicable to what it is people do, and they need to be frequent. If people cannot put the integration process into the context of what they are responsible for, they won't engage to their full potential.

Leaders must be able to perform as teachers to help develop understanding in their organizations. They will need more formal training than others so that they will be credible in leading change. Familiarization and awareness sessions should be made available to others in the organization. These are relatively simple measures of action. People have either received the training or they have not. But it's not really engagement until cognition is transformed into action. This is measurable as well, by measuring the progress of integration. The integrated knowledge management tool can assist in making applied knowledge visible. Leaders can also make their own observations of individual engagement. As noted earlier, learning by practice is the most desirable method of bringing people up to speed about concepts such as IPL. By combining limited class time with hands-on application, people will see the value of the implementation process and will be able to contextualize the practice faster.

You will always find a couple of people in the organization who just won't come around to the new way of doing business. By all means, work with them and help them understand the importance of integration. But if they can't or won't get it, then it is time they moved on elsewhere. Don't waste too much of the valuable time of the organization because there are others out there who need your leadership as well.

COMMUNICATE FREQUENTLY

An organization cannot communicate too much when it comes to keeping its people informed and knowledgeable about the integration process. Again, this is a means of variation control. By frequently communicating, you help people refine their mental models and improve their understanding about action. At first, IPL will seem abstract to many in the organization, and some will need more facilitation than others. It cannot be assumed that those with gaps in understanding will identify themselves or be identified by their leaders. Plan for ambiguity and uncertainty; it will be there. A structured communications strategy can reduce much of the ambiguity and uncertainty, but the primary responsibility for communication will reside at the local leadership level. They know their people best and can communicate in terms that make sense to them. "Stump" meetings can provide the daily interaction at a local level, whereas simple one-on-one dialogue can provide the individual with greater understanding. Who knows, the leader may learn something as well.

STAY TRUE TO THE PLAN

As I mentioned in the first step, you should truly understand what you are getting yourself into before you engage in a wide-scale change project. To ensure success, a genuine commitment must exist and an understanding that the path may not be without unforeseen challenges. Once a decision has been made and other paths eliminated, stay the course. Stay true to the established plan. If along the way the plan does not fit the needs of the organization, don't throw it away—modify it to meet the changing needs. Once the organization has started this journey, it would be unfair to pull the carpet out from under the members. They have invested their personal selves in deployment and have believed the leadership when value was espoused. This speaks directly to the integrity of leadership. If it makes sense for the organization to engage in action as one, then go for it—make it happen. Besides, frequent changes in course direction can only confuse your customers.

People will fatigue along the way—plan for it. Recognize the need for people to be refreshed, but don't pull them off a project that they are critical to. Find other ways to reenergize people and keep them enthusiastic about the journey. A light at the end of the tunnel, though, is imperative. Help them see it and make sure they know that they are valued and appreciated. Some will decide to opt out of the integration process along the way. Before taking action with them, understand why they have disengaged. It may not be because they are not committed; other influences may be at play, such as issues of local leadership, work design, priorities, or resources. Remember, leadership is accountable for ensuring that people have what they need to get the job done. However, if it does turn out that an individual or a group of people decide to opt out for no other reason than because they want to, deal with that more transactionally and quickly.

SUMMARY

Chapters 2 through 4 on integration, performance, and leadership discussed each of the IPL constructs in depth. It is critical for the success of IPL implementation that leaders understand not only about those constructs but also why they are important and how they are interrelated. Without that understanding, leaders cannot be effective leaders of integrated change. They will lack the believability (*Glaubwürdigkeit*) they need for people to follow them.

In this chapter, I discussed implementing the kind of wide-scale change that will be required to get an organization to perform as one. It won't be easy, but it is worth the investment. And it will take an investment of time, people, and money to make it happen. A single leader should lead the deployment efforts, and a cross-functional team should be created to drive the work of change. The process of change should include the entire value stream, and engagement should be measured. Those who opt out of the implementation process need to be brought back into the fold or asked to find other employment. Problems need to be identified and resolved quickly. It's easier to wrestle a baby alligator than it is a full-grown one.

Sustained effort and commitment will allow the organization to arrive at its desired destination of integration. Set the course, create the team, educate the people, develop the plans, measure and celebrate success, keep people engaged, stay the course, and make it happen! With a plan for action.

6
Conclusion

In the Preface, I shared with you my experience on a journey from one side of the world to the other. Needless to say, it was not one of my more favorable traveling experiences. The only thing that saved the trip was that an airline employee made a choice to perform to a level of professionalism that the organization did not manage for—his name was Nelson. Imagine the possibilities of market share and waste reduction the airline could enjoy if all of its employees displayed the same attitude as Nelson. However, I doubt that even Nelson can sustain his personal commitment to excellence if the systems and environment are constantly at odds with him. As with any environmental situation, you need to adapt to the environment, or the environment will have its way with you. The other option is to change the environment to reflect the expectations of the members, leaders, and most importantly, the customers. As I noted earlier in the book, the only thing we cannot change is the natural environment; everything else is social and manmade.

This book introduces integrated performance leadership as an integrated path of thought and action to help organizations think of themselves as integrated organisms and to provide a framework to structure value creating action. The three major constructs of integration, performance, and leadership are key for all leaders and organizational members to understand, not just as an overarching concept but as components that are interrelated. The greater the understanding of what needs to be done and the greater the appreciation of why it is important, the greater the level of commitment from the organization. This is why the model of integrated knowledge management is included in this discussion (see Appendix B). Leaders must recognize that the true capability and capacity of an organization can be realized only when the cognitive maps of the organization are congruent and pull together in the same direction.

As with any good work an organization undertakes, processes must be sustainable. To allow the organization to remain static is to allow the environment to establish distance from the organization's processes. This is true in every aspect of organizing and process execution. The organization must sustain the design of its processes so that they continue to provide value with the least amount of waste possible. The organization must also sustain its cognitive capabilities by measuring applied knowledge throughout the value stream, and it must all link together. Yes, this is hard work, but it is the work of leadership, and it's their prime responsibility. After all, if a leader is focused on executing work and not on developing people and securing resources for the organization, they are not leading—they are managing.

A formidable challenge for any leader is to stay the course of visionary leadership. This requires a strong will and a true conviction for wanting to lead. The visionary leader must be able to balance the transactional demands for business performance with those of the transformational focus of membership growth, while maintaining a focus on the interrelatedness of their actions and project vision as far into the future as possible. It all starts with a choice. People choose their environments, and they also choose their behavior. If the organization decides it wants to embrace the concept of IPL, then the leadership will need to choose its values and ensure that they espouse such every minute of their professional day.

By far the most challenging aspect of implementing IPL is the realignment of financial performance measures. Because organizations are conditioned to behave within the traditional financial accounting structures that have gotten many companies in trouble lately, they will find it hard to rewire themselves to think in terms of integrated financial accountability. Use the very public examples of corporate misbehavior as the call for change and for more transparency of the real performance measures of the organization. This is really an important aspect of developing an integrated organization. If the organization competes with itself internally for resources more than it competes with external competitors for market share, then there is an obvious disconnect in its financial structure. Alignment of financial accountability by value streams is one way of getting the organization closer to integrated financial performance measures; however, avoid the temptation to suboptimize.

There is typically a wealth of opportunities for sharing resources across value streams, which requires the facilitation of accounting structures that enable and foster collaborative teaming throughout and across value streams. Each organization will require a different solution; you should keep an open mind and recognize that internal competition rarely results in holistic performance.

Please also keep in mind that IPL is not intended to be something mystical or strange, but rather it is a logical perspective that the reason an organization is formed is to get something done for the sake of value. Think in terms of the collective as opposed to the functional department. Think in terms of the process of sense making throughout the value stream and how you can manage communication and thoughtful action as a process. Don't create a department because everyone else has one. Keep the structure and processes simple, and the people will understand them. And above all, don't ever stop.

The following two appendices describe tools that can be helpful in deploying IPL in the organization. VISION center networks provide a structured process for project selection and facilitate the engagement of integrated teams. The integrated knowledge management tool is a visual process of aligning the knowledge capability needs of the business with of its people. It also provides an approach to developing surgical learning to fill gaps in knowledge capability. Neither of these tools is mandatory for developing an integrated organization, but each can help in structuring action and making action measurable.

Appendix A
VISION Center Networks

The power of an integrated organization comes from the synergies it develops through focused action and the intolerance of wasteful action. Yet in order to create and sustain synergies, the organization must have a common understanding of where specific action is needed and of the processes for organizing corrective measures. The more quickly this understanding is created and people mobilized, the greater the opportunity for eliminating waste. When we consider the many initiatives an organization can undertake simultaneously, such as Six Sigma projects, lean projects, quick-response manufacturing (QRM) projects, *kaizen* projects, corrective action plans from audits, product/process corrective action, capability and maturity model integration (CMMI) projects, cost-reduction projects, and so on, we must wonder how we can expect an organization to develop a common perspective and understanding of what is important. In this appendix, I introduce a concept of integrated structures and routines that facilitates an understanding of performance and the application of synergistic strategies for improvement. The concept is to create networked centers of action within value streams to accumulate the right data, make sense of performance, apply standardized tools, and take synergetic action to improve processes and products as one company. Most important, this structural tool has the potential to enable organizational sense-making processes that will lead to learning and increased human capability (see Figure A.1).

THE VISION CENTER CONCEPT

VISION centers are physical locations and structures that perform a hub-and spoke-function for project selection within an integrated organization.

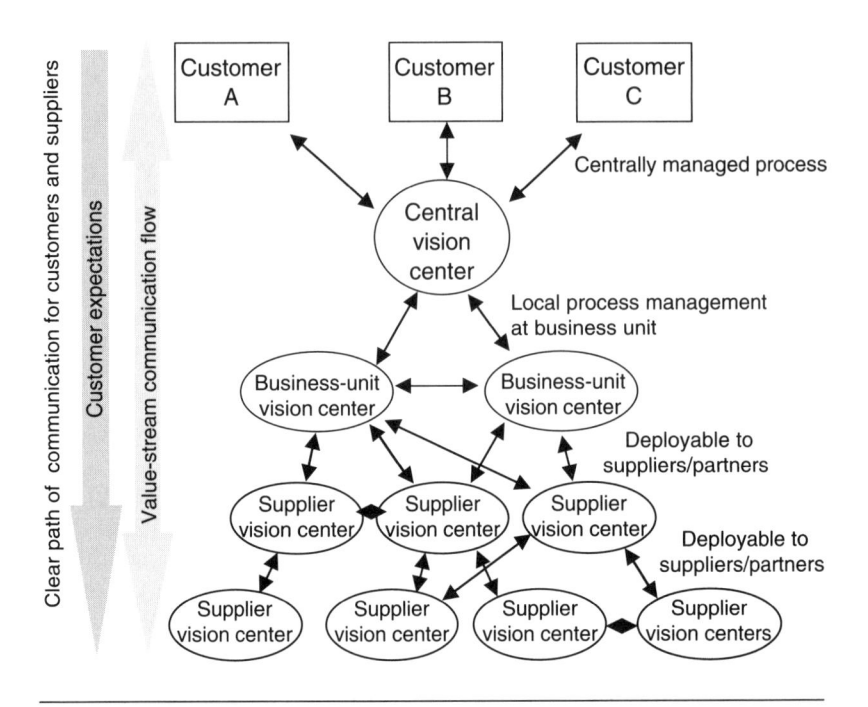

Figure A.1 VISION center network model.

The concept is simple: create a visible process for processing data and directing synergized action throughout the entire organization. When VISION centers are linked together, they can serve as a tool for synergy throughout an enterprise or value stream, or both. The idea is for the organization to have a visual tool of its performance and a structural mechanism that ensures organizational learning. So what does a VISION center look like? It depends on what the organization does to provide value and which tools it has chosen to implement to improve its business. In every case, a VISION center must be visible to the organization and it must be a permanent structure. In a manufacturing environment, it is best located in the middle of the shop so that all can see what is going on. In a service environment, such as an insurance company, it should be located in a high-traffic location such as an entrance to a building. VISION centers should not be tucked away in some corner of the business; they are supposed to encourage engagement and to promote communication. The visibility of the centers also supports the perception of management commitment for improvement. Tools, such as CMMI assessments, earned-value management systems, Six Sigma, supplier accountability, and QRM, should present their data in an organized fashion in the VISION center so that project selections can be made with business priorities.

VISION centers are relatively simple to deploy, and they don't even require an organization to be completely integrated; however, the organization must have a willingness to collaborate. The greater the use of the centers and the linkage as a network, the more powerful they become in eliminating waste and promoting synergy in organizational action. Take, for example, a larger organization that deploys a VISION network and is pursuing the higher levels of CMMI certification. As a localized team creates a new process to further the organization's process maturity, that can be shared through a network in real time, facilitating an enterprisewide solution to a common challenge. The same is true in the application of Six Sigma projects or any other process improvement activity. What makes the VISION process different from other project-planning processes is that the VISION center network is about sharing enterprisewide understanding and being proactive as one company or as a single value stream. The result of a VISION project should not be limited to the local area but shared, or integrated, as changes in business routines and organizational knowledge. However, VISION centers are also about creating local understanding of process performance by creating opportunities for people to see and engage with local projects and comprehend the relationship to the larger organization.

The term *VISION* stands for verify, investigate, standardize, integrate, optimize, and no recurrence. As with all organizational processes, keeping the concept and deployment of VISION centers and networks simple is the key to success. Each letter in the word *VISION* represents an action phase of a project that should provide structure and processes to improving the performance of the organization (see Figure A.2).

In the *verify* phase, the organization substantiates the need for a project using data it derives from the various indicators of performance reporting. For example, CMMI assessments and quality audit data may indicate weak

Verify *the problem or challenge*
Investigate *the true root cause*
Standardize *the solution*
Integrate *the solution enterprisewide*
Optimize *the process*
No recurrence *shall ever occur*

Figure A.2 The VISION concept.

spots in the business processes of an organization. QRM and lean assessments may indicate where opportunities exist for removing waste from the value stream. Quality and service reliability data may indicate design or manufacturing process issues. Earned-value management system (EVMS) data may tell the organization where its programs' cost challenges reside. The more central a VISION center becomes in data management and project selection, the greater the opportunities for assuring synergistic action and reduced competition for organizational resources. In the verification phase, it is important that you define the problem well, but it is not important that you understand the problem at this point. The more data points that direct an organization to a problem, the greater the return when it is solved.

For example, if an area of an organization has performance indicators that suggest it is having problems with its quality (scrap, rework, escapes), cost (EVMS), delivery (QRM and lean assessments), and compliance (audit results, CMMI assessments), then, as opposed to launching multiple projects, a single improvement project should be scoped to address all aspects of performance. After all, a process has a beginning and an end, and going after only bits and pieces of a process may add to waste as opposed to reducing it.

In a more simplistic operation, the center can enact standard project selection rules, such as, "All customer and supplier escapes must be processed through the center." By doing so, the organization emphasizes the two ends of the value stream. I would actually encourage such a standard and immediate rule for two reasons—customer satisfaction and supplier accountability.

The verification phase can take on a more proactive role than just addressing poor performance. Though an organization should consider every problem as a gem to be valued for learning and improvement, it should also recognize what's performing well. All too often, organizations focus only on the negative trends of performance, and, though superior performance is desired and valued, they rarely recognize it. Recognition of desired performance serves two primary functions. First, it provides positive energy and reinforcement of existing behavior, which should increase the potential of sustainability. Second, by recognizing the desired performance the organization should understand why that operating unit is performing in the way it is. Aspects of leadership, work design, knowledge capability, capacity planning, environmental influences, and other attributes should be analyzed in the same fashion as you would any negative performance trend or event, so that understanding occurs. Once the organization understands the desired performance, that learning should be converted into a proliferation of action through the entire enterprise and potentially through the entire value stream. The VISION center network can provide an efficient platform for analysis, learning, and widespread action.

The *investigate* phase is, as the term suggests, the phase in which you analyze the data and processes to ensure you obtain an accurate understanding of the issue. What is important to IPL is who performs the investigation. Integrated product teams (IPTs) or process owners must be held accountable for the performance of their processes and products, regardless of where in the life cycle or value stream the issue resides. In the investigative phase, the IPT or process owner may deploy a number of investigative tools, including design of experiments, fault-tree analysis, Red X, process mapping, or turnback analysis, depending on the issue they are confronted with and the core tools their organization has chosen to deploy.

Having a large repertoire of tools is a nice thing, but having too many tools adds significant variance to the investigative process itself. It is recommended that the organization select the standard tools (toolbox) for the VISION center process and ensure that its people are proficient in their use. By the way, there is no perfect answer that fits all organizations. Each needs to understand the nature of its business processes and select the tools appropriately. However, by standardizing the investigative toolbox, predictability, interpretation, and execution of the investigative process is increased; a common language is created throughout the organization. Also, by establishing rules and standards, the organization is assured that a minimum depth of investigation is performed and that performance data can be collected on the robustness of the VISION center process itself.

Once the root cause of the issue is identified, a corrective action must be taken. Based on my experience, I find that the overwhelming majority of corrective actions fail to address the real root cause of an issue. In most cases, organizations chase symptoms with quick fixes only to relive the issue at a later date. In many other cases, the corrective action may address only the causes for which the investigators have authority (span of control) to go fix. One only needs to review their internal repetitive nonconformance data to recognize this phenomenon. A suggested rule for the VISION center is that not everything should go through it. Only those issues that warrant significant IPT-level interaction should be processed in the VISION centers. This should require those issues that reside within the process to be visible to the leadership of the organization and to command attention in standing reviews.

This forum is the opportunity for critical dialogue to occur—use this rare opportunity! If capital investment or people are needed to implement a corrective action to eliminate a root cause, then put the issues on the table. When help is needed to influence performance outside the immediate organization's span of control, don't ignore it. If the organization opts not to have these discussions, then it is kidding itself about wanting to improve and should forget about integration and real performance improvements. The absence of real commitment to improvement by leaders will send signals to the organization, and the people's willingness to engage will be minimized if not lost all together. When standard work exists, the result of a VISION center case should be a change to the standard work of the organization.

The *standardize* phase is the result of integrating the corrective action with the standard processes and procedures of the organization. This is where the organization changes the way in which it carries out its work on a routine basis. This may include change to engineering design practices, manufacturing process designs, supplier sourcing processes, employee development plans, or any other media that command specific action. These standards become the target against which variance is measured, regardless of whether it relates to product, process, or business activities. For organizations seeking the higher levels of CMMI certification, performance measures relating to these standard processes demonstrate an organization's understanding of its business processes, and actions taken in response to the measures demonstrate continuous improvement. Please keep in mind that standard processes are not intended to add bureaucracy to the organization but rather provide for higher levels of sustained performance through predictable execution.

Maintaining the organization's business process maps and aligned procedures for all to see in the VISION centers will provide visibility of where changes in the life cycle need to occur. The same is true of the organizational knowledge capabilities as managed by a visual tool such as the integrated knowledge management matrix. As with all projects, not only do processes need to be revised from time to time, but so do people.

To *integrate* the standardization efforts throughout the enterprise is to behave as one company or as an integrated value stream. Where the standardization phase develops the integrated change for the organization, the integration phase executes the change. This is where the value of the VISION center network comes in. The network of VISION centers shares learning and measures performance including enterprisewide change. The method of communication in the enterprise or value stream can vary from paper-managed processes to paperless systems. The important point here is that the standardization effort does not remain local, but rather becomes part of the larger system.

There is no reason that an integrated organization should need to learn the same lesson more than once in any location of its business—this includes the largest of organizations. Once an understanding has been reached about an issue, this must be proliferated throughout the system so that others will prevent similar issues from arising in their area. Some methods of communication may be faster than others, or in some cases, enhance understanding better than others. For example, a computer network can link the VISION center networks together in real time, sharing photos and sound files so that people can better understand the content and context of the information—making the process of sense making more capable. Because the system is networked in real time, enterprisewide action is possible immediately. Such systems can also provide visibility of the status of implementation throughout the enterprise. But an organization should not allow the constraints of not having a networked computer system keep it from deploying a VISION center network. A simpler vehicle can be created to fulfill the need for communication.

Routine conference calls or paper alert processes can be created to accomplish the same objective. Remember, the presence of accurate communication to share knowledge is better than no communication at all. The process needs to be well defined, understood, and managed to ensure enterprisewide action is occurring. When the business processes of an organization have been mapped out and waste has been minimized through the establishment of integrated business processes, the ability for an organization to integrate change has been greatly enhanced. This is significant value of the IPL concept—enabling fast enterprisewide change.

To *optimize* a process is to remove variance and waste from it; this involves quantitative measurement. These are measurements of waste reduction, value creation, and process compliance and should be taken at points that facilitate an understanding of how a process is performing. It does little good to measure only the output of a business process when the potential causes of variance are in the inputs. I am not advocating that a meter should be applied to every aspect of the business, but if a process has a history of misbehavior, it may warrant more measurement then others. If the improved process was a former case dealt with by the VISION center, then it certainly should be monitored for optimization to the point that the maximum amount of waste is removed from the process. Processes critical to business performance, customer satisfaction, or compliance to regulatory requirements should automatically be selected for enhanced performance measures. Additionally, those processes that incorporate a higher degree of human discretion may also warrant greater performance measurement attention—after all, humans are typically the greatest cause of variance in organizations. Also keep in mind that as process improvements are realized in one aspect of the process, that may call for modification in another—no process functions in isolation of the system.

The proof that all of your good work in the VISION center has been effective is when the organization realizes *no recurrence* of past problems. As an inherent process, the VISION center network should be on the lookout for recurrences. If they do pop up swift action needs to be taken to understand why. To invest the time and effort in eliminating a cause and

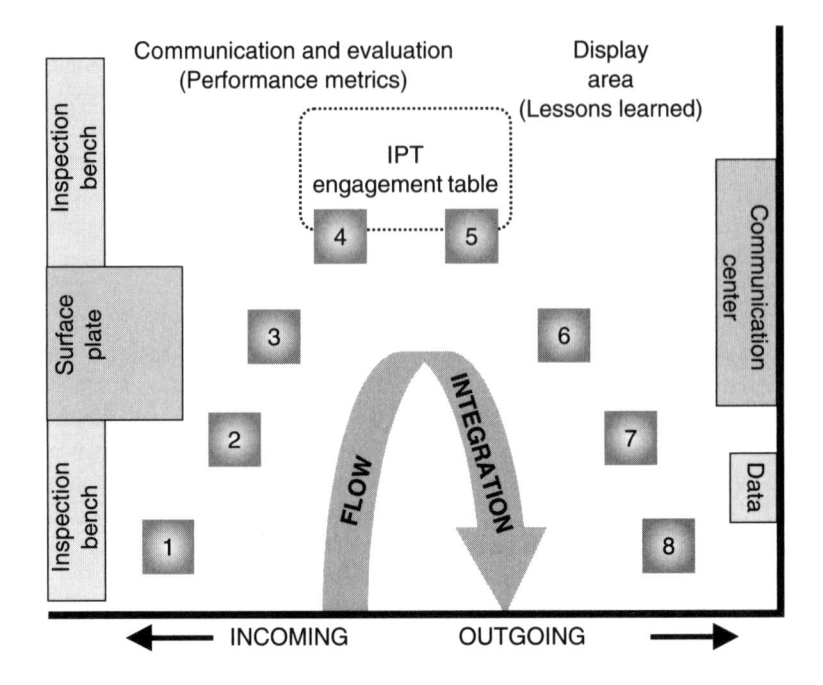

Process Flow
1. <u>Verify</u> the problem
2. Log into VISION center network data entry for cost recovery and cost avoidance
3. <u>Investigate</u> the true root cause
4. Quarantine suspect population
5. Implement the <u>standardized</u> corrective action
6. <u>Integrate</u> the solution enterprisewide (changes to standard work and capture lessons learned)
7. <u>Optimize</u> the process by reducing variation
8. Monitor process to ensure <u>no recurrence</u>

Figure A.3 VISION center product evaluation process.

sharing this learning throughout the enterprise, only to have it come back, is an indication that one of the upstream VISION center processes was not robustly executed. If that does occur, analyze not only the issue but also the robustness of the VISION center process. Figure A.3 depicts the VISION center process.

SETTING UP A VISION CENTER NETWORK

As with any new process an organization employs, the easier it is to understand, the more people who will be prone to use it. Minding these words of simplicity, it is recommended that a phased or modular approach is used in deploying VISION center networks. The experience an organization has had with deploying process improvement tools should influence how much should be bitten off at once. If an organization has a history of using quality improvement tools, it will be comfortable in the basics of a VISION center network. If an organization has applied the concepts of Six Sigma, ACE (achieving competitive excellence), or DIVE (define, investigate, verify, and ensure) together with an (integrated product development) IPD–type structure, then it may be more comfortable taking the more sophisticated approach of integrating all of the performance measures we spoke of earlier. This allows the organization to absorb the concepts within a manageable process. Regardless of how the organization chooses to deploy a VISION center process, the process must engage the process owners and the IPT. Without exception, once the rules are established for the VISION center process, they must be complied with. Otherwise, there will be variance in the process, reduced process predictability, and potential erosion of employee trust in the process. If the rules no longer meet the needs of the business environment, they should be modified. But it is critical that all VISION centers that are connected to a network comply with the same set of performance expectations and process rules; otherwise the ability for the centers to interact will be significantly compromised.

Here are some rules that should be considered:

1. Set the maximum number of projects that may reside open within a center at one time.

2. Set the maximum time allowed for a project to be open.

3. Set the maximum time before a customer receives feedback.

4. Control all products that enter a center or network so they don't reenter production without the appropriate disposition.

5. Maintain effective inventory on all products that enter the centers or network.

6. Use standardized investigative tools.

7. Document the results of every project in a standardized fashion.

8. Ensure that people performing the VISION center processes have the skills necessary to do the job right.

9. Ensure that all projects result in a change to process, design, or standard work. (Where standard work resides for the entire design and production process, all projects should result in a change to standard work.)

10. At the initiation of a project, consider all possible performance measures to ensure that all benefit and none are sacrificed.

The staffing of VISION centers should depend on the size and volume of the centers themselves. At a minimum, it is suggested that a full-time VISION center technician manage the processes of each individual center. This person should be fluent in the processes of project selection, root-cause investigation, and documentation of the project so that the learning can be shared throughout the enterprise. For technical environments, a strong quality or manufacturing engineer should have the core competencies to build upon. In business and public-sector environments, individuals who have a good grounding in their line of business and possess a process improvement mind-set should do quite well. In all cases, the core VISION center technicians should be good facilitators in sharing the understanding of the VISION center process with others. Establishing a community of practice is strongly recommended with the technicians coming together frequently, formally and informally, to share knowledge.

One of their primary roles is to facilitate IPTs and process owners in the phases of the individual projects and to ensure the integrity of the process. (see Figure A.1) So these technicians must have the ability to help others learn the VISION processes through active participation. Assignments as the VISION center technician could be a rotational opportunity for high-potential employees, providing an excellent opportunity to learn quality improvement tools and the interrelatedness of business processes. From a leadership perspective, members who stay in these positions for long durations may find themselves becoming specialists, reducing their opportunities for career advancement. It is recommended to move people through these positions at approximately two- to three- year intervals. Ideally, participation on VISION projects will advance the skills of an organization's membership and promote an understanding of the breadth of the organization. A by-product should be higher recognition of these capabilities—for example, as a Six Sigma Black Belt or as a Red X master.

Table A.1 Sample roles and responsibilities of a VISION center technician. The processowner/IPT has the responsibility for performing investigations and taking action.

Product focus	Process focus
• Confirm issue	• Monitor process performance
• Input to data system	• Analyze multiple measures for high-impact opportunities
• Notify process owner (IPT)	
• Mentor investigation process	• Engage process owners/IPT in project selection
• Ensure standardized documentation	
• Communicate through network	• Input project into data system
• Validate root cause/corrective action	• Mentor investigation process
	• Ensure standardize ddocumentation
• Ensure preventative actions–integrate into standard work and business processes	• Communicate through network
	• Validate root cause/corrective action
• Capture/disseminate new knowledge	• Ensure preventative actions—integrate into standard work and business processes
• Monitor effectiveness/performance	
• Sound a loud alert when the slightest indication of slippage occurs	• Capture/disseminate new knowledge
	• Monitor effectiveness/performance
	• Sound a loud alert when the slightest indication of slippage occurs

As the VISION center increases in size and in the volume of projects it can manage, it is suggested that the number of full-time technicians be increased to meet the desired flow speed. As with any process, you get what you pay for. Anyone who manages an operational business should appreciate the concept of capacity planning. The challenge for many organizations will be getting past the mental block against having indirect employees and the perceived value, may or may not create. If the processes and products of the VISION centers are of value, they should be worth the sustained investment. It is not uncommon for a manufacturing organization with approximately 1,100 persons to have a VISION center with five full-time technicians who focus only on product issues. As business processes are brought into the centers, an additional two to three persons can generate significant value to warrant the investment. For service type and public-sector centers, the number of full-time technicians will drive the number of projects that can be effectively managed at one time. But keep in mind that these full-time VISION center technicians are facilitators and mentors of the VISION center processes. As organizational capability increases in the application of the VISION center processes, the dependency of process owners and IPTs for such facilitation and mentorship should decrease. However, the realities of organizational change will always need to be addressed. As people move in and out of the organization, new capabilities in this process will need to be created. So before an organization downsizes the number of people working in the VISION network and centers, understand what impact that will have on the overall process capability—especially with regards to knowledge capability. Table A.2 provides examples of work which would reside within both product and process focused VISION centers.

The physical dimensions of the VISION center again depends on the product that will reside there. The larger the products the more space that may be needed. The same is true regarding the number of people. There should be ample space for the investigative processes that transpire within the center. For example, some product-focused centers may have coordinate-measuring machines and surface tables to perform measurements on products. These require much more space than simple layout inspection benches. The layout of the centers should preclude crowding of projects residing there. The worst thing that can happen is that products are lost

Table A.2 Example of VISION center work—product focus versus process focus.

VISION Center Work	
Product focus	**Process focus**
• Establish visibility of product performance	• Integrate all improvement initiatives (Six Sigma, CMMI, QRM, lean, IPD, etc.)
• Engage integrated product/process teams (IPT's) in project selection	• Make what's important visible to the entire organization
• Engage IPT's in ownership of product improvement processes	• Scope projects to address multiple performance measures (heavy hitters)
• Integrate learning into organizational memory (standard work, design, procedures, etc.)	• Deploy standardized tools for investigation
• Market successes	• Create and share new knowledge around the business processes
• Send heightened commitment message to employees and customers	• Market successes
• Ensure integration of change throughout all business units	• Ensure integration of change into business processes and standard work throughout all lines of business

within the VISION center process or networks. A well-planned flow process to manage the movement of the product within the center will facilitate visual control of work. Being able to walk into a center and immediately determine the volume of work and capability of the process should be an inherent trait of the VISION center process. The same is true for those VISION centers that focus primarily on business processes.

The organization should establish standards for what charts are displayed on which wall to create a sense of common process throughout the centers. Workstations and conference tables should be organized without obstruction so that collaborative teaming can occur in the VISION center processes.

MODULAR ASPECTS OF THE VISION CENTER PROCESS

An *escape* is a nonconformance that has left the established quality system of an organization. By definition, an escape is a breakdown in an organization's business processes. Even escapes that can be linked directly to human error are a deficiency of the organization's systems. Those escapes that make it to customers are especially troubling because they bring not only added cost to the organization but also the potential for customer dissatisfaction. When it comes to deciding what projects should be undertaken by a VISION center, customer and supplier escapes (nonconforming products and services) should figure prominently in the selection.

The term *escape* is intended to denote any product or service that does not meet requirements and leaves the quality system that created the condition. In the earlier discussed example of quality escape reduction at a major aerospace company, a VISION center–like process was deployed and networked that facilitated the reduction of 45 percent of the escapes within a year. One of the simple rules the organization established was that all customer and supplier escapes must be processed through the centers—without exception and regardless of an escape's impact on performance. This provided a number of benefits. The easiest to recognize is the reduction in escapes and happier customers. But the cost of poor quality that was avoided was well over a hundred million dollars in the first year alone. At the time, the organization was still growing into its new integrated structure, and the teaming that was required on the individual projects taught the organization how to bridge some of the gaps between the various disciplines. The IPTs became stronger as integrated teams and more intimate with their product and processes; the lines between engineering and manufacturing became blurry. Reducing the number of supplier escapes also increased the velocity of product flow, which reduced inventory requirements and delivery delays. Thus, a simple rule can bring about a potentially huge payback if executed robustly and with discipline.

Within the VISION center, the IPT or process owner owns the determination of the root cause. The center that focuses on product issues should have all the tools necessary to perform geometric inspection and, potentially, some simple testing. The closer at hand the equipment is to the team, the more quickly the results feedback gets back to the team. However, it is impractical to expect that every center will have every piece of equipment that could possibly be needed. This is where the VISION network provides additional value. When establishing the VISION centers, an inventory of available equipment should be made visible to the entire network to facilitate the sharing of capital equipment. Additionally, VISION labs may need to be created or existing capabilities specified as such to provide in-depth investigation using unique or expensive equipment. Imagine the team applying the specialized tools of a medical examiner in determining the true cause of a disease. In practice, a VISION lab can be an existing failure analysis laboratory, a material control laboratory, or an engineering laboratory, so long as it deploys the standard investigative tools of the VISION centers and contributes its data and knowledge to the VISION network using the standard processes. It is important that VISION labs do not do all of the investigation work themselves, depriving the IPT and process owners of the opportunity to learn and to own the issue. The VISION labs should only provide services to the network, and their product is data/knowledge sent back to an IPT and process owner. The IPT or process owners must be the owner of the root cause determination and proposed solution as well as be held accountable for the quality of their work.

SUPPLIER ACCOUNTABILITY PROCESS

The *supplier accountability process* fits well into the VISION center process, especially if all supplier escapes are already being worked in the centers. In my years of practical experience, I have found that most traditional supplier quality methods are relatively ineffective in modifying behavior. The primary reason is because the problem is perceived as a quality activity, and traditionally folks in quality manage quality activities. So what you get is one quality engineer talking to another, and neither owns the process. At most, the senior quality leader, or possibly even the general manager, gets called in to explain what they are going to do to fix the issue. However, even with follow up there is rarely a hammer that ensures sustained performance. In the context of IPL, those who cause cost must be accountable for it.

Given that most of us work in a capitalist society, the most influential means to adjust organizational behavior are economic means. Charge those guys back for the pain they gave you! Only be careful in doing so. You will need to ensure that the existing purchasing or contract documents allow for chargeback for poor supplier performance. Withholding payment when you don't have the contractual right to do so can get the organization into even greater issues. Also, keep in the forefront that the primary objective of the process is not to make money but rather to influence the behavior of suppliers to perform as expected. The money is simply the motivator, albeit an important one.

Again, caution is advised. Frequently the organization is part of, if not the total, problem. Releasing designs that are not producible, having unclear work instructions, having conflicting engineering standards, or making unrealistic schedule demands can be a catalyst for trouble. Before assigning blame and accountability to the supplier, it is important to make sure the organization did not cause the problem.

Personally, I have had considerable success with the deployment of the supplier accountability process, recapturing the cost through real cash payments or same value in services. In my responsibilities as a quality leader, I found that my greatest ally in deploying a supplier accountability process was an internal legal department. The collective teams of quality and legal mapped out the process of problem investigation and determined when the appropriate notification and review actions should occur. Additionally, we established standards for documenting cost so as to ensure substantiation of our claims if we were ever challenged.

A lesson learned in my first endeavor was that not all communities within the organization were excited about the process. The procurement organization's initial perception was that we were creating a process that would drive up the price of procured products. At that point our financial accounting systems were not integrated to hold everyone accountable for their piece of cost generation. In this case, procurement was sliding the cost of poor supplier quality performance over to production. The procurement organization wanted to ensure its healthy relationships and not compromise future negotiations. My reply to that emphasized supplier integrity: we didn't want to do business with organizations that wouldn't stand behind their work.

The supplier accountability process also received some resistance from those who would have to document their time to add to the cost recovery claim. Their issue was that they had too much work already in the queue and we were adding more. The lesson—educate the organization more and often, and don't allow any gaps for individuals to slide through. Though we initially had some challenges in data fidelity, we drove the process hard and ensured that top executives clearly saw of the process. Seeing that cash could be coming back certainly developed a higher level of interest from top leadership.

To drive the process hard, I found one of the most intelligent, professional, social pitbulls I could find. Her job was to ensure that at all levels of the organization, people understood the process and were submitting their data in a timely manner. If they did not, they had to deal with her. I eventually used this remarkable talent to manage some of our performance reviews with the local military customer; without going into too much detail it was a nice choice. Our meetings were well planned and flawlessly executed. However, one very important success factor here is empowerment. For a position such as this, the person must be empowered to run with the process and make informed decisions without having to go to management for approval. This is one of those jobs where too much management will hurt the effectiveness of the process. The individual must also be a self-starter, be a quick learner, and have endless energy. Find this person in your organization, give them the process, stand behind them with support, and the process will work.

Continuity of the players is also critical. For the first two years of this process, we had consistent leadership from the quality and legal communities. These two disciplines effectively ran the process with a great deal of success. However, given that there was significant turnover in representation from the other functional disciplines, the process found itself in a continuous training mode, which somewhat affected productivity. For the board leadership, you should pick leaders of a very high position—in our case they were all vice presidents—and ensure that they will be able to perform the function for at least a couple of years. As leaders rotate out, the new leaders must understand the process, the value of the process, and why it is important to make sure the team remains true to the process. Otherwise, the process will suffer from too much variability and not hit its intended mark, performance improvement.

The networked VISION centers provided visibility to every case and provided the functionality of a collector of cost data. IPTs would, either online or manually, fill out costing information as they invested time and materials. If investigative or support functions had to be farmed out to other aspects of the business, the cognizant center would provide a collector charge number for the outside help. Once a case was closed, all foreseeable charges were documented, and then the data package was submitted to the Supplier Accountability Board. In our case, it was jointly lead by legal and quality and also had representatives from procurement and finance. Each had an equal vote in determining final action.

What was rewarding in this endeavor was that the board exercised the full management discretion of the company on any matters that came to it, meaning whatever they determined as the appropriate action with the supplier was the one that was engaged. In the case review, the cognizant leadership of the IPT would present the background and make recommendations for remediation. The board's responsibility was to ensure that the entire organization benefited from the process, not just the one presenting. A process aspect that we had to defend a few times (especially at the end of financial quarters) was that any recoveries had to go back to the department that incurred the cost. This is a critical aspect of the process and must be protected without compromise. The functions of the organization can respond quickly to issues only for as long as they have resources to do so. If the recoveries go elsewhere on the financial ledgers, the support measures of the organization may become depleted. The same is true for those who may want to come to your aid. If there is a chance that they will get the funds back at a later date, they will be more prone to jump in and help out. These are all realities of an organization that is not integrated in its financial accounting processes, and they would become moot if cost and accountability were structurally aligned. This also goes back to empowering the organization to do the right thing without punishing it with our archaic financial systems.

In the first year of deployment of this process, we enjoyed a 100 percent success rate in case recovery and recovered approximately 80 percent of costs. We are talking tens of millions of dollars here and the process cost practically nothing to deploy. We had one full-time supplier cost recovery manager and a couple of fractional-time paralegals, the costs of which were absorbed within the existing resources. Add to that, of course, the time of the board members, who were all executives and lived for work, so their time doesn't count. The time spent in the centers managing each case was included in each recovery, so the process became self-funding. By the way, sending a bill to a supplier gets a lot more attention than a rejection tag. Supplier quality performance improved significantly—quickly.

Now, I have to admit that not all supplier escapes could possibly go through this process of cost recovery. The process of legal documentation is far too laborious. We limited our cases to those that exceeded a specific amount so that we could concentrate on the major issues that were driving cost. If we thought a case would go over the threshold, it immediately became a board item and subject to all of the special controls that ensured recovery. For all others, we established a simpler method for offsetting supplier-induced cost and affecting their behavior. For every escape under the threshold, the supplier was automatically charged a fee for administrative costs associated with the escape. If the escape got to a customer, then the automatic charge was slightly more. These issues were also administered through the VISION centers, as were overall supplier measures such as supplier problem PPM (problem parts per million—based on delivered population).

One final note on supplier accountability: the primary purpose of the process is to influence supplier performance; the money is a great by-product. But be careful—the organization can become seduced by the potential of recoveries. Fairness must be ingrained in the process as well as good business sense. A large company can easily put a smaller company out of business for one tragic mistake in product or service quality. These questions must be asked: is that what the organization desires? And is it improved performance?

SUPPLIER-FUNDED OVERINSPECTION

Because of the high costs associated with having to perform source inspections due to chronic supplier quality performance issues, organizations may find it beneficial to establish a *supplier-funded overinspection process.* The costs associated with supporting poor supplier performance can easily and quickly add up to significant amounts of money. The overinspection process can take the form of contracted supplier quality assurance support, expediting charges, excessive inventory, and many other things. This represents valuable cash that the organization has to spend because suppliers are unwilling to perform to contracted expectations. Again, using the VISION centers as a focal point, as supplier escapes are documented they create a problem PPM measure. Establish some fair rules and make the suppliers pay for their own poor performance. The rules should be simple: if your defective PPM measures are too high, you (supplier) will be required to pay for any required overinspection activities. At a minimum, there now will be a greater assurance that the product that arrives at the organization's door is conforming—but unfortunately through tailgate inspection in most cases. A list of qualified sources for inspection support should be provided to suppliers, and an initial problem PPM threshold should be set. For example, 4000 problem PPM. But keep in mind that this is a measure of delivered product quality, as measured within your systems, and not a measure of the supplier's work in progress. A critical aspect of any measurement is reliability in the measurement itself. Be careful, and ensure your own house is in order prior to deploying a process such as this. If your data feeds for supplier performance are not reliable, fix them first.

In your analysis of supplier performance data, establish the problem PPM threshold at a manageable level. To be excessively aggressive and place a large majority of your suppliers on supplier-funded overinspection may overtask your organization's ability to manage the process. You may find that the majority of your supplier problems reside with about 10 percent of your supply base and it might be best to focus on them first. As your supplier's performance improves, the problem PPM threshold should be ratcheted down year after year. Also, rules should exist that require a critical review of a supplier that fails to improve over time, and in many cases the business relationship may need to be terminated as a result of inadequate improvement. From the VISION center and network perspective, these are the actions that show value and credibility and that must be displayed so that the organization recognizes the value.

QUALITY IN DEVELOPMENT PROCESSES

Quality improvement in development processes for both products and processes should be a further evolutionary step in the VISION center's maturity. The organization reaps a huge value when it implements a quality improvement process prior to errors occurring. This can be routinely realized when VISION centers are integrated into the organization's product development activities. For new designs and production processes, apply failure modes and effects analysis (FMEA) to project where potential failures may occur and estimate the value of intervention in risk mitigation. In addition, we frequently find that during the development production process, things don't always go the way they were intended to go. These are examples of where standard work processes need to be reviewed to ensure that they are adequate for the current work scope.

Processes should also be addressed to ensure that their designs are robust, and this includes their associated work instructions. VISION centers can be an effective tool in ferreting out problems to truly understand their cause and to prevent their introduction into production. They provide the calm in the storm of schedule demands where reason and true investigation can occur. Again, not all issues should go through the VISION center process, only those that are significant in nature or whose complexity requires the interaction of the IPT and the rigor of the VISION center process.

A few years ago, I had the privilege of visiting the engineering validation center at Panasonic's headquarters in Japan. They used a process of design validation that ensured that when a product line was turned out for production, it was ready to go and generate revenue, not problems. All engineering designs, tooling, and work instructions were completely assessed for their ability to support a high-volume production line with the highest reliability. This may be a cultural phenomenon, but I believe that most of us understand the concept "You either pay me now, or you'll pay me later." And those who understand the cost of poor quality models can appreciate the magnitude of how much more must be paid later. The product development VISION center could be a stand-alone center, and it would be designed to enhance the visibility of the various performance measures that are important to that specific product or the overall product development process. But it must be part of the network to ensure that product problems realized in the field are effectively communicated back into design.

In addition to the integration of VISION centers into the product development processes, they should also be used to dive deep into chronic design and process issues. Selection of potential projects should be driven by the various metrics the organization uses to manage its business—focusing on the heavy hitters first, resulting in high-impact results. Or equally important, irradiate the plaguing issues that seem to fester for long periods of time and become a nuisance to the organization. These long-standing problems, though not necessarily costly, are bad from the perspective that they serve as a constant reminder to the organization that no action is being taken to fix them, which can potentially erode some organizational process engagement. If nothing else, such issues should be addressed for the social and mental well-being of the workgroup. The more fragile, positive work environment is subject to the contagion of a negative work environment. It is more important to remove the negative signals than it is to cultivate the positive ones. A negative work environment is a cancer to organizational collaboration and learning.

INTEGRATED PROJECT SELECTION

The next module that should be considered is the *integrated project selection process*. I am sure that most of us have at times had to compete for limited internal resources to improve a performance characteristic of a business process while another team is trying to improve another performance characteristic within the same business process. In Chapter 2, we discussed the value of road maps at the macro level to focus the organization in a sense of synergy around specific action. VISION centers can provide the same type of consolidated focus on a more local level and in a more timely fashion. When VISION centers are used as a central focal point for the business's performance improvement practices, such as Six Sigma, lean, QRM, ACE, CMMI, and so on, they can organize project selections so that the competition for resources is eliminated.

As mentioned earlier in this appendix, you should bring in all of the performance measures that are important to the organization and effectively display them in the VISION center so that the data speak to all that enter the Center. Keep the display of data simple, standardized, and relevant to the needs of the business. For example, if there is excessive inventory in the system, show it by part number and location. Also show where the excessive touch and queue times are in the organization with visual indications on a facility layout. Quality data should also be visual; display not only the data but also scatter charts on the facility layout indicating where the issues are occurring. Again, the concept is the alignment of priorities and bringing the organization to work together. If the organization wants to decrease cost (inventory), increase flow (faster turn times), and improve quality (reduced turnbacks), overlay the data to find the biggest opportunities and go after them as an IPT by specific part number, process, and/or location. This thought process can be used in any environment. Consider a customer service call center and the volume and quality of work that can flow through a single workgroup. As a matter of fact, given all the challenges I have had with some call centers, most notably my cable provider, I would challenge them to consider themselves as cells that should contain all of the capabilities to produce the required service for any appropriately placed call. This would require a call center to think in terms of capability realignment of resources that may not currently reside within their workgroup. Given technology that currently exists, this should be a simple endeavor.

The VISION center can provide the venue for these types of discussions if integrated performance improvements are sought. Radical changes (*kaikaku*) occur only when the whole is looked at from every angle and perceived in ways not previously grasped. The solution is something new, something integrated, and something that creates greater value at less cost than the previous condition. And it is most likely something that would not have been thought of if perceived through a nonintegrated lens.

DEMONSTRATING VALUE

Leaders should always ask, if not out loud then at least to themselves, "So what?" We are engaged in this or that intervention—"So what?" What value does it bring to the organization, or better stated, to the customer? The value concept is itself a tricky animal to understand. As beauty is frequently in the eye of the beholder, so is value. Who is willing to pay for it? As we discussed this in some detail in Chapter 3, I won't rehash it much again here. But value must be defined before projects are selected. What is the expected improvement of the outcome variable? What is that outcome variable or variables? Additionally, input and throughput performance measures must be identified and targeted for process improvement to truly influence the output variable.

Assuming your projects are successful, and I trust they will be, the performance improvements must be broadly communicated. This communication serves a number of purposes. It puts value in context for the workforce, so that they will understand better why the projects are important and possibly be more prone to support the efforts.

When the projects demonstrate a track record of success, those who control the capital of the organization should be more willing to invest in future projects or even expand the process itself to engage more people and create more centers. Most important, value must be communicated to the customer periodically. If the customer does not hear anything relative to improvement efforts, they typically assume that nothing is going on. Caution is advised, however. Don't flaunt the creation of internal value when none is provided to the customer. Ensure that what is reported to the customer is meaningful to them. And how do you know what is meaningful to the customer? Ask them.

A typical method of displaying value internally is through some sort of financial savings to the organization. If you read the literature on quality costing, you will find many models for displaying financial benefits as a result of intervention. Table A.3 shows an example of a lost cost–avoidance model; however, prior to embracing this example, be sure it meets the needs of your own organization.

This specific cost-avoidance model is relatively simple and projects savings for one year. Savings for multiple years can be calculated by changing the value for A to reflect the volume of parts that would be realized in whatever time period you desire to project. Some very important things that this model does not calculate are lost customer sales, lost customer loyalty, cost of field recalls, loss of credibility, increased oversite by regulatory authorities, and any other external costs that typically don't show up in a financial ledger. My recommendation is to create two values: one that is

Table A.3 Sample cost-avoidance formula—does not estimate potential loss of market share.

$$[A \times B\{C+((D \times E)+F+G)\}]$$

A—Predicted demand/number of units in service for one year

B—Presumptive failure rate

C—Material cost if scrapped

D—Labor rate (establish a standard hourly rate)

E—Time to rework, repair, or replace

F—Cost to process paperwork (establish a flat rate, for example $100 per case)

G—Cost of shipping (example: ground $.34/lb., domestic air $.89/lb., international $1.80/lb.)

tangible and easy to touch as in the model example, and a second that is the intangible, that is difficult to project but needs to be understood. In all cases, the formulas must be standardized and not subject to frequent change. So take your time to figure out what is important to calculate and stick with it.

For organizations that perform to U.S. government contracts, the CMMI level is becoming increasingly important, primarily because the level at which an organization is certified is an indication of the maturity of its business processes. The assumption is the greater the maturity of the business processes of an organization, the less the potential risk in doing business with that company. So the value proposition in this case is to show the customer that the selected projects are reducing the risk of doing business with your company. As projects are completed, share with your customer the improvements in process maturity levels and how they will contribute to reducing risk. This should be done often and presented in such a context that the customer understands what you did and what it means to them. Remember, in most cases the customer will not be as familiar with your business processes as you are and may not understand some of the terms or processes that are in place. Keep it simple, and attempt to use terms that will have universal meaning.

Six Sigma values are widely standardized in many organizations today. The value that is frequently communicated is either one of process capability enhancement or one of a waste reduction, which is normally stated in financial terms. The rule of thumb today is that the minimum a Six Sigma project should yield is $100,000 of benefit. My suggestion is to pay attention to many other variables, such as employee fulfillment, customer satisfaction, and safety enhancement. Though these tend to be soft measures, they are just as important to the organization in fostering the environment that will lead to superior performance. So don't get stuck in the requirement that you have to save X amount of dollars to justify a project. Project selection should be, as stated earlier, based on a number of performance measures. Just make sure you consider all of the value and apprise to all stakeholders of what was achieved.

I could go through a number of other measures, such as lean, QRM, *kaizen*, and so on, but I think that would provide little value. The short of it is that unless there is a good reason for engaging in a project, such as creating some measure of value, don't do it. And when you have concluded a project, publish your results widely. The VISION centers should provide the focal point for displaying these successes as well as for showing where other potential projects stand in priority. The VISION center network should be used widely to share successes and to market the need to absorb learning throughout the organization. In many cases, it is cheaper to share knowledge than to develop it locally time and again.

SUMMARY

The VISION concept focuses on the application of standardized tools to understand organizational performance, facilitate organizational learning, drive action, ensure integration, optimize performance, and prevent recurrence of poor performance. As with most process improvement methodologies, VISION applies standardized tools to remove variation. However, VISION applies these tools not only to work processes and product issues but also to the routine business processes of the organization. It also focuses on sustained improvement through the integration of change into the organizational DNA—meaning structure, processes, training, standard work, design, leadership behavior, and ultimately, culture. When deployed through a VISION center, the VISION process becomes more visible to the organization and facilitates engagement of process owners and IPTs. Where the VISION process differs from most other investigative and problem-solving methodologies is in its enterprisewide application of improvement. When the organization engages in the *standardization and integration phases,* it is no longer looking locally but is taking enterprisewide action.

VISION centers are geographical locations within the business that provide the synergy for focused action in deploying the VISION process. The objective of the VISION center is to act as a sense making funnel of the organization's performance measures and to ensure that the organization concentrates on the issues that are influencing customer satisfaction or create value, or both. The VISION center should be staffed with a trained technician who acts as a facilitator to the process owners and IPT members to enable them to understand the performance of their processes and product and who take ownership for improvement. VISION centers should be located in prominent areas so that they can share their activities with the broader organization as well as demonstrate leadership's commitment to the improvement process. When linked through the networks, the centers enable enterprisewide learning.

VISION center networks provide the structure for multiple VISION centers to interact as one to pool resources and to share learning. VISION center networks can represent a value stream, a large cost center, a collective of suppliers, or any other collection of knowledge and action centers that makes good business sense. The objective of the networked structure is to lend speed to action in the business and to prevent the same lesson having to be learned more than once. It also provides an excellent platform, through which we can recognize, understand, and proliferate superior performance.

Appendix B
Integrated Knowledge Management

*Unless an organization objectively knows
how much it knows, it really doesn't know.*

Let's assume the organization has aligned its business processes to create value for the customer while removing waste from action. The integrated product teams (IPTs) are deployed in a cost-efficient manner. Teams and individuals are held accountable for performance. Let me throw out this question: How does the organization know that its people have the knowledge capability to execute the processes of the business? Unless there is some means for identifying knowledge expectations and measuring capability, the answer is it doesn't. For an organization to effectively work together in integrated teams, significant consideration must be given to the knowledge requirements of all its processes and the capability of its members. Otherwise, the organization is operating on the assumption that because an individual holds a specific job title, they have the appropriate knowledge to fulfill the corresponding responsibilities. It is also operating on the assumption that no gaps exist in the knowledge capabilities of the organization if all positions are filled.

All assumptions contain a measure of risk, and the more authority and responsibility an individual or team has over organizational performance, the greater the assumed risk. Take, for example, the engineer who makes a product design change that they perceive as minor. If the engineer fails to understand the interactive impact of that change, they could potentially affect public safety. For example, let's say the material properties of an electrical box in a building installation end up causing a fire because the box cannot resist the heat it experiences. One could say that the engineer should have known better; however, the organization has the responsibility to ensure that the employee has the ability to execute the assigned work or design the work so that it is mistakeproofed and human error is not possible, or better yet, both. If you don't believe that the organization has this responsibility, just pick up a newspaper and note the judgments against companies in product liability suits.

To minimize the risk in regard to knowledge, or better stated, applied human capability, it must be treated as a process and measured to ensure that capability meets expectations. This is true for all levels of the organization, recognizing that risk increases with the level of discretion an individual has in decision making. The challenge of managing knowledge capability or ensuring that it is sufficient is magnified when organizations empower teams to lead the organization. As the organization performs as integrated teams, it needs to make sure the collective human capabilities are aligned and adequate to get the job done correctly. In this appendix, *integrated knowledge management* (IKM) is introduced as an integrated tool to provide the organization a structured process by which to manage its human capability and knowledge requirements.

IKM builds upon much of the research already done in the field of knowledge management. But where the IKM model differs from other knowledge management models is that it focuses on the integration of the business processes of the organization and the knowledge residing within organizational members. Many knowledge management models focus on the organizing of data and information within the organization, and some depend heavily on information systems to facilitate that. Those foci are very important; however, more important is ensuring that your people not only have the knowledge they need to do the work of the organization but that they can actually apply it.

Though the greatest value in deploying a management tool comes from its integration throughout the organization, IKM offers the organization the option of implementing aspects of the model to gain a better understanding of human capability whether the organization engages in integration through IPL or not. This will become clear as we discuss the IKM matrix tool, which can be deployed at any organizational level or function to provide immediate value and transparency to knowledge capability. The process of knowledge measurement is also a requirement of ISO 9000, and of other industry standards, and IKM can provide an effective means of meeting and exceeding that requirement.

As is discussed in this appendix, the major components of IKM are the following:

- Taxonomy of knowledge capability
- Identifying types of knowledge
- Macro knowledge mapping
- Integrated knowledge management matrix

- Knowledge management measurement

- Evaluation of capability

- Capability development

- Value-stream knowledge assurance

TAXONOMY OF KNOWLEDGE CAPABILITY

The notion of IKM is derived from the field of education and the process of educating children. As various local education officials have struggled with establishing a robust process for managing the transference of knowledge, so have government officials at the national level. In the 1950s, Benjamin Bloom was sponsored by the U.S. Department of Health, Education, and Welfare to study various methods of measurement, evaluation, and assessment relative to comprehension of subject matter by individuals. One of the outcomes of Bloom's work was a *comprehension scale* that is based on six points, from a low score of one to a high score of six. At the low end, the person has the ability to recall, to bring to mind the appropriate material—more or less—and has an awareness of the subject. At the high end of the scale, the individual has the ability to judge the value of ideas, procedures, and methods and modify the process or the known knowledge. It could be said that they have a mastery of the specific knowledge requirement. The value of using a scale such as Bloom's is that it is a linear scale, is grounded in educational theory, and has a wealth of research associated with it, and it integrates well into work design and training development. His six levels of cognition, which I will refer to as *knowledge capability* as follows are: level 1—knowledge; level 2—comprehension; level 3—application; level 4—analysis; level 5—synthesis; level 6—evaluation. When I first explored the development of a tool like IKM, I applied Bloom's work exclusively. Though my efforts to manage organization knowledge capability were very successful, Bloom's terms and concepts were cumbersome for the larger organization to understand and apply.

In 2001, Anderson and Krathwohl expanded upon Bloom's work and revised many of the terms to reflect the language of today and to better associate the knowledge expectations into forms of action. Their revision of Bloom's work makes the application of a taxonomy simpler by making each level (they refer to levels as *categories*) a verb that requires the organization to assess what action is occurring as a result of knowledge application. (see Figure B.1)

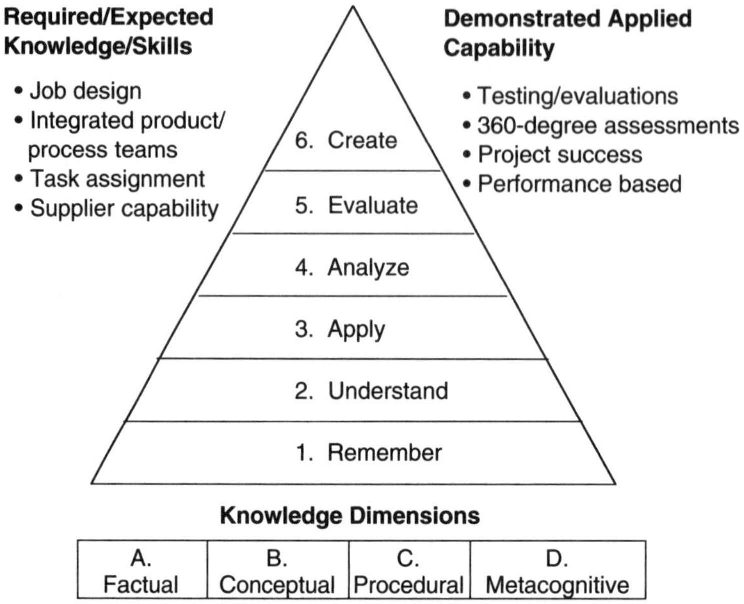
Required/Expected Knowledge/Skills
• Job design
• Integrated product/ process teams
• Task assignment
• Supplier capability
Demonstrated Applied Capability
• Testing/evaluations
• 360-degree assessments
• Project success
• Performance based
6. Create
5. Evaluate
4. Analyze
3. Apply
2. Understand
1. Remember
Knowledge Dimensions
A. Factual
B. Conceptual
C. Procedural
D. Metacognitive

Figure B.1 The integrated knowledge management model (based on Bloom 1956 and adapted from Anderson and Krathwohl 2001).

Level 1: *Remember*. At this level the individual has an awareness of the subject matter, but that awareness is relatively shallow. The retrieval of this knowledge is from long-term memory. They recognize and recall the terms and can repeat what they have read or heard but have no real ability to apply it to a process. Level 1 knowledge is usually the result of communication sessions, briefings, reading, or everyday language and has little applied use other than awareness.

Level 2: *Understand*. The person understands the subject matter but may not be ready to apply the knowledge to a task. They can understand or grasp the meaning of what is being communicated and make use of the idea. Level 2 knowledge may come from reading, short training sessions, or observation.

Level 3: *Apply*. At level 3 the individual has the ability to use ideas, principles, and theories in particular and concrete situations. They are applying what they know to practice, but at a basic level, and are dependent upon procedure to guide them through the process. People who possess level 3 knowledge capability can be peer trainers in executing the defined process.

Level 3 knowledge usually is the result of training and some supervised interaction in application of the knowledge.

Level 4: *Analyze*. The test for this level is communication. Does the individual understand the subject matter to the extent that they can engage in discussion of the various elements? The person has sufficient depth of knowledge to break down a communication into constituent parts to make the organization of the idea clear. The issues must be conveyed complete and organized. The person should also be able to recognize bias in the content. They can, for example, determine when something is subjective rather than objective. Level 4 knowledge comes after the individual has been trained (formally or on the job) and has interacted with the application of the knowledge for some time so that they understand how and why the process works.

Level 5: *Evaluate*. This level requires the person to be able to put together parts and elements into a unified organization or whole and make judgments based on criteria and standards. They have a true understanding of the subject matter and can effectively make sense of the complexity of the applications for the knowledge. To be judged to have capability at this level, people will need to perform all the abilities of the previous levels and be able to organize their understanding around the issues the knowledge is intended for. Those with level 5 knowledge capability have the ability to check and critique the work of others as well as to judge which method is best when more than one option is available.

Level 6: *Create*. At the highest end of the scale, one expects mastery of a subject. The individual should have the ability to judge the value of ideas, procedures, and methods using the criteria for evaluation inherent in the knowledge of the subject. They have a clear understanding of what *good* looks like and can easily engage in double-loop learning in application of the knowledge. A characteristic of level 6 knowledge is the ability to understand the concept to sufficient depth to select alternate methods, change existing processes in the application of the concept, or create something completely new. At this level, people should be able to speak on behalf of the knowledge to others so as to generate activities for new knowledge creation. Level 6 knowledge capability is never a result of attending a formal training session. It is obtained only through extensive hands-on application of the knowledge.

In all of these levels, understand that it is one thing to have the knowledge in one's head and is another to apply it. As we discuss the application of levels and knowledge types, please keep in the forefront the consideration for execution.

Table B.1 The major categories of knowledge (adapted from Anderson and Krathwohl 2001).

MAJOR KNOWLEDGE TYPES	EXAMPLES
A. FACTUAL KNOWLEDGE—The basic elements organizational members must know to be acquainted with a discipline or to solve problems in it	
A.a. Knowledge of terminology	Technical vocabulary, engineering symbols, acronyms
A.b. Knowledge of specific details and elements	Standards and specifications, reliable sources of information
B. CONCEPTUAL KNOWLEDGE—The interrelationships among the basic elements within a larger structure that enable them to function together	
B.a. Knowledge of classifications and categories	Forms of business ownership, regulatory approval requirements
B.b. Knowledge of principles and generalizations	Law of supply and demand, psychological needs
B.c. Knowledge of theories, models, and structures	Theory of evolution, structure of government
C. PROCEDURAL KNOWLEDGE—How to do something, methods of inquiry, and criteria for using skills, algorithms, techniques, and methods	
C.a. Knowledge of subject-specific skills and algorithms	Skills applied in machining, computer programming
C.b. Knowledge of subject-specific techniques and methods	Cost accounting, design validation, auditing practices
C.c. Knowledge of criteria for determining when to use appropriate procedures	Criteria used to know when to apply a certain natural law, criteria used to assess the quality of a program plan
D. METACOGNITIVE KNOWLEDGE—Knowledge of cognition in general as well as awareness and knowledge of one's own cognition	
D.a. Strategic knowledge	Knowledge of outlining as a means of capturing the structure of a unit of subject matter in a resource text, knowledge of the use of heuristics
D.b. Knowledge about cognitive tasks, including appropriate contextual and conditional knowledge	Knowledge of how to substantiate a design, knowledge of the cognitive demands of different tasks
D.c. Self-knowledge	Knowledge that providing critical feedback is a personal strength, whereas being quiet is a weakness; awareness of one's own knowledge level

IDENTIFYING TYPES OF KNOWLEDGE

Anderson and Krathwohl introduced an added dimension of knowledge management by recognizing that there are various types of knowledge. For use in this model they identify four: factual knowledge, conceptual knowledge, procedural knowledge, and metacognitive knowledge (see Table B.1). Incorporating these types of knowledge into the model allows for greater definition of the associated action. It also facilitates greater alignment of expectations of knowledge capability with the design of learning opportunities and with work design. For example, in a manufacturing setting, individuals may be applying machining, grinding, deburring, coating, and inspection processes in accordance with engineering requirements. For this example, there are a number of verb applications to nouns. The verb apply gives us an idea of what capability level is to be applied—level 3, apply. The noun phrase machining, grinding, deburring, coating, and inspection processes in accordance with engineering requirements tells us that there are expectations that work be performed to documented criteria, which implies that procedural knowledge will be required. Those applying procedural knowledge will need to understand how the work is defined and the expectations for compliance to specified norms. Such knowledge-type recognition is necessary for the effective management of the integrated knowledge management process—specifically in regard to doing something to improve the levels of knowledge capability. Depending on knowledge type, leaders will implement different training and learning methods and make work assignments.

Factual knowledge is the knowledge of discrete, isolated content elements—"bits of information" (Bloom 1956). It includes knowledge of terminology and knowledge of specific details and elements (Anderson and Krathwohl 2001). An example is an engineer's knowledge of symbology for drawings or of the periodic elements in a specific metal alloy. Another example could be a government official who has the responsibility of managing the natural resources for a specific area or ensuring the safety of a specific process; among other things, they require knowledge of the written law.

Conceptual knowledge is knowledge of more complex, organized knowledge forms (Bloom 1956). It includes knowledge of classifications and categories; principles and generalizations; and theories, models, and structures (Anderson and Krathwohl 2001). An example is the engineer who, due to an understanding of theory, knows how and why certain chemicals interact. Or the government official who understands the concept of lawmaking and the theory of democracy and applies them in determining what laws are necessary.

Procedural knowledge is knowledge of how to do something (Bloom 1956). It includes knowledge of skills and algorithms and techniques and methods, as well as knowledge of the criteria used to determine and/or justify when to do what within specific domains and disciplines (Anderson and Krathwohl 2001). An example is an engineer who selects certain design characteristics because the engineering standard work specified them as appropriate for the specific application. Or the government official who processes the request for a new law in a certain order and in a specific format as directed by established norms.

Metacognitive knowledge is knowledge about cognition in general as well as awareness of and knowledge about one's own cognition (Bloom 1956). It encompasses strategic knowledge; knowledge about cognitive tasks, including contextual and conditional knowledge; and self-knowledge (Anderson and Krathwohl 2001). Metacognitive knowledge may be one of the more challenging types of knowledge for organizations to learn to manage. This is mostly because it's knowing how we learn. In addition, much has been written about metacognitive knowledge, and not all of it is consistent. For the purposes of this model, we will use Bloom's (1956) definition and keep it simple: cognition awareness and knowing where to obtain knowledge.

This means that in our engineer example, the engineers understand the limitations of their knowledge around specific designs and material but also are aware of how to expand their knowledge base. The same is true for our government official example—if there are aspects of the lawmaking or enforcement processes officials are not familiar with, they should know how to recognize those gaps and know where to gain such knowledge. When it comes to managing metacognitive knowledge, I suggest that the organization focus on the processes of self-evaluation and knowledge acquisition.

Figure B.2 adapts Anderson and Krathwohl's major knowledge types for application in organizations. While keeping the knowledge types intact, an organization could reproduce this table and insert examples that have meaning for it so that the following assessment processes are more easily understood for their application.

MACRO KNOWLEDGE MAPPING

What if an organization were to ask itself, "Do we have all of the human capability we need to be successful?" As noted earlier, if the organization has not treated knowledge capability as a process that is continuously measured against the needs of the business and the changes in its environment, then there is no objective way for it to answer such a question. Without measurement you have speculation. Also, consider whether an organization can perform as one integrated team when it potentially has conflicting

Integrated Knowledge Management **163**

**Integrated Knowledge Management Model
Training and Work-Scope Development**

Training/learning objective or workscope requirements: Clearly stated what the resulting capability should be.

Noun: State the knowledge content (e.g., thermodynamics, environmental policy, contact review).

Verb: State what capability is expected. What will the person do with the knowledge?

Knowledge dimension: What types of knowledge need to be considered?

Knowledge dimension	Knowledge capability/measure					
	1 Remember	2 Understand	3 Apply	4 Analyze	5 Evaluate	6 Create
A. Factual						
B. Conceptual						
C. Procedural						
D. Metacognitive						

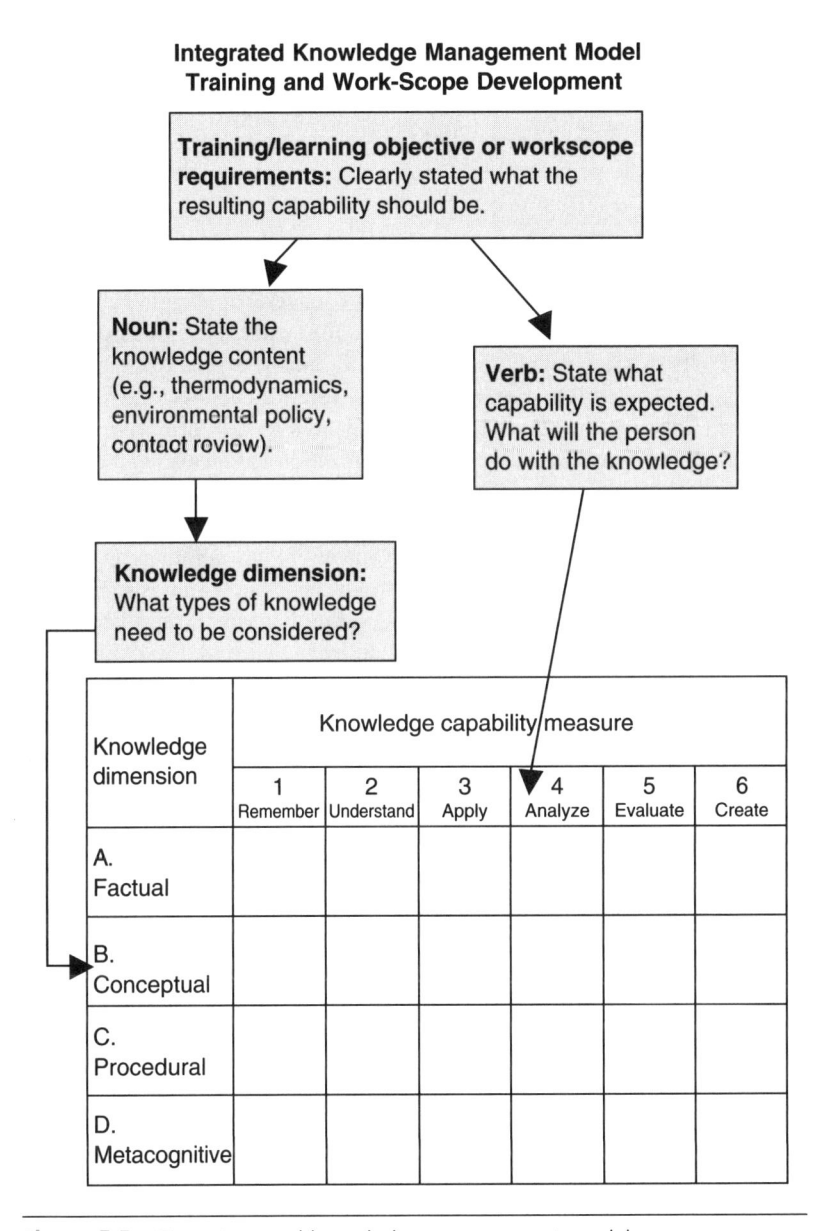

Figure B.2 The integrated knowledge management model worksheet (based on Bloom 1956 and adapted from Anderson and Krathwohl 2001).

understanding and interpretations of processes and gaps in knowledge. The reality is that organizations can perform without specific knowledge management processes in place, but not as one integrated team and with considerable waste and risk. The goal of the knowledge-mapping process is to identify all of the organization's major knowledge requirements and to assess at a high level the needed depth and distribution of capability for each knowledge element.

Assuming that the organization has mapped its value streams and its business process life cycle, as discussed in Chapter 2, it should be able to identify major knowledge and capability requirements in the value-creation processes (first-order value) and its enabling business processes (second-order value). At the highest organizational level of the knowledge management map it is suggested that you use the business process life cycle map as the overarching template. Therein, the organization has identified the major activities and processes that it expects to be performed as its standard for the creation of value in all of its products. For example, in the *design* phase of the business process life cycle, the organization may define as an expectation that the process of design failure mode and effects analysis (FMEA) be performed on each product. For those unfamiliar with design FMEA, it is a process of recognizing design characteristics that have the risk of failure. The objective is to reduce or eliminate risk through design changes or redundancies.

In the creation of the macro-level knowledge management map, the process of design FMEA should be identified as a knowledge requirement that needs to be managed. The question, "Who should have this knowledge and to what level of capability?" can also be asked. As for the, "Who needs it?" question, each aspect of the organization can be identified on the macro knowledge management map and aligned with the knowledge requirement if it is required for that function. As discussed earlier, levels of ability can vary depending on the need of application. For example, an engineer in design or quality may need greater capability than a buyer from procurement. Still, the buyer will need a level of awareness, such as level 1, so that they can support the technical functions of the organization when interacting with suppliers.

The value-stream process map should identify not only what is being done to create value but also who is creating specific product or service value. Identification of the specific value creation for each product or service will provide the context for the process. So if the organization ensures knowledge capability in the process of design FMEA, is there a difference in applying this knowledge from product to product? The answer is probably yes. There certainly is a difference in the design of a car bumper versus a piston in an engine. Therefore, so the expectation for product knowledge should flow into the major business processes of the organization as contextualized process knowledge. It does little good if the knowledge capability of the process resides in one person and the product knowledge resides in another.

To keep the process mapping from becoming overly complex, it is suggested that only the major or critical product or service knowledge requirements flow to the macro knowledge process map. As the knowledge management is deployed at levels closer to execution, the major components of product knowledge can be managed in greater definition. This process sounds simple, right? In reality, the process is usually one of discovery for the organization, which rarely comes without some frustration. On the other hand, the reward can be greater alignment and synergy in action.

During the development of the macro knowledge management map, the organization should determine the *what* and *who* of the processes. That is, what is being done, and does that activity provide value? What knowledge and capability is needed to execute the process? Who is doing it, and what knowledge capability is required to execute the process? This is an excellent opportunity to challenge the current process design and to ask why the organization is doing this or that. In addition to improving the efficiency of a process, you should consider ways of mistakeproofing it to increase its robustness and to minimize human influences. Organizations that have struggled with the deployment of initiatives like IPD may find that this tool solves many of the conflicts they have experienced with process alignment and work execution. An additional benefit is greater workforce flexibility because of the standardization of knowledge expectations and capabilities.

Imagine an organization that can move people around simply by recognizing where business needs are and aligning knowledge capabilities. If gaps exist, they can be managed in a variety of ways, depending on the situation. That certainly is better than laying people off only to hire others to do a similar job elsewhere in the organization. This sort of leadership action helps develop trust and fosters the engagement and performance cultures organizations seek. By the way, for organizations that are deploying Six Sigma or CMMI, the process of managing human capability in the organization could make for an excellent project to reduce waste and increase measured effectiveness and capability.

This question may still remain: How much knowledge does an organization need? It depends on where the products or services of the organization are within their life cycle. If a product or service is early in its design development phases, it will need more knowledge capability in design-related processes than if it were a mature product or service that required only periodic updates in design. However, please do not confuse capability with capacity in this knowledge management process. It does little good to have a few people with the appropriate levels of knowledge capability when the workload requires a dozen. This is where those leaders of the value stream must understand and recognize the knowledge needs of the business and ensure capability and capacity are at the levels of expected execution. As discussed in the Chapter 4 "Leadership," to consider knowledge management as an important business process is a matter of choice. It is suggested that in the capacity-planning activities of the organization knowledge capability be given required consideration. As a test of the capacity-planning efforts, challenge your assumptions of work scope and volume by looking at the expectations of knowledge capabilities aligned with the work. The greater the capabilities of the people, the greater the complexity of the scope of work and efficiency of performed work. Be careful though; this does not mean that if you throw a bunch of folks with level 5 knowledge capability at work that is designed for level 3 knowledge capability, you it will get it done any faster. It does mean that if an organization takes the time to understand what specific knowledge capability is required for a given work scope, it may find opportunities for broadening the capabilities of individuals to complete a broader work scope. This may allow organizations to streamline processes and redeploy people to other areas of the business as needed.

Also, a note about sustainability is offered. If anything is constant, it is change. As the environment changes, the business processes of the organization need to be addressed. The amount of effort to maintain a knowledge management process will depend on the frequency of change—this includes environmental changes, product changes, process changes, and attrition in people. It is suggested that the process ownership be assigned to a single owner in the business—possibly the business process organization. Their responsibility would be to ensure that the process is well defined, is executed, and remains capable. The leaders of the business are responsible for the application of the process and the leadership to ensure sustained process capability.

THE INTEGRATED KNOWLEDGE MANAGEMENT MATRIX

To be managed effectively a process must contain quantitative variables of performance measures. The integrated knowledge management (IKM) matrix is a tool that provides quantitative measures of knowledge capability. The objective is to create an integrated measurement system that will provide the employee, leader, and organization with an understanding of knowledge expectations and measures of the current state relative to human knowledge capabilities. Up to this section, this appendix has focused on ensuring that the knowledge capabilities of the organization are aligned and manageable at the organization's top levels. However, the IKM matrix is a tool that can be deployed in organizations that have not yet undertaken integration efforts. If leaders in an individual segment of the organization desire to manage the knowledge capabilities of their business, there is no reason for them not to create their own IKM matrix. In the remainder of this section, we will discuss the IKM matrix in the integrated context, but I strongly encourage those internal change agents, including functional discipline leaders, to take charge and manage their organization's knowledge capability.

At the macro level, the knowledge management maps identify what knowledge is expected within the organization. They may also address the depth as far as capability is concerned for the major disciplines. Depending on the structure of the organization, the IKM matrix can be deployed in any fashion an organization desires. The matrix can be designed to address the functions of a discipline such as engineering, manufacturing, or quality. It can be deployed organizationally, such as at a facility level. Or it can be deployed as a complete value stream. Given the current state of organizational experience with value stream structures, my recommendation is to create IKM matrices by major functional disciplines. This only allows a specific focus on the sciences related to that function, but it also facilitates the reorganizing of the data into any other organizational form desired—including value streams. To do so, individuals would be tagged accordingly and sorted to provide the desired perspective.

The structure of the IKM matrix should be standardized throughout the organization, with only the individual knowledge expectations varying among the functional disciplines. We'll use the discipline of quality in our example of developing an IKM matrix. Let's assume the organization contains various jobs for quality practitioners, such as laboratory technician, shop quality engineering, quality planning, contract review, supplier quality, software assurance, auditing, and various others. Each of these roles require a unique application of quality training; however, an overarching foundation of knowledge capabilities is expected from any quality practitioner. This foundation could be called the quality basics. Other disciplines would have the same. Regardless of which discipline we're talking about, this is where people may voice various opinions about what these foundational capabilities are.

The best bet is to go to the most recognized professional homeroom for the function and seek out the body of knowledge that has already been identified. In the case of a quality practitioner, if the organization is a U.S. company, it may find what it is looking for at the American Society for Quality (ASQ). For the quality practitioner, ASQ currently maintains about

10 identified bodies of knowledge, designed around professional certifications such as Certified Quality Manager, Certified Quality Auditor, Certified Reliability Engineer, and various others. These certification processes are designed to test the knowledge of a quality professional with regard to a certain application. To keep the matrix process simple, any of these bodies of knowledge can be selected and used without modification to identify knowledge expectations.

However, do not miss the opportunity to tailor knowledge expectations to meet the real needs of the organization, as well as to align them with other disciplines. A discipline should use the ASQ bodies of knowledge as a good starting point to identify what knowledge it would expect a quality practitioner in its business to have. Again, you should use the macro knowledge management map as a guide to ensure that the review team maintains focus on the needs of the business. It is suggested that people outside the discipline not perform this review. Rather, the review should be facilitated by someone trained in the area of professional learning and knowledge management. The facilitator should ensure that the integration processes are adhered to and that there are consistent interpretations of the classification process. The identification and classification of specific knowledge expectations should be completed by the widely recognized leaders of the discipline in the organization; they have the ability to see the organization as an integrated entity.

When I say widely recognized leaders in the discipline, I do not mean positional managers. Those people who choose to be involved in the growth of their discipline and who have demonstrated significant ability should determine the content for this process. The ability to see the organization as an integrated entity is very significant. If those designing the system are capable only of seeing in the traditional sense, what the organization will end up with is a repackaging of the old.

Typically, professional bodies of knowledge do not contain much in the order of leadership attributes, and they rarely provide levels of cognition based on a professional's point in their career. For example, we should expect a person who has been in the profession for 10 years to have a greater breadth and depth of professional abilities than someone with only two years of experience. We would also hope that the seeds of leadership have been planted during the individual's career so that they can become a future leader of the organization. In creating the matrix, the discipline leaders should use good judgment in assessing what levels of cognition are expected at various "grade levels" (for example, entry level, specialist, professional, manager) as well as what the general expectations are for personal leadership. This should be tested against the type of work that could be assigned to the individual at a specific grade level.

The structure of the matrix should provide for the certainty that there will be people in the organization who have a great interest in the depth of the discipline and will gravitate to its technical capabilities. Others will demonstrate a great ability to lead others in the discipline and may require less depth of knowledge but greater breadth of the discipline. The entry point for both career paths should be the same, but at some point there should be a crossroads that allows for growth in one direction or the other. Very few people may possess the capability to be masters of both characteristics—leader and technical expert. These folks typically will be the first to lead very challenging issues—with success.

Regardless of the discipline, the requisite basics will always need to be addressed. These are basic knowledge expectations that every employee of the company should meet, such as knowledge of company ethics, sexual harassment policy, quality policy, and so on. Because of their binary nature (such as attendance in a standardized course or nonattendance), these are easier to manage, and they are frequently managed well in most companies. However, integrating the management of such basics into the various knowledge management matrices gives you a more balanced overview of the knowledge management process in the organization and in individual disciplines. Given the realities of business, frequently priorities need to be set for what gets addressed first. Having a visual tool that shows the entire spectrum of knowledge requirements at once allows you to better set priorities and manage gaps as organizational risk. For example, to reduce risk for the interim, the organization may choose to provide short briefings to ensure awareness but not necessarily go to the level of investment to create a higher level of knowledge capability.

The career paths and grade structure of the discipline should make up the columns of the matrix. The rows of the matrix should represent the actual expected knowledge capabilities, using the six levels of knowledge capability. By grouping knowledge requirements into knowledge sets, you can do an assessment by major capability categories. For example, the basics would make up a stand-alone knowledge set row category. The collective rows would represent all of the basic expectations. In our quality practitioner example, we would identify the major knowledge categories of quality. Using ASQ's various bodies of knowledge, we may come up with the following categories: basic quality; statistical management; inspection and testing; technical basics; standards and regulations; and possibly others. We'd compare these basics to the macro knowledge management map to ensure alignment. And as we desire to plant the seeds of leadership early, we should also develop a category for leadership and team. Each major knowledge set would allow for capability measurement within the set. As new capabilities become needed, we'd simply add to the existing knowledge sets or create a new set if there are a number of like new knowledge capability requirements. But be mindful that by adding to an existing knowledge set, you may be making an adjustment that will affect the knowledge management of the total discipline. If the unique addition does not have general applicability to all within the discipline, keep it out of the knowledge set and manage it as unique and specific to a limited work scope or project or smaller group.

Recognizing that there are specialties within the discipline is very important. For example, in our quality example, we said that there are at least seven specialties, if not more, that need to be addressed, such as laboratory technician, shop quality engineering, quality planning, contract review, supplier quality, software assurance, and auditing. Some of the specialties will have much in common with other specialties and these common knowledge requirements should be grouped within the common aspects for the discipline. However, where there are significant differences in specific job related knowledge expectations, as for example in contrasting software and laboratory quality engineers, the specific job related or field related knowledge expectations should be defined in knowledge sets unique to their field. This will provide more accurate visibility and accounting for the various specialties within a discipline. It is very important to use "professional" sense when creating the knowledge sets. The objective is to standardize as much as possible, but not at the expense of missing critical knowledge requirements.

KNOWLEDGE MANAGEMENT MEASUREMENT

Now that we have a standard spreadsheet method of accounting that lists the requisite knowledge and capabilities of a discipline and stratifies the knowledge capability by grade structure and career paths, we need to establish the measurement system. The measurement of knowledge and capability by grade level should be grounded in a robust numerically based model. Hence the application of Bloom's taxonomy and the six-point scale.

Now it's time to determine what are the appropriate levels of capability for each grade level for each knowledge requirement. Again, someone trained in the area of professional cognition and organizational development should facilitate this to ensure consistent application of the measurement process. However, the recognized leaders of the discipline should be the ones to set the expectations for each grade level, based on the noun and verb combination. My recommendation is to place the bar high when it comes to the alignment of grade structure. Human nature is to meet expectations. If expectations are low, they will be met with little challenge; however, if expectations are high but fair, people will be more apt to continue their personal development.

Take each knowledge row and work from right to left. If at the highest grade level, we expect an individual to have a capability level of X in a certain knowledge requirement, the organization needs to understand when the development of that capability should take place and plan for it in growing measures of capability earlier in the grade structure. Be mindful that level 6 knowledge capability is not always the right measure for your most senior people. Depending on their responsibilities and the requirements of the business processes, a lesser capability level may be appropriate. In addition, unless a broad band exists within a grade level that allows for growth within that grade, you should not expect people to jump in capability many levels from one grade level to another. Government employees experience something similar to this in their General Schedule (GS) structure. A government employee can remain at the same grade level for a considerable amount of time, yet they are expected to grow in capability. A GS-13, step 8 should have greater capabilities than a GS-13, step 1. If not, leadership has failed in its expectations of the organization and in its management of processes for growth.

So enough with the conjecture; let's talk more process specific. For each knowledge requirement, consider the six levels of knowledge capability as verbs and determine at what grade level such capability would be expected. If a person "applies" a specific knowledge, then the level should be a 3 for that specific grade level. As expectations increase or decrease, they should be so reflected in the matrix. It is recommended that you use a worksheet as displayed in Figure B.2 for each grade level and for each knowledge requirement. This worksheet can facilitate the discussion about capability assessment and the determination of the required knowledge types. Identifying knowledge types becomes crucial when developing strategies for capability development and when work design is discussed. The worksheets will also serve as a valuable tool for communicating the meaning of capability assignments at various grade levels. Imagine having a discussion with an employee about the expectations of a knowledge capability. The worksheet provides some structure for that discussion and may provide an understanding of the various dimensions and will aid appreciation of why the knowledge is important. If nothing else, the discussion should help employees better understand how their skills are applied to a process and the connection to the macro business processes.

Once you have completed this phase of the knowledge management matrix, the discipline should have a matrix (see Figure B.3) that outlines all of the expected knowledge requirements for the discipline and that is scalable in capability measures for individual growth. Depending on how

Appendix B

widely the organization deploys the matrix process, there should also be an integrated knowledge management matrix that provides the same level of detail for all functional disciplines within the organization and that guards against potential capability gaps in the macro process. Ideally, the organization establishes a recurring process of interdiscipline review that ensures that

QUALITY PRACTITIONER SKILLS ASSESSMENT
Sample Composite Roll-Up For Organization XYZ

	Practitioner Level	Assoc 1	Assoc 2	Tech	Analyst	QE	QE Spec	Sr. QE
	Number of Quality Professionals	4	5	11	23	87	184	13
TOPIC	**SKILLS REQUIRED**							
Quality	Continuous Improvement	1.3	1.8	2.6	3.6	4.0	4.5	4.5
	Customer Relationships	2.8	3.2	3.8	4.6	4.7	5.0	5.3
	Metrics	3.0	0.6	2.5	3.5	3.3	3.7	4.4
	Process Management	2.8	2.4	2.1	3.4	4.1	4.3	4.1
	Project Management				2.0	2.1	3.1	3.6
	Quality	.8	2.4	2.43	.6	3.8	4.5	4.5
	Quality Audits		2.4	2.3	2.0	3.3	3.6	3.6
	Quality Control	0.5	1.8	2.5	3.5	4.1	4.5	4.3
	Quality Costs		1.6	0.9	1.7	2.1	2.2	3.2
	Quality Function				1.7	2.2	2.9	4.6
	Quality Planning	0.8	2.0	1.0	2.2	2.5	2.9	4.4
	Quality Function Deployment				0.4	1.2	1.3	3.6
	Supplier Relationships	3.0	2.4	1.9	2.6	3.6	4.2	4.5
	Total Quality Management			0.7	0.9	1.8	2.1	2.4
	Subtotal	16.0	20.8	22.7	35.7	43.0	49.4	57.0
Standards and Regulations	International Standards		1.4	0.9	1.5	2.2	2.2	2.3
	Industry Technical Standards			.3	1.9	3.3	4.1	4.6
	Industry Quality Standards	0.0	0.8	1.5	0.8	2.0	1.7	3.2
	International Regulations			0.8	0.8	1.2	1.7	2.3
	National Regulations		0.0	0.7	0.7	1.5	1.8	2.4
	Product Specific Regualtions		0.0	0.3	0.6	0.8	0.7	1.2
	Subtotal	1.0	2.2	5.3	6.3	11.0	12.0	16.0
Leadership and Team	Leadership				1.5	2.3	3.4	4.2
	Meeting Organization				1.9	2.5	5.4	5.1
	Time Management			3.0	4.6	5.2	5.3	5.2
	Communication			2.4	4.4	6.0	5.2	5.6	5.3
	Organizational Dynamics	0.3	.2	1.7	2.4	2.9	3.6	4.2
	Teaming	2.8	2.6	3.6	4.8	4.4	5.0	5.4
	Training/Development				0.7	1.3	1.8	3.5
	Subtotal	3.1	9.2	14.3	22.6	23.8	30.1	32.9
Statistical Techniques	Statistics and Probability		1.2	1.81	.7	2.1	2.7	3.5
	Correlation/Regression Analysis				1.4	0.8	1.3	1.4
	Statistical Decision Making				1.0	0.9	0.8	1.4
	Statistical Process Control		0.4	0.8	1.2	1.7	1.8	2.9
	Reliability and Risk Management			.5	0.3	0.6	0.7	1.4
	Design and Analysis of Experiments					0.5	0.3	0.6	1.1
	Subtotal	0.0	1.6	3.16	.1	6.4	7.9	11.7
Inspection and Test	Inspection and Test		0.9	1.9	2.2	3.3	3.9	4.6
	Inspection Methods		1.2	2.2	2.2	3.6	4.4	5.3
	Measurement Systems		1.2	2.2	2.3	4.1	3.8	4.2
	Acceptance Sampling		1.2	1.5	2.2	2.6	3.1	4.7
	Subtotal	0.0	4.5	7.8	8.9	13.6	15.2	18.8
	TOTALS	21.9	51.9	77.4	106.9	127.8	148.9	171.6
	%6	8.4%	56.4%	53.4%	56.9%	55.8%	58.9%	269.0%

Education/Experience Required

		Assoc 1	Assoc 2	Tech	Analyst	QE	QE Spec	Sr. QE
	Quality Tech Certification/Community College	5 years (D)	8 years (D)					
	Associate Degree	(D)	2 years (D)	3 years (D)	5 years (D)			
	Bachelors Degree			(D)	2 years (D)	4 years (D)	6 years(D)	10 years (D)
	Masters Degree/MBA				(D)	2 years (D)	4 years (D)	7 years (D)
	PhD Degree					(D)	2 years (D)	4 years (D)

LEGEND	SKILL ASSESSMENT
6 = Create	Proficiency Requirement Satisfied
5 = Evaluate	Proficiency Partially Satisfied >50%
4 = Analyze	Proficiency Partially Satisfied <50%
3 = Apply	Skill Gap
2 = Understatnd	Proficiency Rating determined from QE Skill Assessment Questionnaire
1 = Remember	

(Left axis label: **Subject Matter Knowledge Expectations**)
(Bottom axis label: **Capability Expectations**)

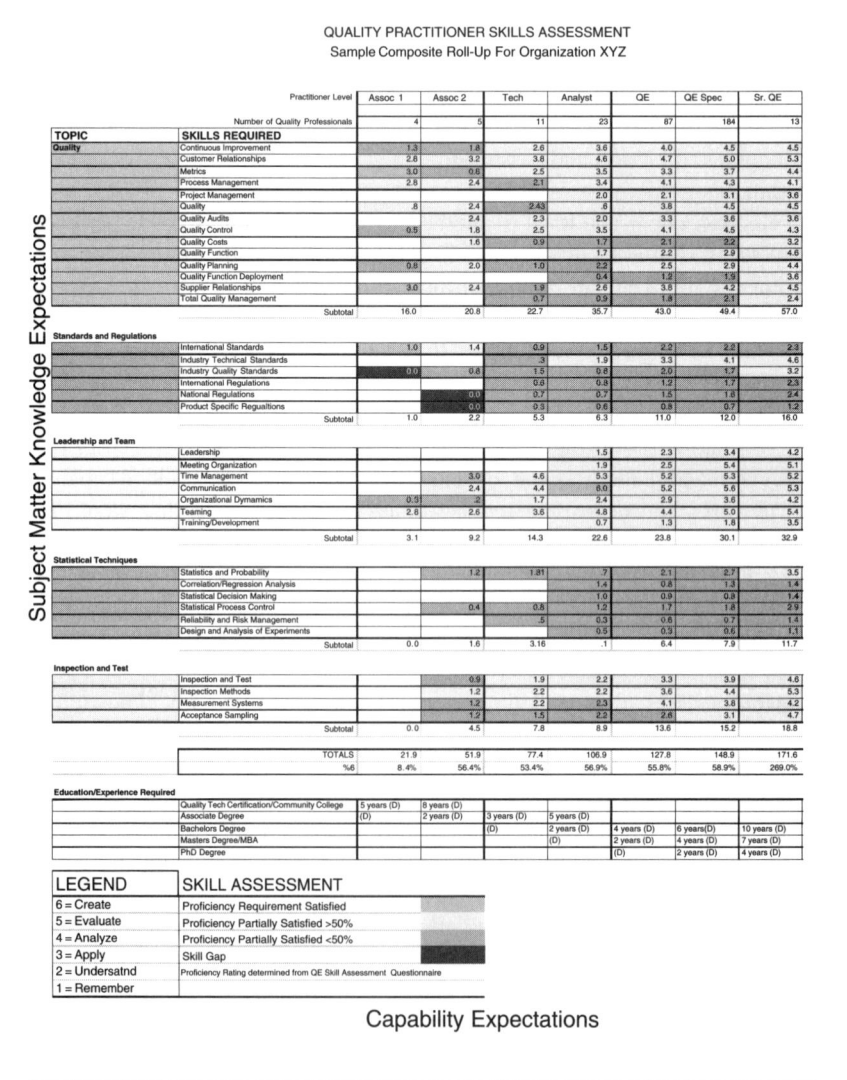

Figure B.3 The integrated knowledge management matrix provides a structured measurement process for managing knowledge capability. (Sample.)

the top-level macro knowledge management map and all corresponding functional discipline IKM matrices reflect current business needs and are aligned with one another. Additionally, knowledge capability should be a required consideration as the processes and procedures of the organization change.

EVALUATION OF THE CAPABILITY LEVEL

This is by far the toughest part of the integrated knowledge management process, and I strongly suggest that professionals who know how to assess and evaluate knowledge levels facilitate this aspect of developing the measurement process. Your human resources generalist will typically not have the skills to help you. If your organization has an organizational development group, it may be capable of facilitating the development of an inventory survey that can accurately determine the capability levels for each of the identified knowledge requirements. However, the truth is that most organizations do not have this type of ability inside because they typically don't manage knowledge and human capability well.

For each knowledge requirement and at each capability level, a set of tangible evaluation questions should be listed that would substantiate the level of capability in that knowledge requirement. It is important that this not be just a self-evaluation but rather an interactive process with either the cognizant leader or development professional that requires substantiation of the capabilities. Ask the question, "How do we know this person has this knowledge or capability?" Examples of successful projects and responses to questions should provide some insight. The objective evidence for the capability will be different for every discipline and for every knowledge requirement. This process will need to be accomplished for every grade level and every career path within the discipline. This extremely important part of the knowledge management process will represent a substantial investment in time and money.

If the organization does not invest sufficient resources to do it correctly, it calls into question the value of the process. Now please do not allow these words of caution to suggest that it is too hard or requires too much effort and should be left for only the large organizations to apply. That is not at all true. The evaluation process can be accomplished in a simpler fashion. Evaluation criteria may be designed less rigorously and still provide a rough order estimate of the current status. One means of application could be the identification of key knowledge characteristics. The organization will need to understand the level of potential variance in the data and use it accordingly. For example, in one of my earliest applications of this concept, I had a real business need to quickly understand the knowledge capabilities of my organization. Essentially, we created an IKM matrix as a functional discipline that was to manage approximately four hundred professionals. We took the time as a collective leadership team to identify the skill expectations and assign capability levels. The evaluation was a tougher prospect.

Using Bloom's level structure, we created questions directed at the expected capabilities. It was not perfect, but it did provide for a rough order estimate of resident capabilities. Over time, the evaluation process was improved. By the way, this was done with no budget or additional head count and in a relatively nonintegrated knowledge management structure. It was simply a leadership choice to do something. A lesson learned was that one success factor is important to recognize when getting started. We appointed a very capable individual who, as his primary job, was to lead and manage the knowledge management process of our functional discipline and work across organizational lines. Time was spent with this process manager to develop an understanding of Bloom's work and the concept of evaluation reliability, and I facilitated his engagement with quality professionals outside the organization so as to ensure that we were looking outside our own pond and were assessing potential future needs as well. We also took the time to train the leaders to minimize, as much as possible, evaluator variance. To facilitate the process and, again, to minimize evaluation variance, the knowledge management process manager was present at most, if not all, evaluations of the practitioners.

Taking planned action, even if it is not perfect, is better than taking no action. As a collective organization, we were able immediately to concentrate our collective efforts on closing the knowledge gaps so as to establish a higher level of organizational capability. At the individual level, we gained a better understanding of whether we had people in the right roles as well as of what we needed to do as leaders to help close the gaps. A word of caution is offered: ensure the credibility of the process. If you take the time to develop a process like this, and ask your people to support the evaluation, then as a leader you must do something with the data. Use the data to ensure that capabilities are aligned and to take action in knowledge growth. If the data indicate you have people who need to develop certain capabilities, and they are asking for such, and leadership does little or nothing to make it happen, that is a major failure of leadership.

ASSIGNMENT OF WORK IN ACCORDANCE WITH KNOWLEDGE CAPABILITY

Once a standardized measurement system is in place for ensuring knowledge capability throughout the organization, work scope and assignments can be aligned to match knowledge capability. This is actually quite simple once the capability processes have been established. Following the same process as outlined in Figure B.2, identify the verb in the work scope, and assign the appropriate levels of capability. Also, understand the noun and the context of application to identify the knowledge type. There is a substantial difference between someone who has level 3 procedural knowledge capability and someone who has level 3 conceptual knowledge capability. Procedural knowledge means that we expect someone to work in a linear way according to defined requirements. Conceptual knowledge means that we expect someone to work in accordance with the established procedures of the organization but that the assigned work may be more ambiguous and requires the application of knowledge around theories. Thus, it is important to truly understand what it is we are asking of our people and to ensure that they have the aligned capabilities to be successful.

My recommendation is to ensure that for every major work or job assignment employees have expectations clearly documented and an assessment is performed of knowledge capabilities. This should happen prior to an individual's being given any significant responsibilities—this includes senior leaders. It certainly would not be fair to the organization or employee if the work scope did not meet expectations, and, even worse yet, if the employee's knowledge capabilities did not match the desired performance. As part of the periodic review process, both the work scope and individual knowledge capabilities should be reviewed together. Take as much subjective influence out of performance reviews as possible and keep them data driven. This includes potential social issues. If teaming capabilities are a potential issue, make the data tell the story, not the gut.

CAPABILITY DEVELOPMENT

As gaps in knowledge capability are identified or as people seek growth in their career, you should provide opportunities for them to develop their abilities. Here are some of the ways in which growth of knowledge capability can occur:

Leadership mentoring. Leaders can take an active role in growing their people, especially if they know where growth is needed. The simple process of engaging in dialogue allows for learning to occur. Some researchers (Schön 1983) claim that most professional learning occurs through dialogue and not necessarily in formal training settings. The leader can also create a sense of openness in the work environment and encourage workers to engage in knowledge sharing.

Rotational assignments. By being exposed to new work scope and challenges, people may learn new techniques and capabilities. However, most rotational assignments are too brief for people to gain any higher levels of capability; they are typically useful for developing up to level 2, and rarely, level 3, knowledge capability.

On-the-job training. On-the-job training (OJT) can be used at lower levels of knowledge capability requirements; it requires supervision in the execution of work. OJT can be designed as a method of learning in action at higher levels of knowledge capability, but it requires more supervision or process checks as the complexity of the process increases. Organizations that rely solely on OJT as a method of learning usually spend more in lost productivity than they would if they structured a combination of learning opportunities (for example, combine OJT with formal training).

Internships. Depending on the length of an internship, very high level of knowledge capability can be established. Take, for example, the typical internships for a medical doctor. It lasts from two to six years depending on the specialty, and it is designed specifically to ensure that knowledge can be applied capably. Corporations also have internship programs, some lasting as short as a summer. The knowledge capability value of internships depend on the focus and length of the process.

Professional society membership. With any investment opportunity, if the investment has a potential of return, you will get what you put into it. The same is true of professional societies. Some are better than others, and you should understand why you would join. I strongly believe that in order to call yourself a professional, you must be contributing to a professional discipline. This could be through engagement in a professional society and driving the evolution of the discipline toward the creation of new knowledge or methods. The professional society also offers you the opportunity to engage with other professionals outside the organization who can increase your awareness of developing theories and practices. On the other hand, simply paying annual dues and not participating in the professional society does little for knowledge capability growth. My recommendation is to get involved and lead.

Traditional educational settings. Universities and colleges can provide foundational knowledge, but rarely is that applied knowledge. They can be used to establish entry-level knowledge capability and align with internal opportunities for application. The rate of demonstrated capability and potential greater responsibilities and authority will depend on the individual's ability.

It will also depend on the leader's determination to ensure that application opportunities exist. This type of knowledge should not sit on a shelf too long before being applied. It will go stale.

Trade schools. Trade schools are unique in that they typically focus on learning in action, which is applied knowledge. Depending on the scope and length of a trade school, a high level of knowledge capability can be developed, but typically in fields of labor application.

Training courses. Organizations should consider training as the surgical application of knowledge development. Many create training courses in a shotgun approach, scattering bits and pieces of information in the air and rarely enabling learning. Based on the work of Anderson and Krathwohl (2001), adapted for organizational use in the IKM model, it is suggested that you consider four major organizing questions in developing learning opportunities:

1. What is important for the individual to learn or know in the specified training or instruction time? (the objective question)

2. How do we plan to deliver the learning so that the learning objective is consistently achieved? (the instruction question)

3. How can learning and application be consistently evaluated? (the assessment question)

4. How can it be assured that objectives, instruction, and assessment are aligned and consistent with one another and with the needs of the organization? (the integration question)

The questions will keep the organization focused on tangible learning actions and aligned with the needs of the business.

USING THE INTEGRATED KNOWLEDGE MANAGEMENT MATRIX

The integrated knowledge management matrix can be used at various levels of the organization. At the level of the individual, it can provide both employee and leader with tangible direction for the employee's development. It adds little value to the organization to send someone off to a training course that does not address an identified need for knowledge capability. For example, some larger corporations will pay for higher education for any employee in any subject matter. I know of people who have gone after degrees in horticulture, yet their business was in aerospace manufacturing, and they certainly had development needs in their present profession. Some discretionary education should be provided for outside an employee's current work assignments, but whatever the training may be, it should relate back to some value proposition for the organization—even if it's in the future.

At the individual level, the knowledge management matrix should become the individual development plan and a quasi-contract with leadership. As an employee, if I have a gap, I should take the initiative to close it. As a leader, I will make learning opportunities available to you. Additionally, industrial learning experiences need to afford students the opportunity to immediately apply their new knowledge in the workplace so that they can contextualize the meaning of the learning, putting it into the context of value creation.

At the organizational level, the knowledge management matrices should be aggregated up to the organizational levels of the organization. For example, a leader could roll up by grade level the aggregate capabilities for their cells, business units, business centers, or the facility. The roll-up can go to any degree needed, but be mindful that as the data blend together, a strong area of the organization can carry a weaker one and provide the leader with a less-than-precise understanding of the real organizational knowledge capability. When rolled up by organization, the data are most useful when they are aggregated to organizational levels that are actionable to specific leaders. The use of range and standard deviation data will also provide the leader with an understanding of capability variance.

From the customer's perspective, management of the human capabilities in their value streams is very important. This is also the perspective that most program managers would be concerned with. The matrices should provide incremental roll-ups at the various stages of the value stream. Though we have not yet discussed suppliers and partners in regard to knowledge management and knowledge capability, they are equally important. I am not saying that your company's knowledge management matrix needs to be deployed into every one of your suppliers or partners, but the organization certainly needs to know the human capability of all those who contribute to the creation of value in its value stream and have an influence on organizational performance. Again, this is an issue of risk management, and we will discuss this in more detail shortly.

Considering the aspects of the organization that can be assessed as part of the value stream, an understanding can be established of where the program stands relative to capability to support execution to the customer. The simplest method of organizing these data is by "tagging" the individuals who contribute to the various processes that execute the value stream and rolling up capabilities—possibly focusing only on key characteristics. Given the dynamic nature of organizations, this would provide the program manager with an accurate understanding of impact as people move on and off the program. Depending on the scale of any program or value stream, a computer-based management tool may make management of this process more efficient. Again, as data blend, they have a tendency to flatten and bring little value to meaning. It is recommended that the organization use statistical tools to understand the variation of knowledge throughout the value stream so that accurate assessments can be made.

Discipline leaders, such as of quality, finance, engineering, procurement, legal, human resources, and so on, have a primary responsibility to ensure that the capabilities of their discipline meet the needs of the organization. They should also be looking forward and projecting future needs of the business. By rolling up to the discipline level, the discipline leader can better understand where disciplinewide action needs to be taken to advance the discipline's capabilities. This is where the discipline homeroom can provide immense value to the organization—by providing learning opportunities for the discipline, developing standard tools for application to decrease variability in understanding, and facilitating companywide job rotations so that people can close potential gaps through learning-in-action. By providing standardized foundations for knowledge to the discipline and across an organization's various businesses, common understanding of processes and performance is created. This also supports the development of common vocabulary and the ability to interact, communicate, and share knowledge as one company.

The IKM matrix can also provide value when trying to develop cross-discipline capabilities in individuals. As noted earlier, I am an outspoken critic of organizations that place individuals into leadership roles within any discipline in which they have insufficient capability. I am a critical of that because it usually is done at the expense of the organizational members who will have to live through the incompetence of the developing leader, and that's not to mention the impact on the business when poor decisions are made. In some cases, there may even be a threat to public safety when such unqualified leaders make decisions that affect the products or services that customers use. I don't need to name names—just look at the newspapers to see example after example of leadership making decisions that are outside of their knowledge capability. The matrix can provide an understanding of how great the knowledge gaps are in a individual who is going to jump into a new discipline. With this assessment of capability, the organization can make decisions as to how much authority such an individual should have and what actions it needs to take to minimize risk. The organization may install a mentor or deputy to address the identified gaps. But again, you cannot control what you don't know.

I have personally used the matrix in this way while bringing a talented production leader into a quality leadership role. My long-term intention was potentially keep this individual in the field of quality, primarily because of his ability to think logically and not interject emotion into the process. He also had a very high level of demonstrated integrity. He had some considerable gaps in his knowledge capabilities as a quality practitioner, especially for the grade level at which he was entering the discipline. At the same time, I oversaw another quality practitioner who was growing in his professional capabilities but needed to be exposed in a more routine fashion to the realities of business and the opportunities of applied leadership. To solve the challenge, I teamed the two up in leadership roles where one was responsible to the other in filling certain learning facilitation roles. The savvy production leader was now the quality manager, and the proficient quality practitioner was his deputy. Prior to the assignment, the three of us came to a good understanding of the relationships and responsibilities for learning. We also had some understandings around decision making and authority. These discussions were focused using the knowledge management matrix. The result was that the gaps in both began to close, and they were learning from each other. Thus, going across disciplines for developmental purposes can be done, but it must be planned and managed robustly. I would also add that this should happen in the earlier stages of a person's career so that the risk to the organization is not so high.

As previously mentioned, we all experience change. If the IKM matrix is to provide sustainable value, it will need to keep pace with change. The tools that we apply in our professions eventually become outdated and are replaced by new ones. Regulations may change and require the organization to develop capabilities that it never had. The business model may change and make the current knowledge requirements and capabilities of little value, necessitating completely new ones. And people frequently change jobs, so the roll-up data are as current as the stability of the organization.

The individual knowledge capability matrices themselves need to be reviewed periodically. The frequency of that review will vary from discipline to discipline, from company to company, and from industry to industry. Many factors should play into establishing a skills relevancy review frequency, but consider anything that poses a threat in the form of the creation of gaps between managed capability and needed capability. Then match the review frequency to the potential frequency of those change factors. If there are any significant changes, such as completion of training or successful application of capability in a project, immediate feedback in the form of updating the knowledge capability matrix would help maintain credibility of the process. And as the knowledge and capability requirements change, so must the individual assessments. If someone was carrying a capability measure of 5 in one knowledge element prior to a change, it does not mean they will be a 5 after the expectations change. You should also believe that the old concept "If you don't use it, you'll lose it" applies to skills and knowledge capability. Just because someone had a demonstrated capability six years ago doesn't mean they have it now.

It almost goes without saying, but as new people enter or as existing people exit the organization, the matrix should be updated to reflect the reality of organizational knowledge capability. I would suggest that during any organizational restructuring process, the integrated knowledge management matrix be used to understand where the restructured knowledge capabilities reside—or don't.

VALUE-STREAM KNOWLEDGE ASSURANCE

As organizational business models grow to include broader external sources of services and products, so does the dependency upon those external sources to perform. As we discussed in the Chapter 3, "Performance," all sources of the value stream must be held accountable for their individual contributions—including waste/cost generation. We discussed the concept of supplier cost recovery and accountability in Appendix A. But who is accountable for ensuring that those external to the organization have the requisite knowledge and human capability to execute the work for which they are contracted? Clearly, the organization should be responsible for ensuring that people in the value stream have the appropriate level of understanding prior to adding value, or in some cases waste. After all, it's the organization that owns the knowledge, or at least it is so in most cases. In some cases, an organization may contract with an external source because the organization does not possess the knowledge or human capability to perform the work, but even then, the organization must challenge assumptions and ensure that expectations and any unique requirements are thoroughly understood. In all cases, the organization is accountable to the customer.

Ensuring that your external producers and service providers understand what is required seems to be a simple and logical concept. However, how do you know that they know? What processes has the organization established to ensure that the external producers understand the requirements? And what about sustainability? If your organization is challenged with changing business environments and movement of personnel, why wouldn't those external to your organization experience the same conditions? I would suggest that whatever the procuring organization experiences in the area of change, it is magnified the further one is down in the value stream.

For an organization to completely embrace the concept of IPL, it must see things from a holistic perspective of accountability and responsibility. Measurement and validation processes must be established to effectively ensure that the entire value stream has the requisite understanding and knowledge capability; otherwise, without any doubt, the organization will get burned. As an example, let's look at an organization that had a long-term relationship with a major supplier who was so significant that it participated as a partner in some programs. Over the years, the relationship developed to the point that the organization felt very comfortable about how well the supplier understood the organization's technical and procedural requirements. Because of the longtime relationship, and decent performance, there was an assumption that as the supplier experienced internal personnel changes, it would ensure that new people would be indoctrinated into the requirements of the system to ensure conforming product. After a very expensive product compliance issue, the organization found that its assumptions were not valid, and it ended up recalling a significant amount of product from customers. The supplier was held accountable for cost, but it's hard to recover lost customer confidence.

As a result of this event, the organization launched a review of its knowledge assurance process and found that it was systemically too comfortable in its assumptions of supplier knowledge capability. This was especially true where English was not the primary language spoken by this American company's suppliers. No organization should assume that the process of translating information from one language to another is a capable process unless it has some means of measuring process capability. To prevent the painful reality of failed performance due to knowledge gaps, IPL requires an organization to create processes for validating the transfer of knowledge and understanding to external suppliers and service providers prior to work beginning. Figure B.4 provides some basic considerations when ascertaining the knowledge capability of your suppliers and partners.

Given that all things change, you cannot validate the understanding of an external source and think it will remain that way forever. Ongoing assessments are essential to ensure that the understanding and human knowledge capability remains at acceptable levels. Incorporating a process of knowledge management assurance into periodic audits or evaluations of external sources is one way to measure this important process. But if the subject matter content is not represented on the audit team, the knowledge assessment process itself may not be capable.

Another challenge to measurement through audit is that many companies are opting to use third-party auditors, who are not knowledgeable about the organizational processes. The execution of third-party audits also tends to be generic and typically rather shallow. Recognizing that IPL expects the IPT, or

Considerations for Supplier/Partner Knowledge
1. Ensure that the external source has access to all applicable data.
2. Engage the IPT (process owners) with the external source to ensure that understanding of the requirements is present.
3. Ensure that the external source has internal processes/procedures for ensuring that those who interact in your value stream have the requisite understanding/ human capability.
4. Ensure that the external source has means for demonstrating that understanding exists (e.g., tests, leader sign-offs, peer reviews, and audit processes).
5. Implement periodic reviews to ensure that people have the requisite knowledge (make sure that the supplier does this as well as the organization).
6. Periodically test the system to ensure that it remains capable (e.g., in-depth spot reviews for understanding and capability).
7. Have a process that flags the external source as a potential knowledge management risk when there are significant changes (e.g., management changes, financial challenges, external changes, personnel changes).
8. If there are multiple languages in the process, make sure that translations are validated and that visibility is maintained regarding updates and changes. Ensure that translated changes flow to all points in the knowledge flow needed.

Figure B.4 A sample checklist for ensuring suppliers and partners have the knowledge capability you expect.

process owners, to account for all aspects of performance of its part of the value stream, the organization should develop processes whereby the IPT reviews knowledge capability. The organization may find that multiple IPTs are interacting with one supplier. In this case, there should be one person in the organization who is accountable for coordinating interaction with the external source.

Internally, the organization should coordinate and synchronize its supplier interactions, especially the messages it sends. Otherwise the supplier's sense-making process can become overly complex and suffer from extreme variance. Additional consideration should be given to the number of customers your suppliers do business with. Again, a number of conflicting signals from multiple customers (see Figure B.5) can cause a supplier to form its own interpretation of messages, which may not be consistent with what you may want.

A more manageable process for managing knowledge capability in the value stream can be implemented by creating a modified knowledge

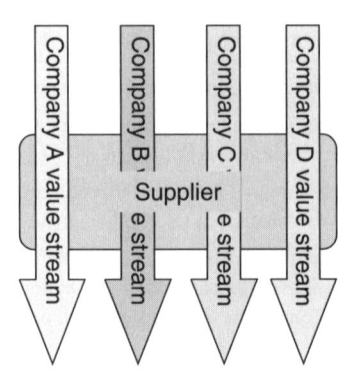

Figure B.5 Organizations must be aware of the multiple value streams flowing through suppliers providing diverse messages.

management matrix for key suppliers. For those suppliers that are critical to the performance of the organization, you would perform a knowledge process mapping exercise. To support all of the work that a specific supplier has from your organization, what knowledge would your organization want to make sure is at the appropriate levels of capability—key knowledge characteristics? Given that larger organizations usually have very large supplier populations, the knowledge elements should kept to the important or critical elements. For example, design change processes, special process controls, and a materials review process could be considered significant if the organization is a manufacturer. The same process of matrix deployment can then be followed as was done internally, and capability measures can be assigned to people in within the supplier's organization. The secret to success in this is keeping the number of elements to the important few and the deployment to those who are critical in the work execution.

In the case where a supplier fails to perform because of a gap in understanding, who bears the responsibility for the added cost? I say both the organization and the supplier do. However, if the organization fails to treat this process as an important aspect of business success, then the majority of the responsibility should rest on the shoulders of the organization.

SUMMARY

Leadership can choose to treat the organization's knowledge capability as a valuable commodity and establish structure and processes to ensure the company's investments, or they can choose to ignore knowledge capability as a process and assume it will happen on its own. Either way, the organization that reduces waste and delights its customers best and first will be the one who captures the market share. As we have discussed in this appendix, by aligning organizational processes with expected knowledge requirements and managing the process of knowledge execution to capability, the organization can realize greater efficiencies in execution and consistency in action.

One thing that needs to be mentioned is social responsibility. If the organization is going to have a sustainable future, it must make commitments in the present. Some organizations have recognized that there is significant benefit providing young people the opportunity to become exposed to the professions at an early age. This could be done through the development of educational relationships with local school systems or with trade schools. The earlier the seeds of knowledge are planted, the greater the potential harvest. One thing is absolutely clear: if a community (whether local, state, national, or industrial) does not treat the concept of learning as an important process, the community will not yield the performance we desire or need to sustain it. So there can be great value in organizations considering an education-based perspective to long-term organizational success.

Glossary

Achieving competitive excellence (ACE)—The quality program developed and deployed by the United Technologies Corporation. ACE applies the concepts of process control, JIT, and lean to provide a comprehensive portfolio of quality tools and methods.

Capability and maturity model integration (CMMI)—A structured measurement method for measuring the maturity of organizational processes. Developed by the U.S. government and Carnegie Mellon University, CMMI's initial focus was on measuring the maturity of software but has expanded to include an organization's business processes. When combined with IPL, CMMI provides an excellent measurement framework for the organization to understand its journey toward and status with regard to integration.

Component-level integrated product/process teams (CIPTs)—These teams are the integrated management teams at the component or business-unit level. They manage IPTs and report to IPMTs.

Conceptual knowledge—The knowledge of more complex, organized knowledge forms (Bloom 1956). It includes knowledge of classifications and categories; principles and generalizations; and theories, models, and structures (Anderson and Krathwohl 2001).

Contextual leadership—Leadership capabilities within a professional discipline. The leader truly understands the profession that they are leading.

Cost center—A cost center is an aspect of the organization that provides services to a program (IPMT) and may actually support a number of value streams. A cost center does not have a profit-and-loss statement but rather a budget that is allocated to it.

DIVE—Define, investigate, verify, and ensure is a methodology applied to investigating performance issues.

Escape—A nonconformance to design, process, or procedure that leaves an organization's established quality system.

Factual knowledge—The knowledge of facts (for example, the sky is blue, smoking leads to lung disease, and titanium has a certain hardness).

IAQG—The International Aerospace Quality Group is an international forum of aerospace quality leaders who have come together to self-manage their industry. The IAQG is an excellent example of how an industry can influence its environment.

Integrated knowledge management (IKM)—The structured process of ensuring that the organization has the appropriate levels of knowledge capability to produce sustainable value for the customer. IKM aligns organizational knowledge capability with business processes and product/service requirements.

Integrated knowledge management (IKM) matrix—A quantitative measurement tool that provides measurement of aggregate knowledge capability at the individual and collective levels.

Integrated performance leadership (IPL)—Combines the perspectives of various sciences to provide a comprehensive path of thought that addresses the need for organizational integration in structure, resources, accountability, vision, knowledge, action, and communication. It recognizes the need for visionary leadership with interrelatedness perspective capabilities. The objective of IPL is to provide a balance of performance for immediate objectives while taking the appropriate actions to ensure long-term sustainable success.

Integrated process and program development/deployment (IPPD)—Grew out of concurrent (or simultaneous) engineering in the 1980s. The objective of IPPD is to engage multifunctional teams of design and manufacturing engineers to develop the manufacturing process concurrently in the product life cycle. Ideally, IPPD expands on the technical integration employed in a disciplined, systems engineering approach to integrate business functions as well as technical functions. IPL provides a structured approach to developing organizational systems and processes that will enable an organization to perform as integrated program/product teams with assignable accountability throughout the value stream.

Integrated product development (IPD)—The conceptual framework of integrated teams focused around a specific product, process, or value stream.

Integrated product/process teams (IPTs)—Teams that represent the combined functional disciplines and business interests of a specific product or process.

Integrated product/program management team (IPMT)—The highest level of leadership over a product line and/or program. The IPMT should be responsible for all funding considerations, strategy development and deployment, and the health of their value stream.

Integrated project selection—The process of aligning the various performance metrics of the organization and developing a project scope that addresses a multiplicity of performance attributes. The process is intended to provide high-impact success and eliminate internal competition for resources.

Interrelatedness leadership vision—The ability of a leader to perceive and understand the interrelatedness of actions and organizational connections and appreciate the significance of these relationships.

Just In Time (JIT)— A term that relates to an organization's business processes that ensure material and/or services are provided when needed and are not held in reserve, such as in inventory, and is a characteristic of a *pull system*.

Kaizen—Results in incremental performance improvement and requires only slight modifications in the way people understand and interact with their processes.

Kaikaku—Results in exponential improvement in performance and always requires a hard-wire change in the way people think about a process.

Knowledge capability—The demonstrated capability of an individual with regard to an element of a knowledge requirement. Knowledge capability has six levels of proficiency and can be charted on the IKM matrix as a means of knowledge management.

Lean enterprise—The concept comes from Womack and Jones (1996) and their expansion of thought regarding lean manufacturing. A lean enterprise is one that has removed waste from not only its manufacturing or service activities but also its business processes. It should not be mistaken as a reference to organizational capacity.

Lean manufacturing—The concept of reducing waste through value-stream alignment and process optimization. Though lean manufacturing has its origins in the business of manufacturing, the concept has expanded to include the notion of a lean enterprise, which applies to all business processes, including those of service industries and government agencies. The primary focus is on the elimination of wasteful action and the creation of value for the customer (Womack and Jones 1996). IPL integrates well with the lean thought process, in that the focus of both lean and IPL is on the elimination of waste and the creation of value for the customer. However, IPL puts additional emphasis on the elements of organizational sustainability, such as learning, culture, leadership, and managing the environment.

Life-cycle business processes—The major phases in which an organization's actions occur to provide a product or service (value) to the customer. The major life-cycle phases are conception, design, production, and service.

Macro process mapping—The mapping of organizational business processes at the highest level of work design. It may not include the actual execution instruction of actual work but will capture the major work processes in an organization's business process life cycle.

Metacognitive knowledge—Knowledge about cognition in general as well as awareness of and knowledge about one's own cognition (Bloom 1956). It encompasses strategic knowledge; knowledge about cognitive tasks, including contextual and conditional knowledge; and self-knowledge (Anderson and Krathwohl 2001).

Micro process mapping—The detailed mapping of organizational processes to the actual level of work execution.

Procedural knowledge—The knowledge of how to do something (Bloom 1956). It includes knowledge of skills and algorithms, and techniques and methods, as well as knowledge of the criteria used to determine and/or justify when to do what within specific domains and disciplines (Anderson and Krathwohl 2001).

Pull system—When there is little to no inventory in the work environment, a structured methodology is required to ensure materials and services are provided when required. Hence, when employees *pull* for their materials or services, they are acquiring their resources from a *pull system*. Toyota widely, and successfully, used this practice in its production systems.

Quick response manufacturing (QRM)—A concept of improving organizational performance by structuring capacity to have inherent surge elasticity to address market changes. Like lean, QRM (Suri 1998) focuses on the reduction of queue time between work time (touch time) and can be applied to business processes as well.

Red X—A process of problem analysis developed in the 1940s by Dorian Shainin, which refers to determined root cause as the Red X. One requirement of Red X is that to verify that the root cause has been truly determined, it must be turned on and off.

Six Sigma—A structured methodology for understanding and controlling variation in processes. Six Sigma has grown from a focus on product or process into a more comprehensive tool that integrates knowledge around process capability into the early design phases. In many organizations, it is growing into a core philosophy of controlling variation in all business and leadership activities.

Supplier accountability—A process that accounts for the added cost a supplier causes to the organization and ensures that the cost can be recovered from the supplier. Supplier accountability is a different perspective than the traditional supplier quality paradigms.

Supplier-funded overinspection—A process that places the expense of added quality assurance back onto the supplier because of its poor performance.

Time-span perspective leadership—A leader's ability to perceive future consequences and opportunities. The further a leader thinks into the future, the greater their ability to plan for long-term success.

Transactional leadership—Speaks to the business acumen of a leader and ability to ensure that resources are aligned to meet business objectives. Within IPL, transactional leadership also embodies the aspects of contextual knowledge—knowledge of the specific field or line of business the leader is leading.

Transformational leadership—Relates to a leader's capability and capacity for caring for the organization's people and facilitating their growth for greater abilities.

Value stream—Made up of the collective value-adding activities that are required to bring a product or service to a customer. A complete value stream includes all tiers of suppliers, internal business processes, and servicing activities.

VISION center—A geographical location that provides focused facilitation of understanding organizational performance and the application of standardized tools for investigation and performance improvement.

VISION center networks—A collected group of VISION centers that can represent one or more value streams. The purpose of a VISION center network is to enable enterprisewide and value-stream-wide learning and action.

VISION concept—Provides a structured methodology for understanding organizational performance, process performance, and product issues. VISION stands for verify, investigate, standardize, integrate, optimize, and no recurrence.

Visionary leadership—Combines transformational, transactional, and time-span perspective leadership. IPL adds the component of interrelatedness leadership.

About the Author

We all start our careers at various levels in our selected profession. Michael Dreikorn began his truly at the bottom rung of the ladder and worked his way through leadership positions and responsibilities to the top executive levels of major corporations and government. In his professional journey, he has accumulated experience in various aspects of the high-tech and service industries as well as in government. Much of his experience has come in international operations and managing global supply chains, providing multiple perspectives for approaching situations. His foundational leadership training came while serving seven years in the U.S. Army in helicopter operations. This experience drove home the importance of reliable systems and people.

While employed at the Federal Aviation Administration, Michael was responsible for policy development and oversight of U.S. production systems, from which he gained a thorough understanding of government's influence over industries. He has held leadership positions at McDonnell Douglas, Northrop, and other aerospace companies. Prior to launching his own business performance management firm, The IPL Group, Michael was the vice president of quality assurance and product integrity at Pratt & Whitney, a manufacturer of turbine-powered engines and the largest operating unit of the United Technologies Corporation.

Michael has focused much of his professional inquiry on social dynamics relative to reliable performance. He holds a bachelor of science degree in professional aeronautics from Embry-Riddle Aeronautical University, a master of science in management from Friends University, and is (still) in the dissertation phase for a doctorate in education from George Washington University in the field of human resources development. Michael has held board or council positions at the Society for Organizational Learning, the Performance Review Institute, the technical advisory council for KPMG—

Quality Registrar, the American Society for Quality—Aviation, Space, and Defense division, and the International Aerospace Quality Group (IAQG); he holds a number of professional certificates and licenses as well. He is the author of *Aviation Industry Quality Systems* (Quality Press/TSI, 1995), which provides an understanding of how to develop management systems for the civil aviation industry.

References

Ackoff, R. L. 1981. *Creating the corporate future: Be planned or be planned for.* New York: Wiley.

Anderson, W., and Krathwohl, D.R. (Eds.) 2001. *A Taxonomy for learning, teaching, and assessing: A revision of Blooms' educational objectives.* New York: Longman.

Bedian, A. G. 1980. *Organizational theory and analysis.* Hinsdale, IL: Dryden Press.

Bennett, S., and J. Brown. 1995. "Mindshift: Strategic dialogue for breakthrough thinking." In *Learning Organizations*, edited by S. Chawla and J. Renesch. Portland, OR: Productivity Press.

Bennis, W. 1979. *Organizational development: Its nature, origins, and prospects.* Reading, MA: Addison-Wesley.

Berry, L. L., A. Parsuraman, and V. A. Zeithaml. 1994. "Improving service quality in America: Lessons learned." *Academy of Management Executive* 8 (2): 32–52.

Bloom, B. S. (Ed) 1956. *Taxonomy of educational objectives: The classification of educational goals, Handbook 1: Cognitive domain.* New York: Longman-Green.

Bluth, B. J. 1982. *Parsons's general theory of action: A summary of the basic theory.* Granada Hills, CA: NBS.

Bowles, M. L. 1989. Myth, meaning, and work organization. *Organization Studies* 3 (10): 405–21.

Brown, J. S., and P. Duguid. 1991. Organizational learning and communities-of-practice: Toward a unified view of working, learning, and innovation. *Organization Science* 2 (1): 40–57.

Burns, T. R., and G. M. Stalker. 1978. Mechanistic and organic systems. In *Classics of organization theory*, edited by J. M. Shafritz and P. H. Whitbeck. Oak Park, IL: Moore.

Buzzell, R. D., and B. T. Gale. 1987. *The pims principles: Linking strategy to performance*. New York: Free Press.

Campbell, J. P., et al. 1974. *The measurement of organizational effectiveness: A review of relevant research and opinion*. San Diego: Navy Personnel Research and Development Center.

Cartwright, D., and A. Zander. 1960. *Group dynamics: Research and theory*. New York: Harper and Row.

Christensen, C., 1997. *The innovator's dilemma: When new technologies cause great firms to fail*. Boston: Harvard Business School Press.

Chung, S. 1996. Performance effects of cooperative strategies among investment banking firms: A loglinear analysis of organizational exchange networks. *Social Networks* 18: 121–48.

Coleman, J. C. 1969. *Psychology and effective behavior*. Glenview, IL: Foresman.

Colyer, S. L. 1996. An empirical investigation of self and other perceptions of visionary leadership as related to organizational performance. Unpublished manuscript. School of Education and Human Development, George Washington University: 148, Washington, DC.

Cooke, W. 1992. Product quality improvement through employee participation: The effects of unionization and joined union-management administration. *Industrial and Labor Relations Review* (46): 119–34.

Costello, T., and S. S. Zalkind. 1963. *Psychology in administration*. Englewood Cliffs, NJ: Prentice Hall.

Culbert, S., and J. J. McDonough. 1985. *Radical management: Power politics and the pursuit of trust*. New York: Free Press.

Daft, R. L., 1983. *Organization theory and design*. St. Paul: West.

——1984. Toward a model of organizations as interpretation systems. *Academy of Management Review* 9 (2): 284–95.

Deming, W. E. 1972. Report to management. *Quality Progress* (July): 2.

—— 1980. The statistical control: Part I. *Quality* (February): 32–5.

—— 1986. *Out of the crisis*. Cambridge: MIT, Center for Advanced Engineering Study.

—— 1993. *The new economics for industry, government, education*. Cambridge: MIT, Center for Advanced Engineering Study.

Denison, D. R. 1984. Bringing corporate culture to the bottom line. *Organizational Dynamics* 20 (13): 4–22.

—— 1990. *Corporate culture and organizational effectiveness*. New York: Wiley.

Denison, D. R., and W. S. Neale. 1996. *Denison organizational culture survey: Facilitators guide*. Ann Arbor, MI: Aviat.

Dewey, J. 1916. *Democracy and education*. New York: Macmillan.

——— 1967. *Philosophy, psychology, and social practice*. New York: Capricorn Books.
Dixon, N. 1994. *The organizational learning model: How we can learn collectively*. London: McGraw-Hill.
Dwyer, M. D. 1993. *Building stocks*. New York: Kidder, Peabody.
Faerman, S. R., and R. E. Quinn. 1985. Effectiveness: The perspective from organizational theory. *Review of Higher Education* 9 (1): 83–100.
Fiol, C. M. 1994. Consensus, diversity, and learning in organizations. *Organizational Science* 5 (3): 403–20.
Harris, S. 1994. Organizational culture and individual sense-making: A schema-based perspective. *Organizational Science* 3 (5): 309–21.
Harvey, J. B. 1988. *The Abilene paradox: And other meditations on management*. Lexington, MA: Heath and Company.
Hedberg, B. 1981. How organizations learn and unlearn. In *Handbook of organization design*, edited by P. C. Nystrom and W. H. Starbuck. London: Oxford University Press.
Herzberg, F., and B. Mausner. 1959. *The motivation to work*. New York: Wiley.
Huber, G. P. 1996. Organizational learning: The contributing processes and the literatures. In *Organizational learning*, edited by M. D. Cohen and L. S. Sproull. Thousand Oaks, CA: Sage.
Huber, G. P., and W. H. Glick. 1993. What was learned about organization change and redesign. In *Organizational change and redesign: Ideas and insights for improving performance*. New York: Oxford University Press.
Ishikawa, K. 1985. *What is Total Quality Control? The Japanese way*. Englewood Cliffs, NJ: Prentice Hall.
Janis, I. L. 1982. *Groupthink*. Boston: Houghton Mifflin.
Jaques, E. 1986. The development of intellectual capability: A discussion of stratified systems theory. *Journal of Applied Behavioral Science* 22 (4): 361–83.
Jaques, E., and K. Cason. 1994. *Human capability: A study of individual potential and its application*. Falls Church, VA: Cason Hall.
Juran, J. M. 1969. *Managerial breakthrough: A new concept of the manager's job*. New York: McGraw-Hill.
——— 1974. *The quality control handbook*. New York: McGraw-Hill.
——— 1992. *Juran on quality by design*. New York: Free Press.
Klein, M. I. 1985. Building service cultures: How two regional department store chains have made it happen and lived to reap the benefits. Paper presented at the Fredrick Atkins Annual Operations and Human Resource Executives Conference, March, 11. Scottsdale, AZ.
Kotter, J. P., and J. L. Heskett. 1992. *Corporate culture and performance*. New York: Free Press.

Lawrence, P. R., and J. W. Lorsch. 1986. *Organization and environment: Managing differentiation and integration*. Boston: Harvard Business School Press.

Lewin, A. Y., and J. W. Minton. 1986. Determining organizational effectiveness: Another look, and an agenda for research. *Management Science* 32 (5): 514–38.

Likert, R. 1961. The nature of highly effective work groups. In *Organizational Psychology*, edited by D. A. Kolb, I. M. Rubin, and J. M. McIntryre. Princeton: McGraw-Hill.

——— 1967. *The human organization: Its management and value*. New York: McGraw-Hill.

Lorsch, J. W., and J. J. Morse. 1982. *Organizations and their members*. New York: Harper and Row.

Maslow, A. H. 1943. A theory of human motivation. *The Great Writings in Management and Organizational Behavior*, edited by L. E. Boone and D. D. Bowen. New York: McGraw-Hill.

——— 1943. A theory of human motivation. *Psychological Review 50*: 370–96.

——— 1954. *Motivation and personality*. New York: Harper.

McClelland, D. C. 1970. The two faces of power. *Journal of International Affairs* **1** (24): 36.

McGregor, D. M. 1960. *The human side of enterprise*. New York: McGraw-Hill.

Mezirow, J. 1985. Concept and action in adult education. *Adult Education Quarterly* 35 (3): 142–51.

Miles, R. H. 1980. *Macro organization behavior*. Glenview, IL: Foresman.

Ouchi, W. G. 1981. *Theory Z: How American business can meet the Japanese challenge*. New York: Avon.

Parsons, G. L. 1983. Information technology: A new competitive weapon. *Sloan Management Review*: 25 (1) 3–14.

Parsons, T. 1937. *The structure of social action*. New York: McGraw-Hill.

——— 1951. *The social system*. New York: Free Press.

——— 1959. An approach to psychological theory in terms of the theory of action. *Psychology: A study of a science*. Vol. 3. Edited by S. Koch. New York: McGraw-Hill.

——— 1960. *Structure and process in modern societies*. New York: Free Press.

——— 1983. *Talcott Parsons on institutions and social evolution: Selected writings*. Chicago: University of Chicago Press.

Peters, T. J., and R. H. Waterman. 1983. *In search of excellence: Lesson's from America's best-run companies*. New York: Warner.

Podsakoff, P. M., and D. Organ. 1986. Self-reports in organizational research: Problems and prospects. *Journal of Management* 12: 531–44.

Porter, L. W., and I. E. E. Lawler. 1968. *Managerial attitudes and performance*. Homewood, IL: Irwin.

Quinn, R. E., and J. Rohrbaugh. 1983. A spatial model of effectiveness criteria: Towards a competing values approach to organizational analysis. *Management Science* 29: 363–77.

Reichheld, F. R., and W. E. Sasser. 1990. Zero defections: Quality comes to services. *Harvard Business Review* (September/October): 105–14.

Robbins, A. 2001. *Get the edge*. San Diego: Anthony Robbins Companies.

Rogers, C. 1959. A theory of therapy, personality, and interpersonal relationships, as developed in the client-centered framework. In *Psychology: A study of a science*. Vol. 3 Edited by S. Koch. New York: McGraw-Hill.

Sackmann, S. A. 1992. Culture and subcultures: An analysis of organizational knowledge. *Administrative Science Quarterly* 37 (1): 140–61.

Sashkin, M. 1996. *Becoming a visionary leader*. Amherst, MA: Human Resource Development Press.

Sashkin, M., and K. Kiser. 1993. *Becoming a visionary leader*. Amherst, MA: Resource Development Press.Margaret HafnerSashkin, M., and K. Kiser. 1993. *Putting total quality management to work*. San Francisco: Berrett-Koehler.

Schein, E. H. 1985. *Organizational culture and leadership*. San Francisco: Jossey-Bass.

——— 1986. What you need to know about organizational culture. *Training and Development Journal* 40: 30–33.

Schön, D. A. 1983. *The reflective practitioner: How professionals think in action*. New York: Basic Books.

——— 1987. *Educating the reflective practitioner*. San Francisco: Jossey-Bass.

Schwandt, D. R. 1993. Organizational learning: A dynamic integrative construct. Unpublished manuscript. George Washington University, Washington, DC.

——— 1994. Organizational learning as a dynamic sociological construct: Theory and research. Unpublished manuscript. George Washington University, Washington, DC.

Schwandt, D. R., and A. M. Gundlach. 1992. Organizational learning: The development and implementation of an operational systems model. Unpublished manuscript. George Washington University, Washington, DC.

Scott, W. R. 1977. Effectiveness of organizational effectiveness studies. In *New perspectives on organizational effectiveness*, edited by P. S. Goodman and J. M. Pennings. San Francisco: Jossey-Bass.

Seashore, S. E. 1979. *Assessing effectiveness with references to member needs*. Paper presented at the annual meeting of the Academy of Management, August 20. Atlanta, GA.

Senge, P. M. 1990. *The fifth discipline: The art and practice of the learning organization*. New York: Doubleday.

——— 1990b. The leader's new work: Building learning organizations. *Sloan Management Review* (Fall): 7–23.

Senge, P. M., and J. D. Sterman. 1992. Systems thinking and organizational learning: Acting locally and thinking globally in the organization of the future. In *Transforming organizations*, edited by T. A. Kochan and M. Useem. New York: Oxford University Press.

Skinner, W. 1986. The productivity paradox. *Harvard Business Review*. 64: 55–59.

Smircich, L., and M. B. Calas. 1987. Organizational culture: A critical assessment. In *Handbook of organizational communications*, edited by F. M. Jablin, L. L. Putman, K. H. Roberts, and L. W. Porter. Beverly Hills, CA: Sage.

Smith, K. K., and D. N. Berg. 1987. *The paradoxes of group life: Understanding conflict, paralysis, and movement in group dynamics*. San Francisco: Jossey-Bass.

Steers, R. M. 1976a. *Methodological issues in evaluating organizational effectiveness*. Paper presented at the Annual Convention of the American Psychological Association, September 3–7, 1976, Washington, DC.

——— 1976b. When is an organization effective? A process approach to understanding effectiveness. *Organization Dynamics* 22: 50–56.

Suri, R. 1998. *Quick response manufacturing: A companywide approach to reducing lead times*. Portland: Productivity Press.

Vaill, P. B. 1996. *Learning as a way of being: Strategies for survival in a world of permanent white water.* San Francisco: Jossey-Bass.

Vroom, V. H. 1960. *Some psychology determinants of the effects of participation*. Englewood Cliffs, NJ: Prentice-Hall.

——— 1964. *Work and motivation*. New York: Wiley.

Walton, R. E. 1977. Successful strategies for diffusing work innovations. *Journal of Contemporary Business* (spring): 1–22.

Watzlawick, et al. 1974. *Change: Principles of problem formation and problem resolution*. New York: Norton.

Weick, K. E. 1976. Educational organizations as loosely coupled systems. *Administrative Science Quarterly* 21 (1): 1–19.

——— 1977. Organization design: Organizations as self-designing systems. *Organizational Dynamics* 3: 31–46.

——— 1979. *The social psychology of organizing*. New York: McGraw-Hill.

——— 1993a. The collapse of sensemaking in organizations: The Mann Gulch disaster. *Administrative Science Quarterly* 38: 628–52.

——— 1993b. Organizational redesign as improvisation. In *Organizational change and redesign: Ideas and insights for improving performance*, edited by G. P. Huber and W. H. Glick. New York: Oxford University Press.

——— 1995. *Sensemaking in organizations*. Thousand Oaks, CA: Sage.

Weick, K. E., and R. L. Daft. 1983. The effectiveness of interpretation systems. In *Organizational effectiveness: A comparison of multiple models*, edited by K. S. Cameron and D. A. Whetten. New York: Academic Press.

Womack, J. P., and D. T. Jones. 1996. *Lean thinking: Banish waste and create wealth in your corporation*. New York: Simon and Schuster.

Yuchtman, E., and S. E. Seashore. 1967. A system resource approach to organizational effectiveness. *American Sociological Review* 32: 891–903.

Yukl, G. 1994. *Leadership in organizations*. Englewood Cliffs, NJ: Prentice Hall.

Zeithaml, V. A., et al. 1990. *Delivering quality service: Balancing customer perceptions and expectations*. New York: Free Press.

Index

A

accountability
    importance, 61
    in life-cycle processes, 81–82
    matrix, 44
    supplier, 144–148, 191
ACE (achieving competitive excellence), 187
Ackoff, R. I., 104–105
action
    massive, 123
    planning, 118–122
    and reflection, 18
    theory, 20–23
adaptation, 20–21
aerospace manufacturing industry, 99
airline example, xiv–xx, 1, 127
Amazon.com, 9
American Society for Quality (ASQ), 167–168, 169
Anderson, W., 157, 161
    See also IKM
ASQ (American Society for Quality), 167–168, 169
AS9100 standard, 61
audits, 63, 182–183
authority, through reporting, 42–46

B

belief systems, 46–47

believability, 96–97, 115, 126
belonging, 106
Bennett, S., 106
Berg, D. N., 103
Black Belts, 49–50
Bloom, Benjamin, 157, *See also* IKM
Brown, J., 106
bureaucracy, 105
Burns, T. R., 91

C

Campbell, J. P., 69–70, 71
capability and maturity model integration.
    See CMMI
Cason, Kathryn, 92
centralization, 40–42
certainty in life, 109–110
CFOs (chief financial officers), 57
change
    first- vs. second-order, 102–103
    gradual, 103
    kaikaku, 59, 151, 189
    kaizen, 59, 189
    learning curve/productivity affected by, 83
    resistance to, 60
    time frame for, 118–119
    urgency about, 116–117
chaos/routines, systems of, 52–60
chief financial officers (CFOs), 57

chief organization performance officers (COPOs), 57
chief quality officers (CQOs), 57
CIPTs (component-level integrated produce/process teams), 35, 187
CMMI (capability and maturity model integration), 51, 123, 132–134, 136, 153, 187
Coleman, J. C., 104
colleges, 176–177
commitment, 106
communication, 122, 124–125
communities of practice (councils), 37–39
compliance, 106
component-level integrated produce/process teams (CIPTs), 35, 187
concept phase of life-cycle processes, 28, 29
contribution, need for, 109–110, 111
conviction, need for, 109–110, 111
Cooke, W., 105
COPOs (chief organization performance officers), 57
cost centers, 37, 187–188
councils (communities of practice), 37–39
CQOs (chief quality officers), 57
customers
    engagement/inclusion, 121
    money as coming from, 2
    satisfaction, 68, 72–73
    service, 71, 73

D

Daft, R. L., 71, 96–97
Darwin, Charles. *See* evolution
decentralization, 40–42
decisiveness, 115–116
Deming, W. E., 11, 51, 71–72, 75, 102
Denison, D. R., 105
design, core competencies in, 41
design phase of life-cycle processes, 28, 29
Dewey, J., 96, 103
dialogue, 101–107
direct-charging personnel, 81
direct reporting, 42–43, 45
disruptive technology, 12

dissemination and diffusion, 18
DIVE, 188
Dixon, N., 101
dotted-line reporting, 42–43

E

earned-value management system (EVMS), 134
educational setting, traditional, 176–177
employee satisfaction, 77–78
end-output metrics, 68
engagement, 104, 121–122, 123–124, 124
entropy, 21–22
environment, 12
environmental creep, 17
environmental interface, 18
equivocality, 96–97
escapes, 72, 73–74, 143, 147, 188
EVMS (earned-value management system), 134
evolution, 11, 16, 85, 98–99
expectations/challenges, 170–171

F

failure modes and effects analysis (FMEA), 149, 164–165
fairness, 83, 85
fears, 75, 102
feedback, 27–28, 63, 65
financial accounting development, 121, 128
financial measurement, 69–70
Fiol, C. M., 101
FMEA (failure modes and effects analysis), 149, 164–165
fragmentation/specialization, 18, 20

G

Glaubwürdigkeit (believability), 96–97, 115, 126
goal attainment, 20–21
group paralysis, 103
groupthink, 102–103
growth, need for, 109–110, 111

H

Harris, S., 106
heroism, 78–79, 89
Herzberg, F., 107
homeostasis, 21–22
homerooms, 36–37, 40
Huber, G. P., 96

I

IAQG (International Aerospace Quality Group), 99–100, 188
IKM (integrated knowledge management), 13, 124, 129, 155–175
    defining, 188
    knowledge capability, assigning work in accordance with, 174–175
    knowledge capability, developing, 175–177
    knowledge capability, evaluating level of, 173–174
    knowledge capability, taxonomy of, 157–160
    knowledge capability vs. capacity, 165–166
    knowledge types, identifying, 161–162
    and life-cycle business processes, 27–28
    macro knowledge mapping, 162–166
    matrix for, 156, 166–170, 177–181, 188
    measuring, 170–173
    value-stream knowledge assurance, 181–184
inclusion, 106
indirect-charging personnel, 81
industry groups, 99–100
initiatives, integration of, 49–52, 64
input measures, 68
integrated knowledge management. *See* IKM
integrated organizational structure, 24–39
    communities of practice (councils), 37–39
    cost centers, 37, 187–188
    functional leadership, 36–37
    and knowledge capability, 100
    life-cycle business processes, 26–32, 58–59, 64, 190
    supply chains, 37
    vs. traditional structure, 24–26
    See also value streams
integrated performance leadership. *See* IPL
integrated process and program development/deployment. *See* IPPD
integrated product development (IPD), 189
integrated product/process teams. *See* IPTs
integrated product/program management teams. *See* IPMTs
integrated project selection, 150–151, 189
integration, 6, 15–65
    and action theory, 20–23
    common direction, defining, 46–48
    decentralization, 40–42
    and environmental creep, 17
    feedback and system design, 63, 65
    and fragmentation/specialization, 18, 20
    of initiatives, 49–52, 64
    organizational learning model, 18–19, 20
    reporting lines, 42–46
    and requisite variety, 11, 16, 20, 64
    routines/chaos, systems of, 52–60
    scope, 120
    structural-design decisions, 39–40
    system validation, 60–62, 64–65
    theory, 16–24
    See also integrated organizational structure; value streams
interchange media, 27
internal audits, 63
International Aerospace Quality Group (IAQG), 99–100, 188
internships, 176
involvement, 105–106
IPD (integrated product development), 189
IPL (integrated performance leadership), 113–126
    action, massive, 123

action plan, creating, 118–122
communication, frequent, 124–125
constructs, 5–12 (*see also* integration; leadership; performance)
decisiveness, 115–116
defining, 188
engagement, continuously measuring, 123–124
examples of lack of, 7–8
need for, 8–9, 15
and a new mental model, creating, 117–118
objectives, 113
and operation, 2
the plan, staying true to, 125
scientific grounding, 17
successes, incremental/frequent, 122–123
and systems, 3–5
understanding, 114–115, 126
and urgency, sense of, 116–117
IPMTs (integrated product/program management teams), 33–36, 61, 189
IPPD (integrated process and program development/deployment), 25, 33–34, 51, 188–189
IPTs (integrated product/process teams), 35, 135, 140–142, 143–144, 146–147, 182–183, 189
Ishikawa, K., 71–72, 75
ISO 9000 standard, 61, 63, 156

J

Jaques, Elliott, 92
JIT (just in time), 84, 189
Jones, D. T., 34, 53, 190
Juran, J. M., 71–72
just in time (JIT), 84, 189

K

kaikaku change, 59, 151, 189
kaizen change, 59, 189
knowledge
 conceptual, 160, 161, 187
 factual, 160, 161, 188
 knowledge capability, 95, 100, 189
 metacognitive, 160, 161–162, 190
 procedural, 160, 161–162, 190
 See also IKM
Krathwohl, D. R., 157, 161
 See also IKM

L

Lawler, I. E. E., 107
leadership, 89–112
 assessing capabilities, 121
 contextualized (understanding), 94–96, 187
 in deployment, 119–120
 and dialogue, psychology/motivation of, 104–107
 for dialogue, environment of, 101–103
 equivocality reduced by, 96–97
 fears removed by, 75, 102
 functional, 36–37
 Glaubwürdigkeit (believability), 96–97, 115, 126
 importance, 89
 in integration, 120
 interrelatedness leadership vision, 189
 leaders as teachers, 96–97
 managing leadership abilities, 97–100
 measuring, 120
 mentoring, 175
 misbehavior of leaders, 89
 by novices, 95–96
 overview, 6, 9–12
 and performance, 75, 86
 rewarding performance/behavior, 107–112
 Senge on, 20
 time-span perspective, 191
 traditional role of directors/managers, 25–26
 transactional, 89–90, 91, 97–98, 112, 191
 transformational, 91, 101, 106, 112, 128, 192

understanding by, 115, 126
visionary, 39, 90–93, 128, 192
lean enterprises, 5–6, 33, 68, 98, 190
lean manufacturing, 51–52, 84, 123, 190
Lean Thinking (Womack and Jones), 34
learning, individual vs. collective, 101
Lewin, A. Y., 69
life-cycle business processes, 26–32, 58–59, 64, 81–82, 190
Lindbloom's variant, 103
localization, 40–42
loggerheads, 60
love, need for, 109–110, 111
loyalty, 106

M

macro process mapping, 64, 121, 190
management systems, 52–53
Maslow, A. H., 104, 107
matrix accountability, 44
MBA programs, 97–98
meaning, 18, 104–105
membership engagement, 60
memory, 18, 60
mentoring, 175
micro process mapping, 64, 190
Minton, J. W., 69
mission statements, 47
momentum, 123
motivation, 104–105

N

normative commitment, 106

O

on-the-job training (OJT), 176
operation, 2
organizational learning model, 18–19, 20
organizations
    aligning metrics, 75–79
    aligning resources, 80–86
    complexity, 11
    culture, 46–47, 65, 75, 118–119
    for-profit, 67
    governmental, 67

health of, 67–68 (*see also* performance)
informal, 46
membership engagement in, 60
memory in, 60
not-for-profit, 67
purpose, 67
training/education, 122

P

Panasonic, 149
Parsons, Talcott, 20–23
pattern maintenance, 20–21, 22–23
performance, 67–87
    and action, 78–79
    aligning financial measures, 128
    aligning measures with macroprocess, 121
    aligning metrics, 75–79
    aligning resources, 80–86
    and balance, 76
    and behavior, 12, 75
    and customer satisfaction, 68, 72–73
    and customer service, 71, 73
    definitions/models, 69–75
    and effectiveness, 69–70, 71
    and employee satisfaction, 77–78
    end-output metrics, 68
    expectations, 120
    financial measurement, 69–70
    input measures, 68
    and leadership, 75, 86
    overview, 6, 9
    poor quality as eroding, 72
    road maps, 76–77, 79
    strategic constituencies model, 71, 75–76
    and sustainability, 79, 128
    throughput measures, 68
    and value streams, 69
periodicals, 100
Peters, T. J., 69
P&Ls (profit-and-loss entities), 33, 37–38
Porter, L. W., 107

PPM (problem parts per million), 147, 148–149
preambles, 61–62
presidents, role of, 24–25, 56
problem parts per million (PPM), 147, 148–149
problem resolution, 102–103
procedures and policies, 58–59
process flowcharts, 59
production, core competencies in, 41
production and delivery phase of life-cycle processes, 28, 30–31
professional society membership, 176
profit-and-loss entities (P&Ls), 33, 37–38
psychological needs, 109–112
pull system, 191
purpose, sense of, 104–105

Q

QRM (quick response manufacturing), 52, 134, 191
QS-9000 standard, 61
quality in development processes, 149–150
quick response manufacturing (QRM), 52, 134, 191

R

Red X, 191
Reichheld, F. R., 72
reporting
    combined, 45–46
    direct (solid-line), 42–43, 45
    dotted-line, 42–43
    informal organization, 46
    system (matrix) accountability, 44
requisite variety, 11, 16, 20, 64
rewards, 107–112
road maps, 76–77, 79
Robbins, Tony, 109–110
Rogers, C., 104
rotational assignments, 176
routines/chaos, systems of, 52–60
rule-making processes, 61–62

S

Sackmann, S. A., 101
Sashkin, M., 90, 108
Sasser, W. E., 72
Schwandt, David, 18–19, 20
Senge, Peter, 18, 20
service execution, core competencies in, 41
service phase of life-cycle processes, 31–32
Shainin, Dorian, 191
significance, need for, 109–111
Six Sigma, 49–51, 123, 153, 191
Skinner, W., 107–108
Smith, K. K., 103
social Darwinism, 17, 20
social responsibility, 185
solid-line reporting, 42–43, 45
specialization/fragmentation, 18, 20
stalemates, 103
Stalker, G. M., 91
standards
    AS9100, 61
    ISO 9000, 61, 63, 156
    QS-9000, 61
stock prices, 67, 86–87
strategic constituencies model, 71, 75–76
strategic planning, 47–48
stretch goals, 78–79
structural-design decisions, 39–40
stump meetings, 125
success, 4–5, 9, 122–123
    See also performance
supplier accountability, 144–148, 191
supplier-funded overinspection, 148–149, 191
suppliers. *See* value streams
supply chains, 37
sustainability, 79, 128
systems
    accountability in, 44
    closed, 20
    control/ownership of, 56–58
    deploying, 62
    design, and feedback, 63, 65

entropy in, 21–22
examples, 3–4
executing, 62
homeostasis in, 21–22
management, 52–53
organizational, 4–5
requisite variety in, 11, 16, 20, 64
of routines/chaos, 52–60
validating, 60–62, 64–65

T

Taylor, 69
team members, roles/responsibilities, 121
throughput measures, 68
TQM (total quality management), 49, 50, 114
trade schools, 177
training courses, 177
transactional leadership, 89–90, 91, 97–98, 112, 191
transformational leadership, 91, 101, 106, 112, 128, 192
trust, 12

U

uncertainty for discovery, 109–110
understanding, 94–96, 114–115, 126, 187
universities, 176–177
urgency, sense of, 116–117

V

Vaill, P. B., 104
value, demonstrating, 151–153

value streams
  defining/measuring, 32, 192
  engagement/inclusion, 121
  and integration, 32–36, 53–54, 55–56, 61
  knowledge assurance, 181–184
  and performance, 69
  training/education, 122
  and values, orders of, 54–55, 69, 72
  waste in, 53–54, 56, 64, 69, 72
visionary leadership, 39, 90–93, 128, 192
VISION center networks, 13, 101, 129, 131–154
  concept, 131–138, 192
  defining, 192
  integrated project selection, 150–151
  modular aspects, 143–144
  quality in development processes, 149–150
  setting up, 139–143
  supplier accountability process, 144–148
  supplier-funded overinspection, 148–149
  value, demonstrating, 151–153
vision statements, 47, 48
Vroom, V. H., 104, 107

W

waste, 53–54, 56, 64, 69, 72
Waterman, R. H., 69
water spider resources, 45
Weick, Karl, 41, 71, 96–97
weld councils, 38–39
Womack, J. P., 5, 34, 53, 190